Other Titles in the Psychology of Popular Culture Series

THE PSYCHOLOGY OF HARRY POTTER

An Unauthorized Examination of the Boy Who Lived

EDITED BY

NEIL MULHOLLAND, Ph.D.

AN IMPRINT OF BENBELLA BOOKS, INC.

Dallas, Texas

"What Do Students Learn from Hogwarts Classes?" © 2006 by Robin S. Rosenberg, Ph.D.
"Harry's Curiosity" © 2006 by Susan Engel, Ph.D., and Sam Levin
"Intergroup Conflict in the World of Harry Potter" © 2006 by Melissa J. Beers, Ph.D., and Kevin J. Apple, Ph.D.
"'Have You Got What It Takes to Train Security Trolls?': Career Counseling for Wizards" © 2006 by Shoshana D. Kerewsky, Psy.D., and Lissa Joy Geiken, M.Ed.
"Hogwarts Academy: Common Sense and School Magic" © 2006 by Charles W. Kalish and Emma C. Kalish
"Attachment Styles at Hogwarts: From Infancy to Adulthood" © 2006 by Wind Goodfriend, Ph.D.
"What Harry and Fawkes Have in Common: The Transformative Power of Grief" © 2006 by Misty Hook, Ph.D.
"Harry Potter and the Resilience to Adversity" © 2006 by Danielle M. Provenzano and Richard E. Heyman
"Discovering Magic" © 2006 by Karl S. Rosengren, Ph.D., and Emily C. Rosengren
"The Magical World of Muggles" © 2006 by Carol Nemeroff, Ph.D.
"Time and Time Again: Muggle's Watch, the Wizard's Clock" © 2006 by Peter A. Hancock and Michelle K. Gardner
"The Social Dynamics of Power and Cooperation in the Wizarding World" © 2006 by Nancy Franklin, Ph.D.
"Mental Illness in the World of Wizardry" © 2006 by Jessica Leigh Murakami
"'Dobby Had to Iron His Hands, Sir!': Self-Inflicted Cuts, Burns, and Bruises in Harry Potter" © 2006 by E. David Klonsky, Ph.D., and Rebecca Laptook, M.A.
"The Werewolf in the Wardrobe" © 2006 by Siamak Tundra Naficy
"Exploring the Dark Side: Harry Potter and the Psychology of Evil" © 2006 by Christopher J. Patrick, Ph.D., and Sarah K. Patrick
"Harry Potter and the Word That Shall Not Be Named" © 2006 by Mikhail Lyubansky, Ph.D.
"Evolution, Development, and the Magic of Harry Potter" © 2006 by David H. Rakison and Caroline Simard, BSc., DMV
"Using Psychological Treatment with Harry" © 2006 by Neil Mulholland, Ph.D.
"Defense Against the Real Dark Arts" © 2006 by Patricia A. Rippetoe, Ph.D.
"Resisting Social Influence: Lessons from Harry Potter" © 2006 by Melanie C. Green, Ph.D.
"Harry Potter and the Magic of Transformation" © 2006 by Laurie J. Pahel
Additional Materials © 2006 by Neil Mulholland, Ph.D.

  Smart Pop is an imprint of BenBella Books, Inc.
10440 N. Central Expy., Suite 800
Dallas, TX 75231
www.benbellabooks.com
Send feedback to feedback@benbella books.com

BenBella is a federally registered trademark.

Printed in the United States of America
10 9 8

Library of Congress Cataloging-in-Publication Data

The psychology of Harry Potter : an unauthorized examination of the boy who lived / edited by Neil Mulholland.
    p. cm.
    Includes bibliographical references.
    ISBN 1-932100-88-1
    1. Rowling, J. K.--Characters—Harry Potter. 2. Potter, Harry (Fictitious character) 3. Children's stories, English—History and criticism. I. Mulholland, Neil, 1946-

    PR6068.O93Z835 2007
    823'.914—dc22

                                                                            2006035440

Proofreading by Erica Lovett and Jennifer Thomason
Cover design by Mondolithic Studios, Inc.
Text design and composition by John Reinhardt Book Design
Printed by Lake Book Manufacturing
Distributed to the trade by Two Rivers Distribution, an Ingram brand
www.tworiversdistribution.com

Special discounts for bulk sales are available. Please contact
bulkorders@benbellabooks.com.

Contents

Introduction

SO, YOU MIGHT ASK, what are my qualifications to investigate the psychology of the world-renowned Harry Potter series?

Well, to start, I did grow up some forty miles from where J. K. Rowling wrote her first Harry Potter books. Much like Harry, I once slept in a closet, where just my single bed fit (but not under the stairs). I also used to travel on a train, just like Harry's, to English boarding school, where I wore a uniform like his and was "sorted" into a group or House in a country mansion. Unfortunately, it was not nearly as magical and interesting as Hogwarts, but I seemed to have as much difficulty as Harry in following the rules.

So, after "six of the best" (six whacks on the rear with my choice of the thin cane that stung or the thick cane that hurt), I was soon shipped off home and ended up at St. Mungo's. Fortunately, it was not the infirmary, but St. Mungo's Academy to finish my schooling. Yes, there was a real St. Mungo who was the bishop of Glasgow around the sixth century.

My other connection to Harry these days, aside from my fascination with the books, is that I developed something called Harry Potter Therapy. If you've looked at any of the Harry Potter blogs about a year or so ago, I seemed to have stirred a bit of controversy as I've used and encouraged others to use Harry Potter images when helping young people overcome moderate levels of worry, anxiety, or depressive feelings. If you are interested in how this works, please read my chapter in this book.

My work as a psychologist is in applying sound psychological theories and practices to the treatment of helping those having mental-emotional difficulties. Harry Potter Therapy often fits the bill.

It is my great pleasure to introduce you to a wide variety of psychology professors and their fine contributions connecting various theories and research in psychology to aspects of the people and events that have and could take place in Harry's on-going story. If you are a Potter fan I hope you find these chapters an interesting study, compared to some of the dry stuff that I had to read in my beginning years of study in psychology.

Long may the "magic" live.

Neil Mulholland, Ph.D.

WHAT KIND OF SCHOOL IS HOGWARTS?

The Muggle world is filled with amazing, magical things—rockets to the moon, the Internet, and miraculous medicines, just to name a few. And the way we Muggles develop these amazing things is, as Rosenberg points out, through a careful process of organized curiosity known as the scientific method. At Hogwarts, Rosenberg insists, the scientific method doesn't exist; the students learn how to do magic, but they are not encouraged to find out how magic works. Is that any way to run a school?

ROBIN S. ROSENBERG, Ph.D.

What Do Students Learn from Hogwarts Classes?

Although the world of Harry Potter is engrossing and inventive, the educational system at Hogwarts is filled with disturbing elements: Hogwarts promotes memorization and punishes experimentation, creativity, and critical thinking skills, creating alumni who are truly unprepared to handle calamities. Of course, not all students are unprepared (as I'll explain in detail later); Harry Potter and some of his friends are notable exceptions.

Just what are Hogwarts's educational goals? We can safely assume that its primary objective is to help students learn the basics of witchcraft and wizardry. Less clear is whether the school seeks to help students learn how to solve problems on their own. That is, even after they've mastered wizarding basics, can they properly recognize and define problems, ask relevant questions, obtain useful information, generate approaches to solving problems, and experiment with possible solutions (Bok)? Let's examine what we know of the Hogwarts educational system and see how well it prepares its students for critical thinking and problem solving.

LACK OF CURIOSITY

Neither students nor teachers appear to be curious about the sources of their magical powers—they take magic for granted. The six Harry Potter books are notable for the characters' utter lack of wonder about *why* the magic they observe and learn works as it does. Consider the owls as a means of transporting messages: How do the owls know how to find a message's recipient, when even the message sender does not know where the recipient is? No one in the books expresses curiosity about how this could be. In contrast, in our world, when people hear about a new communication device, such as instant messaging, Voice over Internet Protocol (VoIP), or cell phones, scientists (including psychologists) would hope that people would express some sense of wonder and curiosity about how such a communication method functions. We want them to be aware that there is an underlying, understandable mechanism.

In Harry's world, even the origins of magical powers are unquestioned. There is no mention of curiosity about why some people with Muggle parents are born with magical powers (as were Hermione, Seamus Finnegan, and Harry's mother, Lily Evans), or, conversely, why some people born to parents who are both magical become Squibs (as were Hogwarts's Argus Filch and Harry's neighbor on Privet Drive, Arabella Figg). These flukes of nature—of genes, we can suppose—become part of the landscape in the magical world. Yet who wants to dig into the soil of the landscape to learn its composition?

In the Muggle world—our world—people are constantly digging into the soil to understand the world around us. Many of us Muggles do not take these matters on faith, assuming that the mechanisms that make our world work are knowable and that we should strive to discover them. This is part of what science classes try to impart to students—the underpinnings of how to discover the mechanisms underlying our world.

Hermione stands as a shining beacon of curiosity; she is not just a voracious reader who retains what she reads, but is curious about the mechanisms of magic and understands their importance. In *Harry Potter and the Goblet of Fire*, when Harry realizes that his first challenge in the Triwizard Tournament is to retrieve a golden egg from a dragon, Mad-Eye Moody encourages him to use his broomstick. But in order to get his broomstick, he needs to learn a Summoning Charm. When Hermione's initial tutoring efforts to teach him the charm are unsuccessful, she has Harry read about the theory behind Summoning Charms to help Harry perform them. Hermione's strategy is consistent with what psychologists have learned: applying existing knowledge to solve problems in a new situation is enhanced when students understand the underlying concepts (Gardiner).

Yet students reared in magical families do not appear to be curious about the mechanisms behind their powers. This particular type of apathy seems to be perpetuated at Hogwarts, where teachers appear similarly uninquisitive about the underlying mechanisms—the *who*, *what*, *when*, *where*, *how*, and *why*—of magic. Hogwarts teachers impart knowledge about (magical) content, not about (magical) process. More surprising, though, is that many of the Muggle-born wizards and witches, educated in our world until age eleven (when they begin their wizarding education), seem to suspend their sense of inquiry once at Hogwarts.

LACK OF SCIENTIFIC INQUIRY

Scientific inquiry is the answer to curiosity's questions—it's about systematically attempting to find answers. Our educational system, particularly in math and sciences, imparts knowledge about both content *and* process. Students learn facts and figures, but they also learn how this knowledge is derived and the *process* by which scientific knowledge is produced. This process is sometimes referred to as the scientific method; in psychology, the scientific method has six steps (Kosslyn & Rosenberg):

- *Step 1: Specify the Problem or Question*. This first step involves a curiosity about some phenomenon of interest, often in the form of a question. In psychology, such questions might be why certain types of people seem to be good leaders, or why people forget where they placed their wallets.

- *Step 2: Observe Events.* Once the question or problem has been identified, scientists proceed systematically to observe those events. In the process they collect data in the form of careful observation or numerical measurements that can be recorded and shared with others. Such observations become the springboard for the next step.
- *Step 3: Form a Hypothesis.* Based on their observations, scientists proceed to generate ideas about how changes in one variable appear to be associated with changes in other variables; that is, they develop a hypothesis about the relationship among variables.
- *Step 4: Test the Hypothesis.* Scientists then go on to test their hypothesis about the relationship among the variables in question. They make new observations or collect new numerical data, this time with specific attention to the hypothesized relationship. What happens next depends on the results of this step. If the results do not support the hypothesis, scientists may need to develop a new one and go back to Step 3. Alternatively, if the results do generally support their hypothesis, they proceed to Step 5.
- *Step 5: Formulate a Theory.* Whereas a hypothesis is a tentative conjecture about the relationship among variables, a theory is grounded in data that the relationship exists and seeks to explain the *mechanism* underlying that relationship. Thus, a hypothesis proposes *whether* a relationship exists; a theory proposes *why* a relationship exists and *how* it works.
- *Step 6: Test the Theory.* As with Steps 2 and 4, this step involves careful observations, only this time they are directed at the theorized underlying mechanisms. When the results do not support the theory, scientists may try to test the theory in a different way; if repeated results do not support the theory, scientists may go back to Step 5 and formulate a new theory, incorporating the information they've learned along the way.

To some extent, we are all scientists in our daily lives. Consider the example of having to tell a friend information that you think will upset her. You are likely to:

1. Wonder how she'll respond (Step 1);
2. Mentally review past occasions when you've observed her hear bad news (a retrospective version of Step 2);
3. Predict how she'll respond (Step 3);
4. Give her the bad news (Step 4);
5. Perhaps formulate a theory of why she responded as she did (Step 5); and should you need to give her upsetting information again, you may;
6. Test your theory (Step 6).

Using the scientific method to generate and examine information, you will learn more about your friend—her reactions and apparent motivations.

Fred and George Weasley seem to have intuited the scientific method and use it to test their magical wares. When testing their Fainting Fancies sweets (*Harry Potter and the Order of the Phoenix*), they appear to have:

1. Set out to create a formula for the Fainting Fancies (Step 1);
2. Mentally reviewed what they know about possible ingredients—and their dosages—that should go into the sweets (Step 2);
3. Predicted how people will respond to the sweets (Step 3);
4. Tested the sweets, which helped them to discover that the dosages might not be strong enough (Step 4).

We don't know whether Fred and George went as far as formulating and testing a theory underlying the relationship between the ingredients and their effects (Steps 5 and 6), but their amazing ability to create new magical potions and objects indicates that they may have.

Fred and George seem to have developed their facility with the scientific method on their own, not from their teachers. Teachers and students, except for Hermione and the Weasley twins, don't ask and therefore don't seek to answer questions about the process of magic. Consider that when Harry's name comes out of the Goblet of Fire, teachers express surprise that someone was able to put Harry's name in the cup and eventually attribute it to some Dark Art (*Goblet of Fire*). Mad-Eye Moody proposes that it is a Confundus Charm, but no one is curious to figure out exactly how it might have been done or cares to try to replicate it. How can students systemically aggregate magical knowledge and learn how to think for themselves if they are not developing and testing hypotheses?

Voldemort applies the scientific method to magical phenomenon: "I have experimented; I have pushed the boundaries of magic further, perhaps, than they have ever been pushed" (*Harry Potter and the Half-Blood Prince* 443). Other examples of experimenting wizards are Nicolas Flamel (who invents the Sorcerer's Stone), Dumbledore (who discovers the twelve uses of dragon's blood), and Snape (who experiments with new ways to make potions and creates new spells). Thus, we learn that experimentation can help wizards become more powerful. Yet, rather than give students the tools to add to magical knowledge, Hogwarts teachers only require that students correctly memorize spells, potions, and the powers of particular ingredients. And Hogwarts is the last step in general wizarding education in the United Kingdom; if students are not taught this basic skill there, they are unlikely to learn it later in life.

In the Muggle world, research has found that courses that place an emphasis on scientific reasoning can affect students' subsequent abilities to reason. For instance, college students taking classes in the social sciences improve their reasoning abilities in particular ways, compared with those taking humanities or natural science classes (Lehman & Nisbett). Another study found that undergraduates who took a psychology class about research methods—that is, the scientific method—were better able to reason and think critically about real-life events than students who took a psychology class about child development (VanderStoep & Shaughnessy).

When students are engaged in class material and spend time answering thoughtful questions asked in class, they are more likely to develop critical thinking skills. However, if they aren't asked questions that require conceptual understanding, they are unlikely to learn the material to the level required for true understanding and application (Gardiner). Unfortunately, Hogwarts students are not challenged to develop such conceptual understanding.

MEMORIZING AT THE EXPENSE OF PROBLEM SOLVING AND CREATIVITY

Astronomy, Charms, Herbology, History of Magic, Potions, and Transfiguration—the majority of core multi-year courses at Hogwarts—do not generally require any problem-solving ability or particular creative element. (Psychologists define creativity as devising effective new ways to solve problems. Although the word *creativity* is also used to describe original artistic productions of high quality, I will not focus on this type of creativity in this essay.) Students memorize spells, charms, and potions and practice their techniques. There is no Socratic thinking or intellectual questioning of ideas or assumptions.

The exception to this extended exercise in memorization occurs when a professor who emphasizes creative problem solving teaches the Defense Against the Dark Arts (DADA) class. (This contrasts with other classes, such as Potions, which may require students to respond to a teacher's query quickly, but the desired response pertains to students having correctly memorized a potion or spell.) Professor Lupin is the first teacher to encourage problem-solving skills among students—to become creative in how they use what they already know. Professor Moody is the first teacher to challenge students to be ready for anything—exposing them to the Unforgivable Curses so that they can develop preparation strategies (*Goblet of Fire*). With both of these DADA teachers, the students are energized and thrilled to think on their feet and solve novel (and real world applicable) problems. Even Snape, as DADA teacher, admonishes students that their defenses should be "as flexible and inventive as the arts you seek to undo" (*Half-Blood Prince* 178).

Creativity often involves "out-of-the-box" thinking to arrive at novel solutions, usually to novel problems (Isaksen & Treffinger; Runco). Such problems may range from very specific (e.g., "How can I figure out what the golden egg is saying?") to the general (e.g., "How can I defend myself from spells directed against me?"). Some psychologists propose that, once a problem to be solved has been identified, coming up with a novel solution occurs in two stages: (1) generate a range of possible solutions; (2) select the most appropriate solution. During this two-stage process, normal mental abilities such as memory and mental imagery—forming vivid mental images—combine to yield new solutions (Finke; Finke et al.; Ward).

Problem solving involves two types of thinking (Guilford; Mumford):

- *Divergent Thinking*: Thinking about a problem itself from multiple viewpoints, thus making it possible to generate numerous ways of approaching the problem (Mednick; Reese et al.);
- *Convergent Thinking*: Focusing on only one way of thinking about the problem (that is, *converging* on a view of the problem) and then systematically working out the steps needed for a solution.

Divergent thinking allows people to generate novel—creative—ways of solving a problem, but because an individual can't proceed with all approaches at the same time, convergent thinking helps prioritize and systematize the ideas.

There is no evidence that Hogwarts encourages divergent thinking, except perhaps in Lupin's DADA classes. It's almost as if being able to do magic and living in a magical world have stunted divergent thinking. Hogwarts seems to reinforce this curb on divergent thinking, encouraging students to approach problems in a particular way—the way that the teacher specifies.

Some wizards, such as Mr. Weasley, do value creativity and problem solving: he admires devices we Muggles invent to overcome our limitations. That is, he admires the ingenious, unpredictable solutions we've created to expand beyond our non-magical constraints. In contrast to wizards, we Muggles seem particularly adept at divergent thinking. Whereas Mr. Weasley appreciates these abilities from afar, Voldemort is one of the few characters who seems to possess them in prodigious quantities. He was able to create and develop powers that were not even thought of by other witches and wizards. Voldemort's many talents suggest that he is good at both divergent and convergent thinking.

Except for the Weasley twins, few of Harry's fellow students at Hogwarts who were born in the wizarding world show evidence of creativity and problem-solving ability. One wonders whether Mr. Weasley's fascination with Muggle inventions inspired the twins with their ingenious products. Yet, teachers generally ignore or scold the Weasley twins for experimenting and creating new magical objects such as the Headless Hats (*Order of the Phoenix*).

Are creative problem solvers born or made? Mostly made: such problem-solving ability appears to be primarily due to aspects of the family environment that all children in a family share, such as the number of books in the home and the activities that children are exposed to (Nichols; Simonton). Obviously, children raised in the magical world are exposed to different environments—and thus have different experiences—than those raised in the Muggle world. Are those wizards who are raised in the Muggle world (until age eleven) more creative and better problem solvers? Do the challenges of living in the Muggle world help create individuals who possess more of the qualities integral to effective problem solving? I propose that the answer to these questions is "yes": *this* is what makes Harry and Hermione particularly good at figuring out ways to combat Voldemort and the Death Eaters, and what makes Voldemort the powerful wizard he is.

LEARNED HELPLESSNESS

What must it be like for students graduating from Hogwarts? What must it be like to live in a society where the workings of the world feel truly magical? It's as if the citizens remain toddlers in their understanding of how things work ("If I say this spell, then that will happen"). It comes as no surprise then that when bad things happen, those in the wizarding world don't feel as if they have any control over events. To influence events, they can only use the limited number of existing magical spells and potions available to them from their education; they aren't able to create new ones or to combine what they already know in effective ways. And when they exhaust their repertoire, there's nothing left.

This is what it must have been like in the fight against Voldemort during his reign. Sirius describes those years, explaining that Voldemort could control people, forcing them to do horrible things and leading everyone to be scared for themselves as well as their friends and families: "Every week, news comes of more deaths, more disappearances, more torturing... the Ministry of Magic's in disarray.... Terror everywhere...panic...confusion...that's how it used to be" (*Goblet of Fire* 527).

This sense of powerlessness in the face of negative events can lead to *learned helplessness*—giving up trying to escape from aversive events. In the classic study on learned helplessness (Overmeier & Seligman), a dog was placed into a cage where it received electric shocks through the cage floor. At first the dog tried to escape, but escape was impossible and nothing it did could lessen or stop the shocks; after repeated failed attempts to escape, the dog appeared to give up—it curled up, simply surviving the shocks. When the dog was then put in a cage from which escape was easily possible, it didn't even attempt to leave— it again curled up, as if to wait out the shock.

Humans, too, can be afflicted with learned helplessness during repeated or enduring aversive events over which they have no control, such as chronic abuse. People's expectations of what is possible plummet. Based on Sirius's description of Voldemort's reign, for many wizards that period was akin to the dog's experience in the first cage. Voldemort's evil exploits were like the dog's shocks—inescapable. Though witches and wizards exhausted their repertoire of techniques, nothing could stop Voldemort. So, most non-Auror wizards could only observe the frightening events or become victims. In the years since Voldemort's defeat in his battle with infant Harry, witches and wizards seem to have maintained their learned helplessness. Although the "shocks" stopped, British wizards and witches don't use those shock-free years to find methods of getting out of the cage, should the shocks come again.

To highlight this sense of impotence in the face of negative events, consider these examples:

- When Harry's name pops out of the Goblet of Fire, Dumbledore remarks that even though they don't know how his name could have been submitted, the Ministry and three wizarding schools "*have no choice but to accept it*" (emphasis mine; *Goblet of Fire* 280)—Harry must compete in the games. (Of course, it's possible that, as with breaking an Unbreakable Vow, Harry might die if he doesn't compete, but when *Goblet of Fire* was published, readers didn't know about Unbreakable Vows, and Dumbledore never really explains to the students exactly *why* Harry must compete.)

- When Ron and Hermione find out about what Professor Umbridge has been doing to Harry during his detentions with her, Hermione wants to do something about Umbridge. Ron says, "'[W]hat can we do about [her]?...'S too late, isn't it? She got the job, she's here to stay'" (*Order of the Phoenix* 325).

Yet Harry and many of his classmates who spend their first decade of life growing up in the Muggle world appear less apt to have learned helplessness. Consider Harry's response to Umbridge's punishments: rather than capitulate and give up in the face of her inescapable and sadistic punishments, he views her detentions as a "private battle of wills" (*Order of the Phoenix* 269), which helps him retain a sense of control over events. Similarly, when Harry thinks that Sirius is in danger at the Ministry of Magic, he doesn't throw up his hands, but decides to *act*—to rescue his godfather.

Hermione also does not succumb to learned helplessness in the face of adversity. Contrast Ron's helpless response to Umbridge's sadistic acts to Hermione's response: "[W]e've got to do something about her" (*Order of the Phoenix* 324). Other examples of Hermione's sense of control over her fate—and her perseverance—abound: she makes a batch of Polyjuice Potion so that she, Harry, and Ron can find out whether Draco Malfoy is the heir of Slytherin. And she persists in looking for legal ways to save Buckbeak, the hippogriff, from his death sentence.

WHAT TYPES OF ALUMNI DOES HOGWARTS PRODUCE?

Devoid of the skills that will help them solve novel problems, Hogwarts alumni are unprepared for Voldemort's ascendancy and return. They are not equipped to "try different things"—to experiment with defensive potions, charms, spells, or counter-curses—and they become mired in learned helplessness. In fact, the magical world *needs* witches and wizards like Harry and Hermione—raised in the Muggle world—to invent, to push the boundaries, and ultimately to rescue those raised in the wizarding world from a power that they are helpless to fight. Like Harry and Hermione, wizards born into a Muggle world grow up in an environment more likely to encourage the skills needed for creativity and problem solving: curiosity about magic's underlying mechanisms and knowing how to experiment and invent. Moreover, they are less likely to succumb to the learned helplessness that seems to have pervaded most of the wizarding world.

ROBIN S. ROSENBERG, Ph.D., is a clinical psychologist. She is co-author of *Psychology in Context* and *Fundamentals of Psychology* (introductory psychology textbooks) and *Abnormal Psychology: The Biopsychosocial Approach* (abnormal psychology textbook). She has taught psychology courses at Lesley University and Harvard University. She has a private practice in the Boston area, and is editor of the forthcoming *Psychology of Superheroes* anthology.

REFERENCES

Bok, Derek. *Our Underachieving Colleges.* Princeton, NJ: Princeton University Press, 2006.

Ronald A. Finke, "Imagery, Creativity, and Emergent Structure," *Consciousness & Cognition* 5 (1996): 381–393.

Finke, Ronald A., T. B. Ward, and S. M. Smith. *Creative Cognition: Theory, Research, and Applications.* Cambridge, MA: MIT Press, 1992.

Lion F. Gardiner, "Why We Must Change: The Research Evidence," *The NEA Higher Education Journal* Spring (1998): 71–88.

Guilford, J. P. *The Nature of Human Intelligence.* New York: McGraw-Hill, 1967.

S. G. Isaksen and D. J. Treffinger, "Celebrating 50 Years of Reflective Practice: Versions of Creative Problem Solving," *Journal of Creative Behavior* 38 (2004): 75–101.

Kosslyn, Stephen M. and Robin S. Rosenberg. *Psychology in Context.* Boston, MA: Allyn & Bacon, 2007.

Darrin R. Lehman and Richard E. Nisbett, "A Longitudinal Study of the Effects of Undergraduate Training on Reasoning," *Developmental Psychology* 26 (1990): 952–960.

S. Mednick, "The Associative Basis of the Creative Process," *Psychological Review* 69 (1962): 220–232.

M. D. Mumford, "Something Old, Something New: Revisiting Guilford's Conception of Creative Problem Solving," *Creativity Research Journal* 13 (2001): 267–276.

R. C. Nichols, "Twin Studies of Ability, Personality, and Interests," *Homo* 29 (1978): 158–173.

J. B. Overmeier and Martin E. P. Seligman, "Effects of Inescapable Shock Upon Subsequent Escape and Avoidance Responding," *Journal of Comparative and Physiological Psychology* 63 (1967): 28–33.

Rowling, J. K. *Harry Potter and the Philosopher's Stone*. London: Bloomsbury Publishers, 1997.

———. *Harry Potter and the Chamber of Secrets*. London: Bloomsbury Publishers, 1998.

———. *Harry Potter and the Prisoner of Azkaban*. London: Bloomsbury Publishers, 1999.

———. *Harry Potter and the Goblet of Fire*. New York: Scholastic Inc., 2000.

———. *Harry Potter and the Order of the Phoenix*. New York: Scholastic Inc., 2003.

———. *Harry Potter and the Half-Blood Prince*. New York: Scholastic Inc., 2005.

H. W. Reese, L. J. Lee, S. Cohen, and J. M. Puckett, Jr., "Effects of Intellectual Variables, Age, and Gender on Divergent Thinking in Adulthood," *International Journal of Behavioral Development* 25 (2001): 491–500.

M. A. Runco, "Creativity," *Annual Review of Psychology* 55 (2004): 657–687.

Simonton, D. K. "Creativity, Leadership, and Chance." In R. J. Sternberg (Ed.), *The Nature of Creativity*. New York: Cambridge University Press, 1988. 386–486.

S. W. VanderStoep and J. J. Shaughnessy, "Taking a Course in Research Methods Improves Reasoning about Real-Life Events," *Teaching of Psychology* 24 (1997): 122–124.

T. B. Ward, "Creative Cognition, Conceptual Combination, and the Creative Writing of Stephen R. Donaldson," *American Psychologist* 56 (2001): 350–354.

Engel and Levin beg to differ. Curiosity is not dead at Hogwarts, they argue. What exactly is curiosity? What can we learn about curiosity from studying Harry? And what role does Harry's curiosity play in his efforts to fight Voldemort? Finally, why can't we make our schools more like Hogwarts to really encourage curiosity in all students?

SUSAN ENGEL, Ph.D., AND SAM LEVIN

Harry's Curiosity

Poor HARRY. His curiosity gets him in big trouble. Right from the start, he suffers terribly because he's so interested in answering questions, solving puzzles, and figuring things out. His curiosity causes him endless time locked in a closet, smacks on the head, and other nasty punishments at the hands of the Dursleys: his aunt, uncle, and cousin, who hate him because of his secret past.

Lucky Harry. His curiosity helps him to be smart and appealing, and it launches him on many of his adventures. Right from the start he wants to find things out, and his inquisitiveness leads him on escapades that bring him pleasure, excitement, satisfaction, knowledge, and, in the end, the high regard of all around him.

What is it about Harry and the events, objects, and people around him that make him so curious?

The Harry Potter series tells the story of one child's quest to satisfy his curiosity. Most of the exciting events of the books occur because Harry is trying to figure something out. His curiosity is the invisible backbone to the story, just as it is the invisible backbone to much of children's thinking and behavior. As we watch Harry try to answer questions and solve mysteries, the psychological components of curiosity come to life. Is Harry more curious than other children? If he is, what made him this way? What happens when the Dursleys try to crush it out of him?

Researchers view curiosity as both an internal and stable characteristic (a trait) of a person and also a transitory set of feelings and behaviors caused by specific features of a situation (a state). In other words, Harry is by nature a curious boy, but his environment might make anyone curious. A close look at Harry's curiosity allows us to see what it is about a situation that encourages or discourages inquiry. Finally, Harry's adventures, at home and at school, provide an excellent blueprint for what it would take to create an environment that encourages curiosity.

WHAT IS CURIOSITY?

From the first pages of the first book, Harry is gripped by a powerful urge to find out more. He asks questions, explores the environment around him, closely observes interesting phenomena, and dwells on complex events that he doesn't fully understand. All of these are considered by psychologists to be manifestations of curiosity. But notice that asking questions, venturing into forbidden spaces, and jumping on brooms are all behaviors that express curiosity, while the thoughts and feelings Harry has while lying in his bed are just that—internal experiences. One of the interesting ambiguities of curiosity is that it is both an internal experience and a set of behaviors. Daniel Berlyne, the first psychologist to empirically investigate curiosity, wanted to capture the nexus between the internal feeling, the behaviors that resulted from the feeling, and the features of the environment that elicited both feeling and behavior. His studies, done in the early sixties, showed that when a person encounters surprise, novelty, and complexity, he or she experiences arousal, which leads to exploration. In one of the first experiments involving humans, Berlyne asked subjects long lists of questions about invertebrates and also asked them to rate the questions in terms of how surprising and interesting the questions were. Then subjects were given long lists of randomly ordered answers to those questions. Finally, they were given the original questionnaire a second time. Just as Berlyne predicted, subjects were more able to answer those questions they had rated as surprising or engaging. Berlyne concluded from this that when a subject confronts surprise, he or she is aroused. Getting the answer to a surprising question reduces that arousal. This arousal reduction, which feels good, reinforces the subject's learning of that item. When Harry is asked at Hogwarts to learn about the study of magical plants, the very possibility that plants are magical surprises him. We can predict, based on Berlyne's work, that Harry will learn the information better because the topic is unexpected and novel. Berlyne's work underscores the fact that curiosity is both invisible (an internal feeling) and visible (a behavior).

But of course, not all phenomena are complex or unexpected in the same way. Early in *Harry Potter and the Sorcerer's Stone*, Harry wonders how he got the lightning bolt-shaped scar on his head: "He had had it as long as he could remember, and the first question he could ever remember asking his Aunt Petunia was how he had gotten it" (*Sorcerer's Stone* 20). Harry's curiosity about his scar is a long-term type of curiosity about how something came to be. There is nothing new about the scar, nothing suddenly unexpected. Yet it is unexplained. In this instance, Harry exemplifies developmental psychologist Jerome Kagan's view—that curiosity is the urge to resolve uncertainty. Harry knows that the scar is unusual—no one else has one, people notice his, and he knows it must have been caused by something. He wants to resolve the uncertainty of how he got the scar.

On the other hand, Harry also encounters more specific and momentary kinds of unexplained phenomena. When he travels to Hogwarts for the first time, he is instructed to depart from Platform 9 ¾. Naturally, this defies anything he has experienced or come to expect. Momentary phenomena like this can also elicit curiosity. When he has been rescued by Hagrid, the giant, and wonderful, strange things have begun to happen to Harry, his thoughts turn to inquiry: "Questions exploded inside Harry's head like fireworks and he couldn't decide which to ask first" (*Sorceror's Stone* 52).

The renowned developmental psychologist Jean Piaget described curiosity as the urge to explain incongruity. In other words, children have expectations, what he called "schema," which guide their experiences and behavior. When something happens that doesn't fit a child's schema, he or she wants to find or figure out why. This definition of curiosity helps us understand why babies and toddlers seem so curious so much of the time. They don't have many schemas, nor are their schemas very complex, so they encounter numerous objects and events that don't fit their few simple schemas. This means all kinds of everyday experiences seem incongruous to them and require an "explanation."

Especially during the first book, Harry has some of the wide-eyed wonder we associate with toddlers. Perhaps that is because the world of magic he is introduced to is full of new and incongruous experiences, just as the ordinary world is for Muggle toddlers. In Diagon Alley, Harry sees all kinds of things that violate his expectations: disappearing entrances, magic brooms, stores filled with cauldrons, and very odd-looking people. Everything he encounters there is unfamiliar. Like a toddler, he now constantly has to resolve discrepancies between what he already knows and what he encounters. Nothing he has experienced living at Number Four, Privet Drive has led him to expect that men will dress in long robes with wizard hats, yet here they do. At Privet Drive, animals didn't talk, and sticks could not do magic. From Piaget's perspective, these incongruities should create a state of almost perpetual curiosity and learning.

While all babies encounter novelty almost every day, by the time children are Harry's age, there is less incongruity in their everyday lives, and, perhaps as a result, fewer children over the age of five exhibit curiosity on a regular basis. This may be why some research has shown that curiosity typically wanes between the ages of four and eleven. But unlike other boys of his age, Harry's world is filled with phenomena begging for explanation. If the internal feeling of curiosity is caused by unexplained phenomena or the urge to resolve uncertainty, can we find out what it is about certain environments that elicit or encourage curiosity more than others?

WHAT IN THE WORLD MAKES US CURIOUS?

In the earliest psychological experiments on curiosity, Berlyne showed that more complex problems elicited more curiosity. Since then, psychologists have continued to tease apart and identify the specific features of a situation that are more likely to spark a person's curiosity. In one interesting study, subjects were presented with several items designed to evoke curiosity, such as a small object with windows, lights, and protruding knobs. Some of the children were actively encouraged by the adult to explore the interesting object, while other children were neither encouraged nor discouraged to explore. The researchers measured how long it took kids to come up to the object (or similar item) and investigate it. Children explored the item more quickly when they were encouraged to. When they got no active encouragement, fewer of them approached the object, and those who did took longer. Moreover, the same child would approach the object when encouraged to and hang back when not given active encouragement. In other words, the situation was more powerful than the individual in determining the level of curiosity expressed.

The psychologist Richard Henderson wanted to identify the specific features of an environment that might encourage or discourage a child's display of curiosity. He devised a method that bears just a hint of the kind of invitation to explore that is replete in Harry's world. In Henderson's work, children of various ages were brought into a lab containing a variety of toys and academic materials, including a "curiosity box." This was a small box with a number of drawers on all sides, each of which contained some unusual or novel object. When children entered the lab, Henderson watched to see how quickly they went to explore the box (clearly the most unexpected and complex object in the room). Henderson also counted the number of drawers a child opened, how many of the objects the child removed to examine, and how long he or she spent exploring each of those objects. Taken together, these measures comprised a "curiosity score." Henderson found that while some children opened more drawers and manipulated objects for longer, this was mediated by other factors. For instance, children spent more time on the objects that seemed more exotic and complicated. The younger children in the study were more likely to explore the objects when their parents were present, though both older and younger children were also affected by what their parents actually did and said while in the room. In other words, the children had different levels of curiosity, but they were almost all influenced by various features of the situation.

In one recent study in our lab, we tried a different version of the curiosity box experiment. Instead of bringing the children to the lab, we brought the box to the children's classrooms. In that setting, we learned something new. Previous research had suggested that children's curiosity wanes with age. Given Piaget's definition, it's easy to see why—less incongruity, more familiarity. But the story is not that simple. In our study, when kids were free to approach the box during a regular school day, we found that the older children (nine-year-olds, in this case) were more likely to investigate the box in small peer groups, while five-year-olds tended to approach the box alone. Perhaps what begins as a solitary activity in early childhood becomes a social activity. This is certainly the case for Harry, who, upon arriving at Hogwarts, instantly finds comrades, Ron and Hermione, to join him, willingly and unwillingly, on his adventures.

So, Harry's environment fulfills all the situational requirements for high levels of curiosity. It is filled with uncertainty, violations of expectations, complex phenomena that elicit exploration and cognition, and peers. But in one respect, Harry doesn't, at least at first, get much of what research tells us you need: adults who sanction exploration. He spends his first ten years with a family whose primary goal seems to keep Harry (and everyone else) from finding out their secret. In other words, curiosity is their enemy.

When Harry dreams of a flying motorcycle, he mistakenly tells his uncle, who furiously silences Harry by barking at him, "'MOTORCYCLES DON'T FLY!'" (*Sorcerer's Stone* 25). Indeed, "If there was one thing the Dursleys hated even more than his asking questions, it was his talking about anything acting in a way it shouldn't, no matter if it was in a dream or even a cartoon—they seemed to think he might get dangerous ideas" (*Sorcerer's Stone* 26). The Durselys' worst nightmare is the kind of unexplained phenomena and violated expectations likely to elicit questions and investigations. But Harry is curious even when his curiosity is punished. He doesn't give up wanting to know who his parents are, where they came from, how he got his scar, or what is in the letter that keeps arriving through every hole in his aunt and uncle's house. Is Harry more curious than other kids? If so, why?

IS CURIOSITY A TRAIT?

The answer is yes, and we shouldn't be surprised. A substantial number of studies have shown that there are measurable and fairly stable individual differences in children's levels of curiosity. While environments are more or less conducive to curiosity, some children are also more likely to investigate the world around them, ask questions, and persist in the absence of encouragement than others. Carole Dweck coined the term "need for cognition" to capture the urge to mentally work on something (a question, a puzzle, a topic of thought). When children are presented with complex objects or mental problems, they have the opportunity for greater cognitive activity. Dweck and her colleagues have shown that some children are more likely to choose the challenging puzzle or to stay with a mentally engaging task longer than others, because they have a "need for cognition." Harry clearly has a great need for cognition. He continues to think about puzzles and mysteries long after he goes to bed, is not dissuaded easily by obstacles, and is drawn toward mental challenges.

A wide range of studies have shown that some people are more curious than others, and some of these studies have even tried to explain *why* there might be individual differences of this kind. For instance, Robert Saxe and Gary Stollak observed first-grade boys with their mothers in a playroom. Observers, trained to look for signs of curiosity, found that some of the boys investigated novel objects in the playroom more than others. These same boys tended to be more pro-social than non-curious boys. But even more interesting, the curious pro-social boys were more likely to have mothers who showed positive feelings toward them, restricted them less, and paid them more attention. Other research has demonstrated a link between the strength of mother-child attachment and the child's tendency to explore his or her environment. Harry certainly illustrates part of this construct—he makes friends easily, others like him, and he is concerned for and loyal to his friends. But his mother is dead, so the findings on the importance of the mother's attention and parent-child attachment don't easily apply to Harry. On the other hand, when Harry looks into the Mirror of Erised at Hogwarts, he sees an adoring and warm mother—our impression of her is that she is open-minded and intelligent. Perhaps, in the magical world of Harry Potter, his mother can support his curiosity without even being alive. While there is clear evidence of individual differences in levels of curiosity, it also seems to be the case that people have somewhat different kinds of curiosity.

According to Berlyne, there are two kinds of curiosity, diversive and specific. Diversive curiosity refers to a general itch to find out more, a constant need to ask questions, open lids, take things apart, watch what's going on. One might think that this describes Harry, because he seems interested in everything around him so much of the time. When Hagrid and Harry are school shopping in Diagon Alley, a place filled with strange sights and sounds, Harry seems almost distracted by his curiosity: "Harry wished he had about eight more eyes. He turned his head in every direction as they walked up the street, trying to look at everything at once: the shops, the things outside them, the people doing their shopping" (*Sorcerer's Stone* 71). But Harry does not really exemplify diversive curiosity. Over the years, psychologists have come to think of this type of curiosity as being somewhat aimless and at times actually interfering with more focused learning and investigating. When one looks more closely at Harry, it seems clear that he is better described by the second type, specific curiosity. This refers to the urge to find out more about a particular object, event, or domain. Often this kind of curiosity leads to more sustained, focused search and exploration than the diversive kind. The ultimate specific curiosity is the kind displayed by scientists who doggedly pursue a question for years, often thinking of more questions the more they know about something. In Book Six, Harry accidentally hears a conversation that he was never supposed to hear. But the conversation is missing one word, a word that Harry is sure is the key to something important about the evil Voldemort. This missing word drives Harry crazy. In searching for the missing word, Harry encounters real dangers, and ultimately the search causes Dumbledore's death. But he doesn't give up until he discovers the word ("Horcruxes"), which indeed offers him the way to defeat Voldemort. Harry is capable of sustained search and inquiry, in the face of discouragement, obstacles, and even risk to himself.

Because specific curiosity is so important to a wide range of intellectual endeavors, it is of great interest to developmental psychologists and educators. Why are some children more likely to pursue their investigations over time, until they really get some answers, know more about a topic, or fully understand the complex or unexplained phenomena they first became interested in? What makes someone more likely to experience specific curiosity? Researchers have begun to find some answers.

While one person might seem generally more curious than another (e.g., have more of a curiosity trait), even a very inquisitive person is going to be more interested in some phenomena than others. Harry is certainly more interested in finding out about his past than learning the history of magic remedies, a topic that holds great interest for Hermione. While this may seem obvious, it has only recently been documented by researchers, and the implications are quite important. Suzanne Hidi and her colleagues wanted to test the idea that children are more curious about things they already have an interest in. The researchers presented toddlers with a range of toys and objects to play with and explore. Some toddlers were offered an object or toy toward which they had been neutral in prior encounters, and some were offered a toy that had previously interested them and to which they had shown a preference. The researchers measured the length of time the toddler spent looking at, manipulating, and playing with the toy and also identified the kinds of things the child did to explore and use the toy. They found that children not only play more with a toy they are interested in but, more importantly, use a wider variety of actions on the toy. In other words, when children have a prior interest in an event or an object, they have more curiosity about it and pursue that curiosity more actively (Krapp, Hidi, & Renninger; Hidi). A child who collects rocks, stores up information about them, notices a new rock, and wants to handle it, look at it, and compare it to the ones he or she already has, is likely, according to this research, to show more curiosity about a rock than other objects he or she might be offered. Learning this has presented researchers with a challenge. Imagine you set out to find out, for instance, if there are gender differences in curiosity (is Harry more or less likely to be curious than Hermione?). As a good scientist, you would want to hold everything but their gender constant—each child would be taken to the same lab, given the same instructions, engage in the same kind of activity (investigating a box, for instance), and so forth. But if in fact it is true that a person's curiosity fluctuates as a function of his or her prior interest in the domain or topic, how can you hold the conditions of the experiment constant from one subject to another? Harry will seem very curious if offered a chance to learn more about Quidditch, whereas if Hermione is offered a flying broom she may seem bored and disinterested. But offer her a book on the history of spells and she's likely to ask many questions, read at great length, and pursue her ideas beyond the classroom.

If it is essential to consider a person's specific interests when measuring curiosity, think how vital it is to consider a student's specific interests when trying to get him or her curious enough to want to learn. Children need access to the things and questions that grab their attention if they are to experience curiosity and the good kinds of cognition it leads to. Though research has shown that children's curiosity is more sustained and intense when they are offered things that interest them, this fact is rarely taken into account when schools design curricula. But that is not so at Hogwarts, where Harry (not to mention Hermione and others) finds so much of interest. What is Hogwarts doing right that other schools do wrong?

CURIOSITY IN SCHOOLS

Ever since Plato, those interested in the development of knowledge have assumed that curiosity is a *sine qua non* of the informed mind. Though scant attention has been paid to the development of curiosity, the slender trail of modern work on the topic can be traced back to John Dewey, who argued at the turn of the twentieth century that it was impossible to educate children if their curiosity and interest were not engaged (Dewey). Oddly, educators, who perhaps have the most to gain from understanding curiosity, have not done all that much to find out about it. While many teachers endorse the goal of instilling a love of learning, this is not typically the quality taken as a concrete measure of a school or teacher's success. At the end of a year, students' math ability is more likely to be measured than their curiosity. In one study, teachers were asked to name the five most important qualities they wanted to encourage or develop in their students. Virtually none of these teachers mentioned curiosity. Yet when teachers (including those who named the five qualities) were asked to circle five qualities from a list of twenty, a majority circled curiosity. In other words, teachers passively endorse the quality, but it is not something they actively think about or focus on.

Do most teachers even know whether the children in their classroom are more or less curious than they were at the beginning of the year? The answer is no. In fact, few teachers could offer a concrete definition of what curiosity is or how it manifests itself in classroom settings. One study asked teachers to identify their most curious students. The researchers also measured the students' IQ and their level of curiosity. The results showed that while teachers readily identify those students who seem more curious, what they really are noticing is a child's intelligence. They seem unable to recognize a child's urge to explore and find out, even though research has shown that such an urge is not the same as a child's IQ.

It's even possible that many adults, without knowing it, fear a child's curiosity, much as the Dursleys fear Harry's: "*Don't ask questions*—that was the first rule for a quiet life with the Dursleys" (*Sorcerer's Stone* 20). The Dursleys are terrified of Harry's questions because they are worried he might learn the truth about his parents and his own magical capabilities. The Dursleys are the opposite of Harry. The story begins with their worry that the secret truth about Harry's past will be found out. This leads them to hate questions and open-ended thinking of any kind. But the Dursleys are not the first adults to dread a child's inquisitiveness. Many parents and teachers find children's questions to be overwhelming, rude, tiresome, and, in some cases, worrisome or aggravating. While parents and teachers often answer their children's questions and seem delighted by a child's interest in a topic, it's just as often the case that adults discourage inquiry, even when they don't realize they are doing so. Teachers, who, it might seem, should be the guardian angels of a child's curiosity, rarely encourage inquiry, especially if such inquiry appears to interfere with lesson plans. In one study, researchers recorded all of the exchanges occurring between teachers and their students during a typical school day. The data show that teachers are often resistant to what are called *unscripted questions*. When children asked unexpected questions during lessons, teachers responded by promising to answer later, redirecting the child to focus on the task at hand, or remonstrating with the child for straying from the topic. This was true even when the children's questions were relevant to the lesson topic.

In another sobering study, the developmental psychologists Tizard and Hughes were interested in the kinds of questions toddlers and preschoolers ask the adults in their lives. They found that children asked their mothers and fathers a lot of questions while at home, but that when these same children entered preschool the next year, they stopped asking almost any questions at all. It may be that school is both the perfect place to learn and the worst place to inquire.

This is disconcerting, to say the least, since there is no question that encouraging curiosity at school has concrete benefits. Earlier I described one of the first experiments on curiosity, in which Daniel Berlyne showed that when people's curiosity is aroused they are more likely to remember the information that satisfies that curiosity. In a wonderful demonstration of this with school children, researchers put fifth- and sixth-grade children into small groups to learn about a topic in social studies. Some of the groups were guided to work cooperatively on the task, while others were given the same topic but in such a way that controversy and argument were built into both the material and the instructions. The children in the controversy condition learned the material better and were more likely, a week later, to choose to skip a free period in order to watch a film on the same topic.

From the beginning, children at Hogwarts are learning things that are not only surprising and uncertain, but relevant to them. Kids want to learn what Hogwarts has to offer. And though no teachers explicitly encourage the adventures Harry and his friends go on, there are many instances in which professors implicitly support Harry. At the very end of the first book, Dumbledore invites Harry to ask him any questions he wants to (though he warns that there will be some questions he cannot answer). In addition, the physical school seems built for adventures, with its rambling hallways, unpredictable portals, and endless array of mysterious events just inviting exploration. Hogwarts offers its students materials designed to intrigue and mystify. Compare, for instance, the books required by most schools we are familiar with to the books Hogwarts requires its students to buy: *The Standard Book of Spells, A History of Magic, Magical Theory, A Beginner's Guide to Transfiguration, One Thousand Magical Herbs and Fungi, Magical Drafts and Potions, Fantastic Beasts and Where to Find Them, The Dark Forces: A Guide to Self-Protection.* These certainly seem to promise more complexity, incongruity, and uncertainty than your typical middle school materials.

Kids want to learn what Hogwarts has to teach. Harry overhears Hermione talking to Percy Weasley during the first days at Hogwarts: "'I *do* hope they start right away, there's so much to learn. I'm particularly interested in Transfigurations, you know, turning something into something else, of course, it's supposed to be very difficult...'" (*Sorcerer's Stone* 125). Research has shown us that when kids are motivated by curiosity to learn, they learn well. Moreover, when curiosity is condoned, it is more likely to be expressed. At Hogwarts, unlike many schools, curiosity is rewarded. Almost all of Harry's investigations bring him honor, satisfaction, and the admiration of others.

Hogwarts is a model school. So, while children read Harry Potter because they are curious to find out what happens, adults should read Harry Potter to find out how to make schools where curiosity is nurtured and children can learn easily and happily. The hidden treasure in the Harry Potter books is the picture they offer us of what a really good school should look like.

SUSAN ENGEL, PH.D., earned a B.A. from Sarah Lawrence College in 1980 and a Ph.D. in developmental psychology from CUNY Graduate Center in 1985. She is currently a senior lecturer in psychology and director of the Program in Teaching at Williams College. Engel has taught students from age three to adults. In addition to journal articles and book chapters, Engel has written three books: *The Stories Children Tell: Making Sense of the Narratives of Childhood* (W. H. Freeman 1985), *Context is Everything: The Nature of Memory* (W. H. Freeman 1997), and, most recently, *Real Kids: Creating Meaning in Everyday Life* (Harvard University Press 2005). She is also the co-founder and educational advisor to an experimental school in eastern Long Island, The Hayground School. Engel's research interests include the development of autobiographical memory, narrative processes in childhood, imagination and play in childhood, and the development of curiosity. She lives with her husband and three sons in New Marlborough, Massachusetts.

SAM LEVIN is a student who attends school in rural Massachusetts. His own curiosity has led him to an extensive year-long study of one small pond and all that lives near and within it.

REFERENCES

Berlyne, Daniel. *Conflict, Arousal, and Curiosity*. New York: McGraw Hill, 1960.

John Coie, "An Evaluation of the Cross-Situational Stability of Children's Curiosity," *Journal of Personality* 42 (1974): 93–116.

Dewey, John. *Interest and Effort in Education*. New York: Houghton Mifflin, 1913.

Dai, David Yun and Robert J. Sternberg. *Motivation, Emotion, and Cognition: Integrative Perspectives on Intellectual Functioning and Development*. Mahwah, NJ: Lawrence Erlbaum Associates, Publishers, 2004.

Bruce Henderson, "Parents and Exploration: The Effect of Context on Individual Differences in Exploratory Behavior," *Child Development* 55 (1984): 1237–1245.

Bruce Henderson and Shirley G. Moore, "Measuring Exploratory Behavior in Young Children: A Factor Analytic Study," *Developmental Psychology* 15 (1979): 113–119.

Suzanne Hidi, "Interest and its Contribution as a Mental Resource for Learning," *Review of Educational Research* 60(4) (1990): 549–571.

Nancy Lowry and David W. Johnson, "Effects of Controversy on Epistemic Curiosity, Achievement, and Attitudes," *Journal of Social Psychology* 115 (1981): 31–43.

Renninger, K. Ann, Suzanne Hidi, and Andreas Krapp. *The Role of Interest in Learning and Development*. New Jersey: LEA Press, 1992.

Robert Saxe and Gary Stollack, "Curiosity and the Parent-Child Relationship," *Child Development* 42(2) (1971): 373–384.

Tizard, Barbara and Martin Hughes. *Young Children Learning*. Cambridge, MA: Harvard University Press, 1984.

Do Gryffindors hate Slytherins because of who they are, or because of the school environment? The persistent conflict between these houses goes back to the founding of Hogwarts many years ago. Even the teachers appear to participate in these ancient rivalries. Is this an accident, or has Hogwarts been defined to create just such animosities? Beers and Apple suggest that it has, and point to classic and contemporary research findings in the area of social psychology to show how it could be done.

MELISSA J. BEERS, Ph.D.,
AND KEVIN J. APPLE, Ph.D.

Intergroup Conflict in the World of Harry Potter

For MANY OF US, the groups to which we belong define who we are. For Harry Potter, being a student at Hogwarts and belonging to Gryffindor House are arguably the most important things in his life. However, even the most casual reader of the books has noticed that groups are also the source of the greatest conflicts in Harry's world, particularly at Hogwarts School of Witchcraft and Wizardry. In many ways, Hogwarts seems to be a "perfect storm" in terms of intergroup tension. Knowingly or not, the school administrators have created and reinforced a structure that has all the necessary ingredients to brew some potent intergroup conflict.

Groups are important and provide us with innumerable benefits. For example, becoming a Gryffindor and joining the Quidditch team add more to Harry's life than just labels or new friends. These group memberships change the way Harry defines himself, and for Harry—like the rest of us—group memberships are an important source of self-esteem. Still, there are consequences in identifying with one group over another, as clearly seen at Hogwarts School.

INTERGROUP CONFLICTS CAN ARISE QUICKLY: THE MINIMAL GROUP PARADIGM

Research on social identity theory has found that once people are divided into groups—even randomly divided by the toss of a coin—they start to show remarkable favoritism to their own group members. In a classic study, Henri Tajfel (1970) researched how schoolboys would divide rewards among others. First, boys were divided into groups by guessing how many dots flashed on a screen. Once they all guessed, the researchers told each boy whether he overestimated or underestimated the number of dots and assigned him to one of the groups on the basis of his guess. In reality, though, the boys were randomly assigned to one group or another; their guesses were not used to create the groups. One might think that the reason for creating the groups would have little impact on how the boys subsequently treated one another, but surprisingly, it actually had a very clear impact on their behavior. Even though their assignment to groups was based on a seemingly trivial issue—whether they overestimated or underestimated the number of dots on the screen—once separated into groups, the boys tended to favor other members of their own group. That is, when allocating rewards between the two groups, overestimators favored other overestimators, and underestimators favored other underestimators, even when the boys who were making decisions knew nothing else about the others in their groups.

Social psychologists use techniques like this one to help isolate and identify why groups have such a powerful influence. By randomly assigning people to arbitrary groups, researchers can examine the effects of simply being a part of the group, independent of other qualities, characteristics, or experiences group members may have in common. This technique is called the minimal group paradigm, because the groups are formed on a minimal or trivial basis. Tajfel's idea for studying minimal groups likely resulted from his own experiences as a soldier during World War II. During the war, he was struck by how important group identity was. Tajfel was fighting for the French army when he was captured by the Germans. While a prisoner of war, Tajfel hid his group identity as a Jew. Because his captors never knew he was Jewish, he survived the war. When he returned home he discovered that his family and friends were killed for no other reason than their social identities—as members of the group "Jews." Perhaps because he saw people being brutalized for their group memberships during World War II, Tajfel wanted to investigate the minimal conditions necessary for people to discriminate against each other. Through a series of clever experiments such as the one described above, Tajfel discovered that simply being placed in laboratory-contrived groups was enough to cause strangers, as well as children who used to be friends, to discriminate against each other.

Of course, intergroup tensions are only increased when group members utilize stereotypes. Stereotypes are overgeneralizations, or beliefs that every member of a group shares similar characteristics. For example, to describe someone as a professor conjures up certain assumptions about that person. We may assume, without knowing anything at all about the person, that the person is intelligent, introspective, and probably not very athletic. We might also assume that person to be male. Sometimes, those expectations may be correct. However, more often than not, stereotypic overgeneralizations lead us to incorrect conclusions about people based on their group memberships. Stereotypes act as a filter or screen, biasing the information we notice and distorting our interpretation of another's behavior (Darley & Gross; Dunning & Sherman; Stone, Perry, & Darley).

INTERGROUP CONTACT: A SOLUTION?

Gordon Allport (1954) argued that increasing direct contact between conflicting groups was a critical factor in eliminating stereotypes, prejudice, and discrimination—an idea known as the *contact hypothesis*. Allport's paper coincided with efforts to desegregate American schools on the basis of race, and based on the original contact hypothesis many school districts began bussing children of different racial and ethnic backgrounds to their schools. The reason for the bussing was to increase contact between members of different groups, because politicians and school administrators believed increasing contact would decrease discriminatory behavior. Unfortunately, there is no evidence to suggest that the original contact hypothesis was effective in reducing intergroup bias, and in fact it had counterproductive results in efforts to desegregate schools—prejudice actually increased (Stephan). Since then, research has determined that contact will only reduce intergroup bias under some specific conditions. First, groups must be of equal status and must receive the same treatment. Second, the groups must cooperate, and mutual interdependence and a common goal help foster cooperation. Contact should occur between multiple members of different groups on an informal basis. And lastly, efforts to increase contact should have institutional support—that is, all school administrators and professors must be "on the same page" and support rather than undermine the process (Aronson, Wilson, & Akert).

A study highlighting the importance of intergroup contact was conducted by social psychologist Muzafer Sherif at a summer camp for boys in the 1950s. The researchers divided the boys into two groups and managed to create a great deal of intergroup hostility very quickly by arranging a tournament—a series of competitions involving football and baseball games, tug-of-war, a tent-pitching contest, and a treasure hunt. The boys could earn trophies, prizes, and medals. Boys at this camp were sorted into groups randomly and were kept segregated in two different regions of the camp. They chose names and symbols that represented their group (coincidentally, the "Rattlers" and the "Eagles"), and the symbols were emblazoned on flags and caps. As a result of categorizing the campers into groups and encouraging competition between them, great distrust and hostility developed quickly between the groups. Members of the different groups teased and fought with each other; one group burned the other's camp flag, and a heated food fight was waged in the dining hall. Even if children had been friends before camp began, group membership seemed to take precedence over past friendships.

To reduce the conflict, Sherif and his colleagues introduced superordinate goals that required the campers to work together and ignore group distinctions in order to be successful. For example, when the campers were returning from a trip, their bus broke down (an event staged by the researchers). All of the campers, regardless of group, had to work together to push and pull the bus back to their campground.

Another goal was introduced when researchers staged a problem with the camp's water supply and campers had to work together to restore their access to water. Although the researchers had tried no fewer than seven intergroup contact situations, only when superordinate goals were introduced did the intergroup conflict begin to lessen. By the end of camp, true friendships formed across group lines (Sherif, Harvey, White, Hood, & Sherif; Sherif).

HOGWARTS: A STUDY IN MAXIMIZING INTERGROUP TENSION

Considering the classic research studies described above, if one wished to create an environment that would maximize intergroup conflict it would likely have a few distinct characteristics. First, individuals would be assigned to groups based on distinctive group characteristics. Second, group membership would be made as obvious as possible through team symbols, colors, or uniforms. Third, inequality among groups would be emphasized by showing favoritism to one group over another. Finally, intergroup contact would be limited as much as possible, and when it does occur, the situation should be competitive—not cooperative. This scenario bears an uncanny resemblance to Hogwarts School.

1. *Groups are created based on distinctive characteristics.* The children at Hogwarts are placed in groups with a strong history, and each group is unambiguously associated with specific stereotypes. In our society, we are all aware that stereotypes of different groups exist. However, with practice and motivation we are able to suppress stereotypes and make accurate, individualized judgments about others (Fiske). At Hogwarts, however, students and staff alike seem to have difficulty suppressing the stereotypes about the different Houses, and they have little motivation to do so.

Early on, Harry learns that each House has rather distinctive characteristics, and some groups instantly seem more desirable than others. Once at the school, students are "sorted" into one of the four Houses by a magical hat that can supposedly discern the best-fitting House for the student's personality. Indeed, Harry's first experience at Hogwarts is the Sorting Ceremony. At that ceremony, the Sorting Hat introduces the characteristics associated with each House: bravery for Gryffindor, loyalty for Hufflepuff, intelligence for Ravenclaw, and cunning for Slytherin. The Sorting Ceremony also clearly illustrates the importance of social identity. Harry desperately wants to be part of a group, so his greatest fear at the Sorting is not being chosen for *a* group at all. Ultimately, the Hat chooses Gryffindor for Harry, to his great relief. Almost immediately after his Sorting, Harry is drawn to his in-group members and begins to see the out-group members—particularly the negatively characterized Slytherins—as sharing common characteristics: "Perhaps it was Harry's imagination, after all he'd heard about Slytherin, but he thought they looked like an unpleasant lot" (*Harry Potter and the Sorcerer's Stone* 119).

Given the biasing properties of stereotypes, in such an environment students' expectations will certainly influence their perception of the students in the other Houses. When we assume that group members all share the same characteristics, it often leads us to think "they are all the same." That is, applying stereotypes to every member of a particular group may lead to the conclusion that members of a group are more similar than they actually are. This is a phenomenon known as *out-group homogeneity* (Linville & Jones). We tend to overestimate how similar other groups are compared to our own groups. Moreover, we tend to make more extreme or polarized judgments about out-group members. For example, the Dursleys believe that all wizards are the same. For them, the wizarding community is an out-group, and thus they do not attempt to understand the individual differences that exist among wizards—they are all assumed to be strange and bad. The Dursleys don't appreciate the complexity of the group, and they tend to make extreme or polarized judgments of the witches and wizards who do cross their path. Thus they maintain their beliefs that wizards are strange and magic is bad. To them, there is likely little difference among wizards such as Professor Dumbledore, Ron Weasley, Draco and Lucius Malfoy, Sirius Black, or Lord Voldemort. But to a person who has more individual experience with these characters, the differences among them are unmistakable.

Our increased experience with many members from our own groups helps us to recognize differences among our in-group members. For example, regarding the students in Gryffindor House, there are many subtle differences among them. Hermione is studious, Ron is fun-loving, Neville Longbottom is clumsy and forgetful, Colin

Creevey is diminutive, and Lavender Brown is giggly. They are certainly not all the same, and they aren't always in total agreement with one another, either. Are we to think that Slytherin, Ravenclaw, or Hufflepuff students don't also possess many differences among them? Relatively speaking, we tend to have little or no contact with people who don't belong to any of our groups, so such misperceptions are hard to dispel.

2. *Group membership is made obvious.* At Hogwarts, one's group membership is impossible to miss. Students in the four Houses live in a segregated environment: they live together in separate dormitories; they are required to eat meals and take classes with other students in their own groups; their robes bear distinctive crests in their House colors. In almost every aspect of school life, group distinctions are made clear. If children are willing to discriminate against their friends under minimal conditions, it is not surprising that Hogwarts students perceive and treat each other differently based on their House memberships.

3. *Favoritism and inequality between the groups are prevalent.* At Hogwarts, students are clearly subject to differential treatment on the basis of their group membership. For example, professors and prefects can award points for good behavior or good performance in class, but they can also deduct points as punishment. In their first year, Gryffindor and Slytherin students share Potions class under the direction of Professor Snape, head of Slytherin House. From Harry's perspective, Snape exhibits in-group favoritism. In class, Snape levels criticism after criticism at the Gryffindors. He unfairly deducts House points from Gryffindor while awarding points to Slytherin. Similarly, Professor McGonagall, head of Gryffindor, smuggles Harry a Nimbus 2000 when she sees evidence of his natural potential for Quidditch. Indeed, students in Hufflepuff, Ravenclaw, and Slytherin could argue that Headmaster Dumbledore shows favoritism toward Gryffindor House (Dumbledore's own House as a student) by awarding them just enough points to beat Slytherin for the "House cup" at the end of Harry's first year. Such preferential—perhaps even prejudicial—treatment seems pervasive and unchecked.

4. *Groups compete in a variety of contexts.* Unmistakably, the system of Houses at Hogwarts has created a competitive environment. Opportunities for group contact increase, rather than decrease, ten-

sion and conflict. Almost all intergroup contact is competitive in nature. In classes and in sports, the Houses compete for the annual House cup; indeed, it is not to any group's advantage to cooperate. Houses accrue points throughout the year, and the score is kept in the Great Hall by giant hourglasses bearing each House's colors (yet another mechanism making group distinctions obvious). Quidditch competitions also continuously reinforce social identity and polarize the groups. Indeed, most of Hogwarts's administrative policies seem to be based on separating the students instead of integrating them.

A HOUSE DIVIDED: SPECULATION ABOUT HOGWARTS'S DESIGN

Objectively, the school structure at Hogwarts does little to embrace diversity or encourage positive intergroup contact. This begs the question, why have school administrators chosen this path? The system of Houses was established by the school's four founders (each House bears a founder's name), but over the years school staff perpetuate and augment the problems inherent in such a design.

A flaw in the system that becomes evident in hindsight is that heads of Houses come from the Houses themselves. Perhaps this choice was well-intentioned, and the founders hoped that leaders selected from within each House would best be able to reflect the qualities valued by that founder. However, the resulting effect is that the school can be described as having a *silo* structure—a particular kind of management structure that prevents effective exchange of information between units. At Hogwarts, flow of information and resources among the Houses is limited, at best, and usually takes place in the form of hearsay and gossip.

Another possibility may be that the school design was purposefully chosen by the founders to increase competition. Perhaps they believed that the competitive environment would benefit students' training. Competition, after all, can be a great motivator to improve oneself. The founders may have literally pitted the students against each other to help motivate all of them to maximize their potential, not realizing that they were actually making the school vulnerable to a threat from inside its own doors.

Another alternative may be that Hogwarts was founded on an uneasy truce among the four founders. The founders may have had different goals and preferences in terms of the environment they thought provided students with the best training, but each knew that on their own they were unlikely to successfully build their own schools. Thus, although they were willing to cooperate to a certain extent, they preferred to keep their own students segregated and, in effect, isolated from opposing viewpoints. It is no secret that, for example, Godric Gryffindor and Salazar Slytherin had starkly different views on the training of pure-blood wizards. Indeed, Slytherin ostensibly left Hogwarts after a heated disagreement with Godric Gryffindor over the school's liberal admissions policies. A more sinister possibility is that one (or more) of Hogwarts's founders did not want their school to succeed; they may have ultimately wanted Hogwarts to fall apart into separate schools. Creating an environment in which the Houses do not get along may have been part of an overarching plan designed to cause the school to split into smaller schools. This plan may also explain why Salazar Slytherin left the Basilisk in the Chamber of Secrets. Slytherin knew that the monster had the capacity to destroy Hogwarts. If Hogwarts was destroyed, Slytherin (or his disciples) would be able to create a school focused on his principles—a school probably intended for *pure-blood* wizards only.

Lastly, a final speculation is that perhaps Hogwarts's design was purposefully flawed by Salazar Slytherin to create an opportunity for Voldemort, his heir, to gain power. Perhaps he had some foresight that led him to anticipate Voldemort's rise to power. Could the creation of a divisive atmosphere at Hogwarts have been a strategy intended to weaken the wizarding community, overall? With Voldemort's return and Dumbledore's death, there seems to be little unifying the wizarding world—except, potentially, Harry Potter.

OPPORTUNITIES FOR CHANGE?

At the start of Harry's fifth year, the Sorting Hat attempts to bring the school together with the superordinate goal of defeating Voldemort. This year, the Hat warns students that unity is more important than differentiation between the Houses. Unfortunately, the Hat's plea is not successful in inducing a superordinate goal, as evidenced by Harry's reaction: "'And it wants all the Houses to be friends?' said Harry, looking over at the Slytherin table, where Draco Malfoy was holding court. 'Fat chance'" (*Harry Potter and the Order of the Phoenix* 209).

If the school does survive the imminent threat posed by Voldemort, several changes will be necessary to prevent intergroup conflict from reemerging. First, the school should eliminate the group-based competitive situations that have fueled past tensions. For example, perhaps Quidditch teams could be intramural instead of House-based. Heads of Houses could be rotated so that they do not always represent their own House. Teachers could also facilitate more positive intergroup contact by modifying their instructional styles. If the Hogwarts faculty creates more opportunities for cooperative learning, it could introduce superordinate goals and the contact between the students could be more positive and productive.

IN CONCLUSION

Reading the Harry Potter books is a magical experience. Harry's experiences resonate with readers from many different backgrounds. One important element in the books' appeal is the realistic portrayal of the psychological impact of groups and group conflict. We are all social beings; we have all experienced the sense of belonging to a group as well as the stress that can accompany group conflict. J. K. Rowling's writing eloquently and effectively conveys the importance of groups to her characters and the power groups hold in their lives. By examining these issues from a social psychological perspective, we can better understand the characters in Harry Potter's world—and perhaps ourselves as well.

ACKNOWLEDGMENTS

The authors wish to thank Megan J. Bulloch for her insightful comments on an earlier version of this essay.

MELISSA J. BEERS, Ph.D., is senior lecturer and Psychology 100 Program Director at Ohio State University, where she teaches several courses, including introductory social psychology, statistics, and the teaching of psychology. She is also vice president of the Strategic Research Group (SRG), a research and consulting firm based in Columbus, Ohio, as well as a wife and a very proud mother of a three-year-old son. She received her Ph.D. in experimental social psychology from Ohio University. Had she been privileged to attend Hogwarts, she would have hoped to be sorted into Ravenclaw.

KEVIN J. APPLE, Ph.D., is an assistant department head and associate professor at the department of psychology at James Madison University. He enjoys teaching a wide variety of classes, including general psychology, research methods, and the psychology of the Holocaust. His main research interests include both the intergroup bias and methods for assessing classroom learning. When not teaching classes or doing research, he is most likely reading a Harry Potter book or spending time with his wife and two children. If he had attended Hogwarts, he would have likely been sorted into Hufflepuff, but his co-author thinks he is Gryffindor material.

REFERENCES

Allport, G. W. *The Nature of Prejudice*. Reading, MA: Addison-Wesley, 1954.

Aronson, E., R. M. Akert, and T. D. Wilson. *Social Psychology*, 5th Edition. New York: Prentice Hall, 2005.

J. M. Darley and P. H. Gross, "A Hypothesis-Confirming Bias in Labeling Effects," *Journal of Personality and Social Psychology* 44 (1983): 20–33.

D. Dunning and D. A. Sherman, "Stereotypes and Tacit Inference," *Journal of Personality and Social Psychology* 73 (1997): 459–471.

Fiske, S. T. "Interdependence and the Reduction of Prejudice." In S. Oskamp (Ed.), *Reducing Prejudice and Discrimination*. Mahwah, NJ: Lawrence Erlbaum Associated, Publishers, 2000. 115–135.

D. T. Gilbert and J. G. Hixon, "The Trouble of Thinking: Activation and Applications of Stereotypical Beliefs," *Journal of Personality and Social Psychology* 60 (1991): 509–517.

P. W. Linville and E. D. Jones, "Polarized Appraisals of Out-Group Members," *Journal of Personality and Social Psychology* 38 (1980): 689–703.

Rowling, J. K. *Harry Potter and the Sorcerer's Stone.* New York: Scholastic Inc., 1998.

——. *Harry Potter and the Order of the Phoenix.* New York: Scholastic Inc., 2003.

Sherif, M. *In Common Predicament: Social Psychology of Intergroup Conflict and Cooperation.* Boston: Houghton Mifflin, 1966.

Sherif, M., O. J. Harvey, J. White, W. Hood, and C. W. Sherif. *Intergroup Conflict and Cooperation: The Robber's Cave Experiment.* Norman: University of Oklahoma, Institute of Intergroup Relations, 1961.

Stephan, W. G. "Intergroup Relations." In G. Lindzey and E. Aronson (Eds.), *The Handbook of Social Psychology* (3rd ed., Vol. 2). New York: McGraw-Hill, 1985. 599–658.

W. G. Stephan, "School Desegregation: An Evaluation of Predictions Made in *Brown v. Board of Education*," *Psychological Bulletin* 85 (1978): 217–238.

J. Stone, Z. Perry, and J. Darley, "'White Men Can't Jump': Evidence for Perceptual Confirmation of Racial Stereotypes Following a Basketball Game," *Basic and Applied Social Psychology* 19 (1997): 291–306.

H. Tajfel, "Experiments in Intergroup Discrimination," *Scientific American* 223 (1970): 96–102.

Tajfel, H. and J. C. Turner. "The Social Identity Theory of Intergroup Behavior." In S. Worchel and W. Austin (Eds.), *Psychology of Intergroup Relations.* Chicago: Nelson-Hall Publishers, 1986. 7–24.

What should Harry, Hermione, and Ron do when they grow up? If they figure it out, Kerewsky and Geiken suggest, it won't be any thanks to Hogwarts. The authors take issue with career counseling at Hogwarts, suggesting that a brief interview about careers in the second-to-last year of school at Hogwarts is just not enough. They suggest how career counseling from our Muggle world could be easily adapted to the wizarding world at Hogwarts.

SHOSHANA D. KEREWSKY, Psy.D.,
AND LISSA JOY GEIKEN, M.Ed.

"Have You Got What It Takes to Train Security Trolls?"

Career Counseling for Wizards

CAREER COUNSELING AT HOGWARTS: AN UNDEVELOPED RESOURCE

Congratulations! You are the first witch or wizard born to your otherwise-Muggle family. You received your admissions letter from Hogwarts, your parents nervously but gamely took you cauldron shopping in Diagon Alley, and you followed the kids from magical families through the wall to Platform 9¾. Chances are that when you've gone home for the holidays, you've had a hard time explaining what you're learning to your proud but clueless parents. When your uncle asks what you're planning to do with your fancy degree from your expensive, special school, your parents, ignorant of magical careers, might reply, "Oh, there are loads of magical jobs," or, "Be a magician." Your unconvinced uncle might mutter something about throwing good money away or talk about how he worked his way from the stockroom to CEO of Grunnings: "And I didn't need to learn how to pull rabbits out of a hat for *that*!"

Belatedly, you realize that you don't really know what you're going to do for a living. For the last four years you've told your parents, "I'm going to be a wizard!" without thinking further about what wizards actually do. You envy your friend Ron Weasley. Born into a magical family, Ron surely knows about magical careers. While Ron, a typical teenager, may not be very interested in career exploration, you don't even know your choices. Some nights you wake up in a cold sweat, wondering whether, after seven years at Hogwarts, you'll find yourself at a Muggle university, behind on your basic sciences, unqualified to become a dentist, and forced to work in the Grunnings stockroom after all.

As a first-generation wizard, you are at a great cultural disadvantage when it comes to knowing your career options. Like many students who progress academically farther than their parents or who are able to take advantage of specialized education, you do not have family role models or advisors. You might be entirely disinterested in a life-long career at Grunnings, or you may faint at the sound of a dentist's drill, but it is still helpful to be able to consider and dismiss these possible jobs based on your relatives' glowing descriptions.

Fortunately, you attend Hogwarts, the premiere British school of witchcraft and wizardry, which admits magical students from both wizarding and Muggle families. You assume that career exploration and planning will be readily available, ongoing, and include useful information for Muggle-born wizards who are new to the world of magic. Imagine your disappointment, and perhaps your concern, as you progress through your early years at Hogwarts without hearing a single word about your future opportunities. Whether you are acutely conscious of this deficit or only vaguely worried about what you will do after Hogwarts, somewhere in the back of your mind, you wish that things were different.

Harry and Hermione (both raised by Muggle parents) find themselves in similar circumstances, and even Ron, a young man from a magical family, is not well-served by Hogwarts's meager and inadequate career counseling services. Harry and Ron seem startled to learn that they must attend a mandatory career meeting late in their fifth year (*Harry Potter and the Order of the Phoenix*). Even allowing for the pair's typical obliviousness to almost any Hogwarts events that don't involve Quidditch, there still seems to be little advance notice of this one-time, individual meeting with the students' head of House. This advising session is scheduled oddly late in the students' education, falling after Easter break. This is far beyond the point where learning about careers might motivate students to spend less time at Honeydukes and more time studying. Yet it is also scheduled before students have taken their O.W.L.s, the results of which determine their future classes, advanced study, and career opportunities.

In preparation for this meeting, employment brochures appear in Gryffindor Tower (*Order of the Phoenix*). While these flyers have probably been available every spring, it is doubtful that Harry has noticed them before now, as they are only brought to the attention of the fifth-year students. The brochures give an overview of each career, including the depressing implication that in some cases, it's already too late to get good enough grades for that profession. (We confess that as professionals involved in undergraduate human services training, the authors are dismayed that "you don't seem to need many qualifications to liaise with Muggles" [*Order of the Phoenix* 657], a confirmation that direct service delivery is an undervalued career path no matter what your degree of magical skill.)

Harry's meeting with Professor McGonagall (*Order of the Phoenix*) is probably typical of other students' meetings and may even be more extensive than some. Still, it hardly serves as a ringing endorsement for Hogwarts's career counseling services. Attended by Professor Umbridge in her administrative role, this meeting not only may be little help to Harry, but it may be detrimental. In the power struggle that ensues between his professors, Harry's career counseling needs are lost. Harry leaves the meeting having discussed only the requirements for becoming an Auror. It is still not clear that he understands what an Auror does or what other jobs might be a satisfying fit for him. This single meeting is the extent of the official career advice Harry receives.

It is not clear why Hogwarts's career services are so woefully inadequate. Although it is tempting to assume that the Ministry of Magic has issued a cost-cutting decree, slashing student services in favor of beefing up disciplinary services (e.g., *Order of the Phoenix*), there is no indication that the career advice meetings have changed significantly in recent years. Perhaps most wizards simply look at job announcements in the *Daily Prophet* or enter a guild operating under an apprenticeship model. However, the first-generation wizard, and others as well, would benefit greatly from a more extensive career exploration process.

IMPROVED CAREER COUNSELING AT HOGWARTS

Fortunately for the wizarding world, it's likely that at some point an enterprising Muggle-born Hogwarts graduate will bridge the cultural gap by introducing contemporary Muggle career services to the Ministry of Magic. Improved career services could easily be introduced at Hogwarts, and existing career counseling could be enhanced.

Muggle career counseling is not simply a matter of filling out a few checklists, running them through a computer, and receiving a prophecy about your perfect job. Career counseling ideally includes both an evaluation of the student's (or client's) developmental circumstances, the use of structured instruments to explore the student's preferences, skills, pragmatic needs, and aspirations, and targeted exposure to real people doing real jobs.

DEVELOPMENTAL CONSIDERATIONS

Using a developmental framework serves several purposes. First, it is helpful to understand how students of different ages and socio-cultural circumstances typically think about the work world. Second, it allows the counselor to anticipate potential developmental issues related to career and vocation that may arise as the student reaches, or fails to reach, normal developmental mileposts. These aspects of a developmental approach help the counselor adjust his or her focus and activities, providing services that are the best fit for the student. Third, and most immediately related to our goal of improving wizards' career services, a developmental model suggests institutional programming and opportunities that are developmentally appropriate for students in order to meet their changing needs as they progress to adulthood.

The work of Ginzberg, Ginsburg, Axelrad, and Herma provides a simple developmental vocational model that will help us structure these services before and during the students' education at Hogwarts. This model suggests that career decision-making is a process that occurs over time and reflects the students' growing ability to think abstractly and plan for the future.

In our application of this model, the first step in career planning occurs when children from Muggle families discover that they are magical, and children from magical families learn whether they are magical or Squibs (non-magical people from wizard families). A person's magical characteristics open certain possibilities while precluding others. It is interesting to notice that even in the wizarding community, there are jobs that require more or less magical ability and aptitude. Stan Shunpike, the conductor on the Knight Bus (*Harry Potter and the Prisoner of Azkaban*), does not appear to use magic as a regular job responsibility. However, magical people do not seem to enter primarily Muggle careers, even if they live in Muggle communities. This may reflect cultural bias against non-magical professions rather than a prohibition on non-magical work.

Although the discovery of magical talents takes place mainly in a family context, career counselors could visit Muggle families to describe the educational path and career options available to their magical children. This correlates to the end of Ginzberg et al.'s *fantasy* stage at about age eleven and entry into the *development of interests* stage, when children begin to base their career choices on their developing interests.

In addition, career counselors could consult with magical families whose Squib children may benefit from both career counseling and a referral for personal or family counseling, depending on how the family and child feel about having a non-magical family member. A genogram, a form of annotated family tree that helps in the exploration of multigenerational family issues and values (McGoldrick, Gerson, & Shellenberger), may be a useful adjunct to this consultation. Family career patterns over several generations could be identified, and attitudes toward people who have deviated from the dominant family professions could be discussed. For example, Neville Longbottom's grandmother is clearly very proud of Neville's Auror parents and disappointed in Neville's slow magical development. Constructing and exploring Neville's genogram might lead to the discovery of relatives who are horticulturalists and a discussion of Neville's own interests and strengths. Wizards are already familiar with the idea of a family tree, as we know from the tapestry of the Black family that hangs at Grimmauld Place (*Order of the Phoenix*).

Studies show that increasing numbers of Muggle high school students are indecisive about what they want to do for a career (Gati & Saka), and it is safe to assume that this holds true for magical high schoolers as well. This career indecision is correlated with anxiety as well as a lack of adequate career-related information (Kelly & Lee). In order to help wizard students make more informed choices, career counselors could provide information about the Houses during the pre-Hogwarts family visit. Alternately, information about the Houses (for example, a brochure entitled, "IS HUFFLEPUFF RIGHT FOR YOU?") could be sent by owl post along with the Hogwarts acceptance letter. Using the same owl would be cost-effective and would give students time to discuss their House options with their parents or other magical relatives.

The next phase of career counseling, still falling within Ginzberg et al.'s *development of interests* stage, occurs at Hogwarts, where first-year students are placed in Houses by the Sorting Hat (*Harry Potter and the Sorcerer's Stone*). Though it is implied that character plays a role in the Sorting Hat's decisions, this process includes an element of choice. For example, having heard from Hagrid that "'[t]here's not a single witch or wizard who went bad who wasn't in Slytherin" (*Sorcerer's Stone* 80), Harry silently begs the Sorting Hat, "*Not Slytherin, not Slytherin*'" (*Sorcerer's Stone* 121), while Hermione reports that the Sorting Hat ultimately chose to put her in Gryffindor rather than Ravenclaw (*Order of the Phoenix*).

Hogwarts students cannot be blamed if their career goals seem unfocused. The relationship between required classes, O.W.L. and N.E.W.T. scores, extracurricular activities, and future careers may not be apparent to the students, at least at the outset. Neither does there appear to be any immediate consequence for shoddy academic work up to the point at which students take O.W.L.s. Though detentions are handed out frequently, and Houses accrue and lose points based on student accomplishments and conduct, the magical world does not seem to include the concept of academic probation or being held back a year for unsatisfactory progress. Though assignments are graded (and perhaps courses as well), there is little formative (ongoing) feedback on a student's academic progress. By the time students learn about their career options and take their O.W.L.s, it is already too late for them to make significant changes that would lead to different summative (final) feedback provided by this examination.

We recommend that the head of each House monitor his or her students' progress at the end of each term. Although this might require an administrative assistant in a Muggle school, it is likely that this monitoring could be accomplished magically, especially since House achievements and demerits are already magically accounted for by the House hourglasses. Further, to increase new students' exposure to potential wizarding careers, prefects could hold evening meetings featuring panels of Hogwarts graduates, who would describe their current work and how it relates to their studies at Hogwarts. Although students like Harry and Ron might not prioritize these meetings in their first years at Hogwarts, students like Hermione probably would and might exert some influence on their peers. Prefects might also have higher attendance if they provided food at these gatherings, an ancient bribe that is effective in residence halls serving both wizards and Muggles.

The third and fourth years at Hogwarts correspond to Ginzberg et al.'s *development of capacities* stage. Students at this age may be more aware of the relationship between academic performance and their future careers and better able to reflect on their career interests. At this stage, when students are critically evaluating their own abilities, plentiful feedback and opportunities for academic and extracurricular activities may prove helpful. Although some highly motivated students such as Hermione find ways to take additional classes, first- through fourth-year students typically follow a lock-step curriculum with few electives or choices once they arrive at Hogwarts. The lack of electives and choices does a disservice to the students as they strive to identify their own strengths and interests. Career-focused activities in the third and fourth year could make a real difference for many young wizards. One such example is Informational

Interviewing (Michelozzi), a technique in which students interview people whose work interests them. This helps students to clarify and refine their potential career fields. For example, students wishing to work in the United States can explore specific job information including the job outlook and earnings with the U.S. Department of Labor's *Occupational Outlook Handbook*, though this may be of more interest to North American Muggles.

MUGGLE TOOLS FOR CAREER AND VOCATIONAL EXPLORATION

As students reach the halfway mark in their Hogwarts education, more direct interventions become developmentally appropriate. By their fifth and sixth years, with O.W.L.s looming, wizard adolescents enter Ginzberg et al.'s *development of values* stage. These students are more able to consider their skills, abilities, and values. This is a time when it may be easy to engage Hogwarts students in self-assessment activities. With cultural adaptations (and, of course, norming and validation with wizard-only samples), a career counselor could administer Muggle-derived career assessments to older students. While many Muggle assessment tools, such as the Myers-Briggs Type Indicator (Sharf), may be helpful for career exploration, we recommend that activities that directly relate to career opportunites be implemented first.

Many career-seeking Muggles have encountered Holland's Theory of Types (Sharf). Two typical Muggle tests, the Strong Interest Inventory and the Self-Directed Search, are used to identify a person's Holland Code, which represents his or her work style preferences. The Holland Code helps identify goodness of fit, or congruence, between an examinee's preferences and the preferences associated with a particular career. Although the Strong Interest Inventory and the Self-Directed Search are typically administered on a computer, hand-scored forms are available and could be used at Hogwarts, where electronic equipment does not appear to function.

Holland identified six preferences, any of which may be dominant or most important to the examinee. A person's Holland Code is his or her first three preferences in descending order. However, even the primary (one-letter) code can be helpful in determining a student's general area of career interest. An easy way to begin to explore a student's Holland Code is "The Career Interests Game" (University of Missouri Career Center). Fortunately, this game has been adapted for use with Hogwarts students (Geiken & Kerewsky). In the Hogwarts game, students are instructed to imagine that they have just arrived at a party in the Great Hall, where they see that six conversations are in progress. Students are asked to choose which conversation they would like to join first. Each conversation reflects one of the dominant Holland Code types. Students may choose from these conversations:

- Discuss how to create an accurate magical map of the moving stairs (*Realistic:* A person whose primary type is "Realistic" may enjoy physical demands and may be practical, solution-focused, and action-oriented)
- Discuss how to brew a potion that stumps Professor Snape (*Investigative:* Introspective, rational. The typical primary type for people with a mathematical and scientific bent, as well as those who enjoy research)
- Discuss painting a new magical mural outside the Hufflepuff dormitory (*Artistic:* Creative, open, expressive, and artistic)
- Plan the upcoming Halloween event (*Social:* Interpersonally oriented, flexible, understanding, cooperative, and idealistic)
- Discuss how to get ahead in the wizarding world with a new magic shop (*Enterprising:* Assertive, persuasive, good at selling things or ideas, competitive)
- Talk with the representatives from the Ministry of Magic about improved organizational procedures (*Conventional:* Organized, rule-following, dependable)

Jobs are also given Holland Code types based on the Holland Codes of people who hold those jobs and enjoy their work. Once students know their Codes, they can use Internet resources, such as *Vocational Biographies*, to learn more about jobs that match their Holland Codes. Some cultural translation may be necessary, as not all magical or Muggle careers have exact analogues across these communities. Sadly, at present Hogwarts students may have to go into Hogsmeade, or even to a Muggle population center, to gain access to these resources. (Dentistry, by the way, has an Investigative major code. Fred and George are obviously Enterprising and clearly not Conventional.)

TARGETED CAREER EXPOSURE

Hogwarts students appear to lack even basic hands-on exposure to the world of work. They do not seem to have either term or summer jobs, and, with the exception of the prefects and Head Boy and Girl, do not seem to have opportunities to tutor, help in the library, copy scrolls, brew standard potions used in lessons, or help Hagrid with the day-to-day care of the Blast-Ended Skrewts. Though we hypothesize that an apprenticeship model is used in magical Great Britain, this is only a guess. This lack of experience places wizards at a distinct disadvantage in relation to their Muggle counterparts.

Hogwarts students would clearly benefit from direct vocational contacts. Throughout their Hogwarts education they should be encouraged to participate in job shadowing or internships, where they can gain first-hand work experience and see for themselves whether that job or field is a good match for their interests and skills. For example, though Ron might only serve as a Bludger-boy or Snitch-scrubber during a summer Quidditch internship with the Chudley Cannons, he would have the opportunity to observe the work environment and learn about the realistic demands on the members of a professional Quidditch team, including both players and support personnel.

These assessment and exposure activities, in conjunction with individual and group discussions with their counselors, could be repeated as students receive their O.W.L. scores and anticipate their N.E.W.T.s., entering Ginzberg et al.'s *transition period* in their last years at Hogwarts. The transition period includes the choice between continuing one's education and entering the work world. In the magical world, adolescents become adults at age seventeen. Upon coming of age, some wizards (such as Fred and George) may choose not to complete their Hogwarts degree. Harry has expressed his intention to fight Voldemort rather than attend his final year at Hogwarts (*Harry Potter and the Half-Blood Prince*). This suggests that basic career counseling should be completed before the final year, and that both dropouts and graduates should be made aware that they may return to use Hogwarts's Alumni Career Services at any time.

CAREER DEVELOPMENT NEEDS BEYOND HOGWARTS

Career and personal development do not end at age seventeen. Super and others remind us that the career development process continues through one's work life (Sharf). This is immediately evident in the lives of several of Harry's instructors. Remus Lupin, though by all accounts an excellent Defense Against the Dark Arts instructor, is unable to keep his teaching job at Hogwarts once it is generally known that he is a werewolf (*Prisoner of Azkaban*). Though he assists the Order of the Phoenix (*Order of the Phoenix* and *Half-Blood Prince*), his robes are shabby and he does not appear to be economically stable. Mad-Eye Moody, a former Auror, is engaged as an instructor and later volunteers for the Order. Even Horace Slughorn, who is retired or semi-retired, rejoins the workforce to teach Potions. Assuming that Harry survives the conflict with Voldemort, it is unlikely that he will work in only one field for the rest of his life. Generally speaking, the wizarding world should be prepared for a large number of returning veterans wanting to finish their education, needing retraining, or seeking new careers that accommodate acquired disabilities in the wake of the coming battle with the forces of evil.

FUTURE DIRECTIONS

In addition to the provision of Muggle-based services to wizards, Muggles may also benefit from this cultural exchange. Non-magical students who are familiar with Harry's story may find it helpful to role-play Harry and his friends as a way to explore their own career preferences. Graduate students in psychology may find it easier to learn to administer and interpret career and vocational instruments such as the Strong Interest Inventory using "clients" such as Draco Malfoy or Cho Chang.

Career counseling in the wizarding world is still in its infancy, and much remains to be accomplished. In addition to the suggestions above, wizards need well-trained career counselors, wizard equivalents of both the Muggle *Occupational Outlook Handbook* and the *Vocational Biographies*, and more visible employment services in wizarding communities.

Finally, the needs of non-majority wizards and other magical sentient creatures, such as Veelas and centaurs, should be specifically addressed. The magical world has its own share of racism, sexism, classism, and other forms of discrimination that would be very familiar to any Muggle. All of these aspects of inequality impinge upon both educational and career opportunities and, if unchallenged, ultimately fail both the Muggle and wizard communities.

SHOSHANA D. KEREWSKY, Psy.D., earned her master's degree in counseling psychology from Lesley College and her doctorate in clinical psychology from Antioch New England Graduate School. She is an assistant professor in counseling psychology and human services at the University of Oregon, an adjunct instructor in the Transitions to Success program at Lane Community College, and a licensed psychologist in private practice. In addition to psychology publications, her work has appeared in *English Journal*, *Fiction International*, and literary anthologies. Although she never learned to speak Elvish or Klingon, she may be the only psychologist ever to present to the American Psychological Association in full wizard's regalia.

LISSA JOY GEIKEN, M.Ed., earned her master's degree in counseling, in addition to her graduate work in diversity and disability studies from the University of Hawaii at Manoa. She is currently pursuing her doctorate in counseling psychology from the University of Oregon and specializes in individual counseling regarding relationship challenges, life transitions, and career counseling. Lissa is committed to enhancing the exploration and discovery of life adventures for people from a variety of backgrounds, including both Muggles and wizard-born.

REFERENCES

I. Gati and N. Saka, "High School Students' Career-Related Decision-Making Difficulties," *Journal of Counseling & Development* 79 (2001): 331–340.

Geiken, L. and S. D. Kerewsky. "Life after Hogwarts: A Career Development Lesson Plan." In S. D. Kerewsky, E. E. Cate, A. R. Caban, D. Cohen, L. Geiken, N. T. Kemp, R. V. Lesea, D. Messer, A. Shahane, and K. P. Walters. *Harry Potter and the Clinician's Toolbox.* Poster presented at 113th American Psychological Association Annual Convention, Washington, D.C., 2005.

Ginzberg, E., S. W. Ginsburg, S. Axelrad, and J. L. Herma. *Occupational Choice: An Approach to a General Theory.* New York, NY: Columbia University Press, 2001.

K. R. Kelly and W. Lee, "Mapping the Domain of Career Decision Problems," *Journal of Vocational Behavior* 61 (2002): 302–326.

McGoldrick, M., R. Gerson, and S. Shellenberger. *Genograms: Assessment and Intervention (Second Edition).* New York: W.W. Norton & Company, Inc., 1999.

Michelozzi, B. N. *Coming Alive from Nine to Five: A Career Search Book (Fifth Edition).* Mountain View, CA: Mayfield Publishing, 1996.

Rowling, J. K. *Harry Potter and the Sorcerer's Stone.* New York: Scholastic Inc., 1998.

———. *Harry Potter and the Prisoner of Azkaban.* New York: Scholastic Inc., 1999.

———. *Harry Potter and the Goblet of Fire.* New York: Scholastic Inc., 2000.

———. *Harry Potter and the Order of the Phoenix.* New York: Scholastic Inc., 2003.

———. *Harry Potter and the Half-Blood Prince.* New York: Scholastic Inc., 2005.

Sharf, R. S. *Applying Career Development Theory to Counseling (Second Edition).* Pacific Grove, CA: Brooks/Cole, 1997.

"The Career Interests Game." *University of Missouri Career Center.* <http://career.missouri.edu/students/explore/thecareerinterestsgame.php>.

"Occupational Outlook Handbook (OOH), 2006–07 Edition." U. S. Department of Labor, Bureau of Labor Statistics. <http://www.bls.gov/oco/>.

Vocational Biographies. <http://www.vocbiosonline.com/login.php>.

Is Howarts more like Harvard, MIT, or Yale? Or is it more like the Devry Technical Institute? Kalish and Kalish compare our Muggle educational system to that of Hogwarts and note the strong emphasis on the practical over the theoretical with encouragement for moral and emotional development given by the staff.

CHARLES W. KALISH
AND EMMA C. KALISH

Hogwarts Academy
Common Sense and School Magic

THE HARRY POTTER series puts the reader in a child-like position. We are exposed to an exotic and unfamiliar world, and we must make sense of the strange goings-on in the world of magic. This parallels every child's problem in coming to understand the strange goings-on in what adults appreciate as the real Muggle world. These problems are ultimately unsolvable. Nobody has a complete understanding of the world around us, but most people come to some basic, common-sense understanding. To be an adult member of twenty-first century Western culture involves, in part, knowing about such things as germs, tigers, and presidents. In the world of Harry Potter, common sense includes such things as jinxes, hippogriffs, and Ministers of Magic. Part of the fun of the series is following Harry's encounters with the unfamiliar world of magic. Harry did not grow up in the magic world (he lacks magical common sense), and the readers learn along with him.

It is all too evident that there are many kinds of knowledge and skills that we would like to have as part of our common sense that are not. One of the central questions in cognitive development is why some things seem to be effortlessly learned by almost everyone, while other things take a lot of hard work and are learned by a select few. The classic example is speaking versus reading; almost everyone learns to speak, but we require special institutions and schools to get people to read, and even then not everyone succeeds. A distinctive feature of the Harry Potter series is that the wizarding world also has schools. In the case of British witches and wizards, Hogwarts School of Witchcraft and Wizardy is responsible for instilling what society deems to be important magical knowledge. People would not go to all the trouble (and, we imagine, expense) to establish and attend Hogwarts unless they thought it provided some critical opportunity for learning magic. But what kind of opportunity? What do people learn at Hogwarts, and why do they need to go to school to do it?

The focus at Hogwarts is magic. There are some classes not directly related to magic, notably Professor Binn's course on the history of the wizarding world. It is likely no accident that history is regarded as the worst class at Hogwarts. It is a dry recitation of names, dates, and battles, uninteresting even with the novelty of having a ghost as teacher. Many other classes seem to be missing. It is not clear where wizarding youth encounter the classic "three R's" of reading, writing, and arithmetic. For example, the closest students come to mathematics is the class of Arithmancy, an unpopular elective, regarded as challenging and unnecessary. Those born into the Muggle world, such as Harry and Hermione, learn the basics in Muggle school. Perhaps there is a system of wizarding elementary schools. Even if Hogwarts did offer classes in reading and mathematics, it is hard to imagine they would be great favorites. How could calculus compete with Care of Magical Creatures or Transfigurations? We could imagine the philomath Hermione Granger eagerly signing up for familiar Muggle courses, but anyone else?

The bulk of the Hogwarts curriculum, and the classes that excite interest, are most akin to sciences in the Muggle world. Instead of biology we have Herbology and Care of Magical Creatures. Hogwarts offers Potions rather than chemistry, Astrology rather than astronomy. Charms and Transfigurations deal in magical forces somewhat analogous to gravity or quantum mechanics. Like Muggle sciences, magical studies focus on learning about important forces and relations in the natural (or at least non-social) world. This parallel is evident in that magic serves as a substitute for natural science. Wizards have the Floo Network for travel, but no knowledge of the internal combustion engine. Wands and spells, not electricity, produce light. It is only the eccentric wizard Arthur Weasley who ever expresses interest in Muggle science and technology. After all, magic is so useful, why would anyone want to learn about science? Even most Muggles do not want to study science. At Hogwarts, though, students are eager to learn the wizarding equivalent. Why? How is learning magic at Hogwarts different than learning science in high school?

Though we do not have complete syllabi for the courses at Hogwarts, we get a pretty good sense of what the curriculum is like. The classes are very hands-on and applied. The students learn how to do things: feed hippogriffs, transplant mandrakes, levitate cups, and brew all sorts of potions. Instruction is largely a matter of encouraging practice. The teachers present the students with problems and then let them go, offering occasional advice (or, in the case of Professor Snape, snide criticism) along the way. The instructional model is akin to an apprentice learning from a master. An apprentice shoemaker or weaver makes shoes or weaves a rug under the guidance of an expert. With time and much practice the apprentice becomes a master. This is an effective and time-honored form of instruction (Rogoff). It is not, however, the way learning in Muggle science classrooms is typically organized.

What do students learn at Hogwarts? Is their knowledge of magic comparable to the knowledge of science a Muggle high school graduate might have? The witches and wizards at Hogwarts know how to do magic. The wizard qualifying exams test how well students have mastered the practices and procedures of magic. A question from the O.W.L. Charms test asks examinees to "*describe the wand movement required to make objects fly*" (*Harry Potter and the Order of the Phoenix* 712). They (and we) also have a rough, general sense of the forces and factors that make magic work. Intention, concentration, and wand movement are very important in casting spells. Quantity, order, and consistency of ingredients are important in brewing a potion. We do not see students learning a lot of abstract theories or mechanisms. Nor are students learning methods of inquiry. Why do certain wand movements make objects fly? How could we discover which movements cause particular magical effects? We suspect some of the teachers know the answer to these questions. Such knowledge would seem to be critical for inventing new spells or potions, for example. Though the students know how to work with magic and how to control it to some degree, they do not seem to know why it works.

It is tempting to say that what the students at Hogwarts are learning is very different from science. They just take the action of magic on faith; they use magical tools but do not know or ask how they work (see chapters by Nemeroff and Rosenberg, this volume). The students at Hogwarts are in much the same position most Muggles are with respect to science *before* school. Psychologists describe people as having everyday or intuitive theories (Gelman & Kalish; Gopnik, Meltzoff, & Kuhl). Such theories allow us to work with the forces we encounter, and involve some general ideas of the phenomena involved, but are not detailed, explicit, testable systems. A good example is young children's theory of illness (Kalish). Most American preschoolers know that germs make you sick. They have a basic theory: sick people have germs, germs are little particles or animals, the germs from sick people can get on you, if the germs get inside you, you get sick. The theory allows some prediction and control: stay away from sick people, wash your hands, etc. It does not provide a full explanation; for example, how do germs make people sick? This is the same kind of understanding that most of us have about electricity, weather, or genetics. The average Muggle without formal training is no more "scientific" in his or her knowledge of infection than Harry is in his knowledge of transfigurations.

One of the features of commonsense theories is that you do not need to go to school to acquire them. Of course, some experience is needed: children are not born knowing about germs. But it is not the case that anyone sits a child down and works through the principles of germ theory. One important question that comes out of this line of research is: just what do we need schools for? What characterizes the kinds of knowledge that require explicit instruction and formal institutions to support reliable acquisition (Sperber)? Some understanding of infection, or electricity, or weather we pick up by simply living with these forces. That kind of knowledge tends to be very practical; we know how to use electricity, what to do when we are sick, and how to interpret a weather forecast (all within limits). One of the functions of schooling is to supplement or extend common sense, but in what ways or directions?

Explicit instruction does seem necessary if people are to learn abstract, detailed, formal theories. Though just growing up in twenty-first-century Western culture seems sufficient to lead most of us to develop a functional understanding of germs, we need to create very special circumstances to get people to learn about T cells or ICAM-1. This kind of knowledge goes beyond what is practical or useful in everyday life and involves an array of esoteric objects and forces. One of the reasons that schools are necessary for such knowledge is that we find it difficult to acquire. It is relatively painless, indeed enjoyable, to learn basic number facts, but few people find algebra intrinsically motivating (Geary). The same thing holds with respect to the processes of thinking. Though people intuitively develop ways of reasoning and testing beliefs, systematic methods of critical thinking (e.g., the scientific method, formal logic) seem to require special support (Kuhn). Unfortunately, even the special institutions we create to teach these things are not always very successful.

One goal of school, then, could be to formalize common sense understanding. Science education provides the theory behind our intuitive ideas. Math education systematizes our quantitative intuitions. Much of American education is organized this way. Looking through a high school biology or mathematics textbook reveals a collection of abstract theoretical facts and processes, disconnected from immediate practical utility. (There are four phases of meiosis. To add polynomials, find the matching variables and exponents.) Interestingly, the teachers at Hogwarts do not frame their instruction in this way. We do not learn about the categories of potions ingredients or a symbolic/formal model of wand movement. Very little theoretical vocabulary is introduced in a Hogwarts lesson. As far as we can tell, the purpose of Hogwarts is not to teach the theory of magic. Rather, the focus is on using magic.

The contrast between applied and theoretical instruction is at the heart of a major pedagogical conflict in the series: Dolores Umbridge's Defense Against the Dark Arts course and the D.A. study group. Umbridge is clear that her curriculum is not about doing magic. The title of her chosen textbook is *Defensive Magical Theory*, and her primary course goal is "[u]nderstanding the principles underlying defensive magic" (*Order of the Phoenix* 240). The students are incensed and take the radical step of organizing their own class under the direction of Harry Potter. In part, the students take this step because they know that their qualifying exams will test practices and procedures. However, Umbridge's theoretical focus is also a cue to the students (and the reader) that she doesn't really want them to learn to defend themselves against Dark Arts. At Hogwarts the way to keep the students from learning is to teach them theory.

Just as Hogwarts the institution is a traditional boarding school, underneath all its magical trappings the curriculum is also very traditional. It emphasizes practicing procedures, often derisively described as *drill and kill* (in the case of some of the more powerful spells, this may be a literal description). Why do the teachers teach this way? One of the virtues of the applied approach to magical training at Hogwarts is that the students like it. Though there are plenty of scenes of students grumbling about homework, by and large the Hogwarts students are motivated. They appreciate that working hard in school will allow them to perform new and more powerful spells. In contrast, it is the rare ninth grader who can appreciate the power of adding polynomials. Achievement in a Hogwarts class is relatively objective: either you can turn the cup into a bird or not. Success in a typical Muggle science or math class is less obvious. The students have to take it on faith that what they have learned is correct and potentially useful. It does not seem surprising that the Hogwarts model would be more motivating.

The students like the practical focus, but from what we know about Hogwarts teachers, it is unlikely that they are designing their classes just to be popular. Perhaps the reason for the procedural focus is that mastering the "basics" paves the way for later theoretical material. For example, in mathematics we think that students have to memorize the times-tables as a condition for being able to handle more complex or abstract content (e.g., algebra). Yet research suggests that emphasis on learning procedures may actually hinder learning theoretical or conceptual knowledge, as students become so focused on carrying out the procedures they cannot reflect on how, why, or when the procedures work (Alibali). When you get very good at hammering, every problem tends to look like a nail. There is evidence that the curriculum at Hogwarts builds to more abstract theoretical classes. However, it is only the rare student (e.g., Hermione) who seems to pursue such a course of study.

In addition to laying the groundwork for future learning, a second motive for the Hogwarts curriculum is to provide professional training. Students are getting the instruction they need to begin careers in the magical world. Indeed, the link between school achievement and professions is quite explicit. Harry knows precisely what he must achieve in school in order to qualify for his chosen profession as an Auror (Dark wizard hunter). A virtue of the apprenticeship model of education is that it produces people skilled and ready to take on professions. Successful apprentice shoemakers become master shoe-makers (though not shoe-theoreticians). This link to career and profession is largely absent from contemporary American education. A common question in American high schools is, "Why do we need to know this?" Students at Hogwarts rarely need to ask. One proposal for reform of our Muggle schools is to use the motivating promise of professions to engage students' interest in learning. If students can see the link to careers as doctors, architects, or urban planners, they may be more motivated to learn biology, math, and sociology (Shaffer). It seems pretty clear that it is the promise of accreditation for a profession that keeps Harry at Hogwarts (that and not wanting to live with the Dursleys).

So, Hogwarts is a kind of trade school. The reason young witches and wizards go to Hogwarts is to receive practical training. Wizarding society has recognized the need to prepare its children for careers and has established Hogwarts (and other magical academies) to serve this function. But Hogwarts has an additional function not typically associated with our Muggle trade schools. Most trade schools offer a limited set of programs. Students choose a school after they have identified the kind of training they want: learning to be a chef, or a fashion designer, or a computer technician. First-year students at Hogwarts all take the same classes and learn the same basic set of skills, but as the years go on the curriculum is differentiated. An important part of the Hogwarts experience is identifying an area of focus. Hogwarts functions not just as a place to learn a set of magical skills, but also as a place in which students are sorted into particular professions.

The discriminating function of Hogwarts is apparent from the moment new students set foot in the building. The very first thing a student at Hogwarts does is don the Sorting Hat. The hat assigns each student to one of four Houses in the school. In the fifth year, another kind of sorting ritual occurs with the O.W.L. exams. Based on the results of the exams, students are tracked into particular courses of study for their final two years at the school. Presumably, parents send their children to Hogwarts because they believe in the Sorting function: Hogwarts will get children into the right House and into the right profession. But how? Continuing the question of why young wizards go to school: What does Hogwarts actually do to achieve this sorting? Does it uncover a student's essential pre-existing characteristics, or does it provide a student the opportunity to develop new abilities and talents?

The idea that schools are places where individuals differentiate is not unique to the wizarding world. Muggle schools also have a sorting function as students identify career goals and pursue distinct interests. Schools also sort students "vertically" into higher and lower performers. Psychologists have been very interested in people's ideas about the sorting that goes on in schools. Muggles expect their schools will sort students, and researchers have noted that there are two very different attitudes or beliefs about how that sorting process does or should work.

One attitude is that it is the school's job is to diagnose students' abilities. Each student has a particular combination of talents. Schools uncover those individual characteristics and identify the appropriate educational/career path. The psychologist Carol Dweck (1991) has characterized this attitude as an *entity theory*. People are born with a fixed amount of a trait. Intelligence is the classic example. We often feel that people are born smart or dumb. Geniuses have an exceptional innate ability. Development consists of the unfolding or revelation of one's endowment of intelligence. Dweck describes an alternative view as an *incremental theory*. This view emphasizes achievement and the alterability of personal characteristics. Great thinkers are made, not born, is the motto. School's function is not to diagnose, but to nurture. Schools provide the opportunity for students to apply their efforts to achieve their individual goals. Very roughly, in one view school does the sorting ("You belong here"), and in the other view students sort themselves ("I want to be there").

The strongest version of an entity theory is what psychologists have described as intuitive *essentialism* (Gelman; Medin & Ortony). For example, folk beliefs about animal species hold that each animal has a characteristic essence that determines its kind (e.g., makes a dog a dog and not a cat), is responsible for species-typical attributes (e.g., makes a dog bark and not meow), and cannot be changed (e.g., a dog cannot turn into a cat). Essentialist intuitions also influence thinking about human traits and identities. Many social categories (e.g., race, gender) are assumed to be innately determined and immutable (Haslam, Rothschild, & Ernst; Hirschfeld). Personality characteristics (e.g., shy, mean) also engage essentialist thinking (Gelman & Heyman). Magic clearly has an essentialist component. Some people are born with magical ability, some are not. Although magical ability is not inherited as reliably as species identity, it does seem to be immutable. Squibs cannot acquire magical ability. Similarly, the Sorting Hat seems to divine students' essential identity when assigning them to Houses. Although never stated in the books, our essentialist intuition is that House identity is immutable: a Slytherin could no more become a Gryffindor than a leopard could change its spots.[1]

Despite a strong commitment to equality and achievement, Americans and American schools tend to emphasize innate essence and entity theories. In contrast, Asian schools and societies tend to emphasize achievement (Stevenson & Stigler). The American attitude is that the cream will rise to the top; the Japanese say even the dullest pebble becomes shiny after years of polishing. From what we can see in the texts, intrinsic potential seems to outweigh hard work in the study of magic at Hogwarts.

Ability and effort almost define the relation between Harry Potter and Neville Longbottom. Harry is recognized as a magical prodigy. He has powers far beyond his years or training. Yet, he is an indifferent and unmotivated student. He squeaks by in all his classes, copying much of his work from the talented *and* hardworking Hermione. Harry is also a natural flyer (something equivalent to athletic ability). He is the youngest Seeker ever to play on a House Quidditch team, despite not growing up with the sport. In contrast, nothing

---

[1] Harry Potter seems to be unique in that the Sorting Hat offers him a choice of Houses: Gryffindor or Slytherin. This may be a signal that Harry has a mixed or dual-identity. Dumbledore seems to feel that Voldemort and Harry have a unique connection, with each sharing some of the essence of the other.

comes easily to Neville Longbottom. He clearly tries hard—Neville is a conscientious and motivated student (as one might say in a letter of recommendation). Neville's work ethic and attention in school are much better than Harry's. Neville, though, is a hapless magician. His spells do not function, and he is a poor flyer. We have to conclude he lacks ability; he is low in the magical equivalent of IQ.

An emphasis on intrinsic ability is confirmed by indications in later books that Neville has a talent for Herbology—a magical green thumb. It does not appear that Neville is more strongly motivated or works harder in Herbology than in other classes. Indeed, Herbology seems to be a rather low-status magical specialty; much cooler to excel in Defense Against the Dark Arts. Rather, Neville's success with plants can be credited to a special aptitude. This is one of several indications that magical ability is not unitary. For example, some people have *Sight*, a special ability at Divination (though there is some question about the legitimacy of this gift). Harry Potter, skilled in other areas of magic, is a poor fortune teller. An influential view of cognitive ability is that there are multiple *intelligences* (Gardner). People with different levels or combinations of intelligences have aptitudes in different domains; there are linguistic, musical, and mathematical talents (though Gardner himself does not endorse a fixed-entity view of intelligence).

An entity/fixed-ability view is very consistent with the practical orientation of the Hogwarts curriculum. See which areas students show aptitude for, then prepare them for careers that build on those strengths. In contrast, the abstract, theoretical knowledge often encountered in Muggle schools is, at least in part, motivated by a more developmental and achievement-focused approach to education. We may not expect that most students have a practical need to know the four phases of meiosis, but we may believe that all students are enriched by some exposure to science. This is generally the motivation for including the arts and humanities in the school curricula (subjects notably lacking at Hogwarts). Students take English in school, not just to become better writers (or to identify verbal aptitude), but because we think reading literature is an important part of developing as a person. Muggle schools reflect the liberal arts tradition and the goals of developing a common (e.g., national) culture and educating for values. Schools are recognized as institutions that help children become adults, not just by mastering a set of skills, but also by developing an identity and character.

The Harry Potter series tracks the lives of a group of children from ages twelve to eighteen. Given this subject, development is clearly a major theme in the series. Like any other literature concerned with adolescence, much of the focus is on emotional maturity and the development of character and values. The Harry Potter characters are also developing their magical abilities, and that involves attending school. Acquiring magical powers provides many analogies with cognitive development. In particular, the series engages our intuitions about the nature of knowledge and the significance of achievement versus innate endowment. In Hogwarts we see an example of how society takes responsibility for the development of children. We recognize a common concern with preparing children to be adult members of society and providing an opportunity to acquire knowledge unavailable in other contexts.

In thinking about the role of schools in cognitive and magical development, we also recognize the same questions with respect to emotional and moral development. To what extent is the development of magical ability parallel to the development of character? Are people born good or evil? Can people change? Is school a place where people realize their essential characters—their magical abilities and their propensities to good or evil? Or is school a place where students have an opportunity to develop new talents, to learn to fly, and to become better people?

ACKNOWLEDGMENTS

The authors would like to thank Dr. Laura Dresser and attorney David Austin for their professional contributions to this essay.

CHARLES W. KALISH is a professor of educational psychology at the University of Wisconsin-Madison. His research interests concern the development of inductive inference and intuitive theories. Thanks to this essay, he is now able to look back on all those enjoyable hours spent reading Harry Potter books and realize he was actually working.

EMMA C. KALISH is a sophomore at West High School in Madison. She is an acknowledged expert in all things Potter and the first person we know of to decode R.A.B.

REFERENCES

M. W. Alibali, "How Children Change their Minds: Strategy Change Can Be Gradual or Abrupt," *Developmental Psychology* 35 (1999): 127–145.

Dweck, C. S. "Self-theories and Goals: Their Role in Motivation, Personality, and Development." In R. A. Dienstbier (Ed.), *Nebraska Symposium on Motivation. 1990: Perspectives on Motivation,*. University of Nebraska Press, 1991. 19.

Gardner, H. *Frames of Mind: The Theory of Multiple Intelligences.* New York: Basic Books Inc, 2004.

D. C. Geary, "Reflections of Evolution and Culture in Children's Cognition: Implications for Mathematical Development and Instruction," *American Psychologist* 50 (1995): 24–37.

Gelman, S. A. *The Essential Child: Origins of Essentialism in Everyday Thought.* New York: Oxford University Press, 2003.

S. A. Gelman and G. D. Heyman, "Carrot-Eaters and Creature-Believers: The Effects of Lexicalization on Children's Inferences about Social Categories," *Psychological Science* 10 (1999): 489–493.

Gelman, S. A. and C. W. Kalish. "Conceptual Development." In W. Damon and R. M. Lerner (Series Eds.), and D. Kuhn and R. S. Siegler (Eds.), *Handbook of Child Psychology: Vol. 2 Cognition, Perception, and Language* (sixth ed.). Hoboken, NJ: Wiley, 2006. 687–733.

Gopnik, A., A. N. Meltzoff, and P. K. Kuhl. *The Scientist in the Crib: Minds, Brains, and How Children Learn.* New York: William Morrow & Co., Inc., 1999.

N. Haslam, L. Rothschild, and D. Ernst, "Essentialist Beliefs About Social Categories," *British Journal of Social Psychology* 39 (Pt. 1) (2000): 113–127.

Hirschfeld, L. A. *Race in the Making: Cognition, Culture, and the Child's Construction of Human Kinds.* Cambridge, MA: MIT Press, 1996.

Kalish, C. W. "What Young Children's Understanding of Contamination and Contagion Tells Us About Their Concepts of Illness." In M. Siegal and C. Peterson (Eds.), *Children's Understanding of Biology and Health.* New York: Cambridge University Press, 2000. 99–130.

C. W. Kalish, "Essentialist to Some Degree: Beliefs About the Structure of Natural Kind Categories," *Memory & Cognition* 30 (2002): 340–352.

Kuhn, D. "What is Scientific Thinking, and How Does it Develop?" In U. Goswami (Ed.), *Blackwell Handbook of Childhood Cognitive Development*. Blackwell Publishing, 2002. 371.

Medin, D. L. and A. Ortony. "Psychological Essentialism." In S. Vosniadou and A. Ortony (Eds.), *Similarity and Analogical Reasoning*. Cambridge University Press, 1989. 179.

Rogoff, B. *Apprenticeship in Thinking: Cognitive Development in Social Context*. New York: Oxford University Press, 1990.

Shaffer, D. W. *How Computer Games Help Children Learn*. New York: Palgrave Press, 2007.

Sperber, D. "The Epidemiology of Beliefs." In C. Fraser and G. Gaskell (Eds.), *The Social Psychological Study of Widespread Beliefs*. New York: Clarendon Press, 1990. 25–44.

Stevenson, H. W. and J. W. Stigler. *The Learning Gap: Why Our Schools are Failing and What We Can Learn from Japanese and Chinese Education*. New York: Simon & Schuster, 1994.

WILL HARRY
BE OKAY?

Goodfriend is a bit worried about Harry. She describes the three styles of psychological attachment, which are ways that we learn to relate to others as children. These tend to stick with us throughout our lives. She shows how Rowling has given each Harry, Ron, and Hermione one of these different styles and speculates what this might mean for each of their futures.

WIND GOODFRIEND, Ph.D.

Attachment Styles at Hogwarts
From Infancy to Adulthood

Picture London during the height of World War II. The city was constantly threatened by bombings from above. Parents had only one greater fear than the fear of their own death: the death of their children. To keep its young ones safe, the British government evacuated children to the countryside. After the war, families were reunited. Physically, the children were fine. However, an unforeseen side effect had occurred. The children had been separated from their parents at a crucial time in their development, and, as young adults, they began displaying a variety of psychological disorders. For many of these adolescents, a key problem among these issues was the inability to form strong, loving ties with other people. From this phenomenon, psychology researchers noticed and created *attachment theory*. Attachment theory focuses on how the familial environment during one's formative years affects one's ability to begin and maintain normal, adult relationships—including romantic relationships. Psychologists have now identified three distinct *attachment styles*, or patterns of behavior relevant to how one interacts with potential romantic partners. Perhaps it is coincidental, but these three attachment styles can be seen in almost perfect form in the three main characters in the Harry Potter series: Hermione Granger, Ron Weasley, and Harry himself.

A BRIEF HISTORY OF ATTACHMENT THEORY

Inspired by the emotional troubles caused by mass child evacuations in London, British psychologist John Bowlby began a long line of research into child-parent bonds. Bowlby observed infants with their primary caregivers (usually their mothers) and noted that the infants grew upset when their mothers would leave, even temporarily. Bowlby began writing about the bond that exists between children and their parents and how disruptions of this bond can lead to emotional problems later in the child's life.

It was one of John Bowlby's students, Mary Ainsworth, who pioneered research showing that different people can have different attachment styles. In other words, one child will respond to his or her parents in a very different way than another child. Ainsworth's research, as well as the research of hundreds of people after her, showed that, for the most part, there are three main attachment styles: *secure*, *anxious*, and *avoidant*. Although modern researchers argue constantly about what to call these styles and how to measure them, there is a high level of agreement about what each style means in terms of behaviors. These behaviors are linked to two key times in life: (1) early childhood experiences with one's family, and (2) beginning and—maybe—maintaining adult relationships. Because romantic relationships are so important to our adult lives, the concentration of research has been in applying the attachment style formed in a person's early childhood to how that affects his or her romantic relationships (e.g., Hazan & Shaver).

A good way to understand the different styles of attachment is to see how research psychologists measure them. Although many different measures exist, one of the most popular measures today is a scale called "Experiences in Close Relationships" (Brennan, Clark, & Shaver). Below is a brief version with ten sentences (the actual survey is much longer). How much do you agree with each sentence?

Anxiety Items

1. I'm afraid that I will lose my partner's love.
2. I often worry that my partner will not want to stay with me.
3. I often worry that my partner doesn't really love me.
4. I often wish my partner's feelings for me were as strong as my feelings for him/her.
5. When my partner is gone, I worry that he/she might become interested in someone else.

Avoidance Items

1. I prefer not to show a partner how I feel, deep down.
2. I find it difficult to depend on romantic partners.
3. I don't feel comfortable opening up to romantic partners.
4. I get uncomfortable when a partner wants to be very close.
5. I prefer not to be too close.

The more sentences you agree with, the less secure you are. In other words, if you agree with items 1–5, you would be classified as anxious. If you agree with items 6–10, you would be classified as avoidant. If you don't agree with any of the items, you can rest assured you are secure.

Although some people might argue that the children in Harry Potter are too young to use as examples of people in romantic relationships, I believe they are a perfect opportunity to see young adults attempting romance for the first time. How will they approach each other? How do they attempt to form emotional bonds? How will they end relationships? Fortunately for us, each of the three main characters is quite different, and each is an example of one of the three main styles of attachment.

HERMIONE GRANGER: A CASE STUDY IN SECURITY

All three attachment styles follow the same principle: the behaviors, self-esteem, and trust of others established in someone as a young child will follow that person for the rest of his or her life. The first attachment style identified by researchers is *secure*. Secure is, by far, the most common of the three styles, emerging in about two-thirds of children (Berscheid & Regan). This pattern or style is first established when a child's parents provide reliable, steady, sensitive care—parents who are consistently responsible and loving (Berscheid & Regan). Securely attached children are typically more socially gifted and more competent in social situations. Secure children have high self-esteem and are likely to trust others.

Hermione is a great example of a secure individual. Admittedly, we know the least about her early and family life, compared with the other two main characters. We never see her at home, and she spends little time at home past the age of eleven. However, what we do see is a stable, normal, supportive relationship with both parents. We know they are dentists who are not part of the magical world. However, when Hermione receives her invitation to attend Hogwarts School of Witchcraft and Wizardry, they recognize the opportunity for their daughter and trust that she will be all right entering this new and exciting world. They regularly accompany her to Diagon Alley for school supplies and attempt to get to know her friends' parents. They plan elaborate family trips during school breaks, such as to France and a skiing resort.

We also see Hermione's love for her parents. Even though she is often away, she regularly sends letters home and always thinks of her parents in times of joy and sadness. For example, one of her first thoughts after she is named prefect of Gryffindor is to send a message to her parents. She is considerate of their feelings and knows they will be proud: "'They'll be really pleased—I mean, prefect is something they can understand'" (*Harry Potter and the Order of the Phoenix* 165). Hermione is understanding of their basic ignorance of the magical world but confident in their support. Another example is seen later in the same year. Hermione was planning to spend Christmas skiing with her parents, but she decides to stay at Sirius Black's house over the holidays after Mr. Weasley is injured. She explains to Harry, "'Mum and Dad are a bit disappointed, but I've told them that everyone who's serious about the [O.W.L.] exams is staying at Hogwarts to study. They want me to do well, they'll understand'" (*Order of the Phoenix* 498). Clearly, they are willing to support and trust Hermione in everything she does, while still showing her that they love her and want to spend time with her. When her parents finally get to see her at the end of the year on the train platform, we witness them "taking it in turns to hug" her (*Order of the Phoenix* 868).

This is the parental pattern that results in a secure attachment style: loving and supportive, while encouraging exploration of one's own interests. As a result, Hermione displays classic secure behaviors. A nice comparison of Hermione, Ron, and Harry is seen at their first meeting: the Hogwarts Express. Harry attempts to find a compartment by himself. Ron sits with him but complains about his family and is embarrassed about being poor. What is Hermione doing? She is helping Neville find his lost toad, confident and generous with someone who clearly needs help. Just hours later, Harry and Ron are both completely scared to try on the Sorting Hat that will decide their House assignment, but Hermione is eager and confident, practically running to the stool. And who can forget her secure confidence in all of her classes, always the first person to raise her hand?

Hermione's general confidence is pretty clear. She does have moments of doubt (for example, waiting for her O.W.L. results), but her "doubt" is over not receiving excellent grades in every class—including Divination, which she quit! For attachment theory, however, we must focus specifically on her romantic relationships and examine if this security follows her into that area.

We see Professor Lockhart as Hermione's first crush. Like any twelve-year-old girl with a crush, she exhibits typical girlish behaviors regarding the object of her affection. When Ron asks if she's outlined her class schedule with little hearts, she blushes. She is also constantly defending him to Ron and Harry, who don't understand the attraction. When she receives a get-well card from Lockhart, she keeps it under her pillow. Later it is clear that she sent Lockhart a valentine; when Ron asks her about it, she blushes and tries to avoid the question. It is also in this book (*Harry Potter and the Chamber of Secrets*) that we see the first seeds of a growing relationship between Ron and Hermione, as Ron shows boyish jealousy over Hermione's attentions to Lockhart. This jealous tendency will be a recurrent pattern in Ron's life (see below).

It is not until a couple of years later, however, that we see Hermione's first official romantic relationship begin. (Note: this is two years ahead of her friends Ron and Harry.) In *Harry Potter and the Goblet of Fire*, the entire school is excited about the Yule Ball. It is clear that Hermione would like Ron to ask her to the dance. However, secure people do not wait around forever, pining after people who show no interest. When

Ron doesn't ask her, Hermione moves on to someone who does appreciate her: the famous and talented Viktor Krum. They spend the entire year running into each other in the library, and originally Hermione is annoyed by his presence. Eventually, however, she learns that they have a lot in common and she easily strikes up a good relationship with him. She has a great time at the ball until her fight with Ron.

The fight with Ron also shows us Hermione's character and attachment style. Ron has spent the entire evening being rude and obsessive (again, see below for a detailed analysis of Ron). At the end of the evening, Hermione calls him on his cowardice and true feelings: "'Well, if you don't like it, you know what the solution is, don't you? . . . Next time there's a ball, ask me before someone else does, and not as a last resort!'" (*Goblet of Fire* 432). Hermione has feelings just like any healthy person would. She is hurt by Ron's lack of attention but brave enough to call him on it, and she has enough self-worth to value a relationship partner who will value her equally. Hermione continues to have a relationship with Krum, mostly through letters, but it is clear that their relationship is based on mutual interests and respect for each other.

Throughout the next two years, Hermione's relationship with Ron is mostly characterized by petty fighting. However, their fights are obviously driven by feelings that Ron is not willing to admit and that Hermione is not willing to push. She understands feelings much better than either of her male friends and knows how to get to them. When Ron begins his sickening relationship with Lavender, Hermione goes on a date with McLaggen, Ron's competition for the Keeper position on the Quidditch team. Predictably, Ron is driven crazy by this. However, Hermione ends the relationship with McLaggen within a few hours of their date; she is not willing to use another person for her own selfish purposes, again showing her healthy relationship patterns and understanding of emotional bonds between people. At the end of *Harry Potter and the Half-Blood Prince*, she and Ron finally seem to have resolved their issues, realizing that time is short in the reflection of Dumbledore's funeral. However, their relationship was much more stalled because of Ron's stupidity than because of anything Hermione did. Ron's way of interacting with potential partners is much different from Hermione's, and it is a perfect example of the second major attachment style.

RON WEASLEY: A CASE STUDY IN ANXIETY

The second attachment style identified by researchers is called *anxious*. Anxiety, in terms of attachment, has origins in parents who are inconsistent in their caregiving—sometimes supportive and loving and sometimes absent, distracted, or simply unnoticing of the needs of their child (Berscheid & Regan). Children raised in this environment often have low self-esteem, with no confidence that the ones they love will reciprocate. They seem to scare easily, meaning they are often upset when things go wrong, and they find it easier to pretend to be angry or annoyed with the ones they love, when they desperately want to reunite and smooth things over. In short, the anxious attachment style is characterized by people who have an extreme need for closeness and attention from others and, at the same time, have a constant fear of rejection.

It is easy to see how Ron's home life is characterized by instability and distracted parents. With seven children, Mrs. Weasley understandably can't give each of them the attention a child needs. In fact, when we see Mrs. Weasley interact with her children, it is only in one of three modes: (1) warning them not to get into trouble, (2) yelling at them when they have, inevitably, gotten into trouble, or (3) crying/fussing over them when the trouble has caused injury or potential death. Often her style of parenting is simply to berate them. After Ron steals the flying family car and crashes it, she sends him a Howler that screams at him in front of the entire school: "'I DON'T SUPPOSE YOU STOPPED TO THINK WHAT YOUR FATHER AND I WENT THROUGH…I THOUGHT YOUR FATHER WOULD DIE OF SHAME…ABSOLUTELY DISGUSTED…'" (*Chamber of Secrets* 88). These are not words of loving support, but it's clear that Ron has her attention.

Ron is aware of his mother's challenges—in fact, when he first meets Harry he's a bit embarrassed by her, and explains to him, "'[S]he hasn't got much time…with five of us [still at home]'" (*Sorcerer's Stone* 101). It was likely much worse when Ron was younger and all seven children were home. It is clear that Mrs. Weasley loves her family; she is just stretched too thin. For example, she hand-makes (or wand-makes) sweaters for her children every year. However, she never notices or remembers that Ron hates maroon, the color he always gets. This mixture of loving attention and lack of ability to focus on detail is the hallmark of a parent with an anxious child. Ron's father is equally torn in two directions, but we see this in his work life. Mr. Weasley's entire essence is ambivalence: his job is to bust wizards for misuse of Muggle objects, but his joy in life comes from doing that very thing. He tries to manage the entire family but must constantly be at work to support the nine of them, thus does not have any time to actually spend with his family except on special occasions.

This lack of attention and quality time with either parent leads directly to the most central trait of an anxious person: his or her need for attention and a jealous tendency. We constantly see these patterns in Ron throughout the series. Ron's ultimate goal is to be the most popular and well-liked person at Hogwarts. What is the evidence for this? In the very first book of the series, Ron and Harry stand before the Mirror of Erised, which shows them their deepest, darkest desires. Ron's vision is of himself, standing *alone*, as Head Boy. He has won both the Quidditch and House cups, implying the glory and fame that he seeks. Finally, Dumbledore explains to Harry the importance of these visions: "Ronald Weasley, who has always been overshadowed by his brothers, sees himself standing alone, the best of all of them" (*Harry Potter and the Sorcerer's Stone* 213). Throughout their friendship, Ron is happy for Harry's successes, but Ron also clearly desires the attention for himself. After Sirius Black breaks into Hogwarts and seems to have attempted to kill Ron (he was really trying to kill Ron's rat), Ron becomes an "instant celebrity. For the first time in his life, people were paying more attention to him than to Harry, and it was clear that Ron was rather enjoying the experience" (*Harry Potter and the Prisoner of Azkaban* 270). Similarly, after Ron finally succeeds at Quidditch and wins the game, all he can do is give Harry and Hermione (and anyone else nearby) a blow-by-blow reenactment of the match. Even while trying to study for O.W.L.s, "he was thoroughly enjoying being patted on the back by Gryffindors walking past his chair, not to mention the occasional outburst of 'Weasley is our King'" (*Order of the Phoenix* 703). Ron is clearly in his version of paradise with all this attention.

Importantly, attachment theory suggests that we should see these patterns of jealousy and the desperate need for relationships in Ron's romantic life. Again, attachment theory is supported throughout

Ron's entire young life. He constantly attempts to get attention from girls, but at the same time seems too scared to act on important feelings because of his fear of rejection. We see this clearly in the turbulent relationship between Ron and Hermione.

Ron's jealousy toward Hermione becomes obvious in his reaction to seeing her crush on Lockhart: he's disgusted by her infatuation and begs her to tell him that she didn't send Lockhart a valentine. We see his jealousy again when Hermione goes to the ball with Krum. Ron has no right to be jealous when he waited until the last minute to ask Hermione (and then in a very rude way), but Ron's focus at the time is simply getting the prettiest possible date in order to impress others. He actually asks Fleur out, to everyone's dismay. Ron places no value on Hermione as a possible relationship partner until someone else desires her, thus inflating her public value. It drives Ron crazy that Hermione and Krum continue their relationship after the ball.

What is Ron's way of dealing with this situation? To simply tell Hermione that he has feelings for her? No—anxious people (according to attachment theory) do not have the confidence in themselves to believe that others will return their affection. As stated above, they desperately crave loving relationships but don't have the self-esteem necessary to maintain a trusting partnership. Thus, Ron's solution is to date a non-threatening alternative: Lavender Brown. Lavender offers no real threat to Ron because she is clearly infatuated with him, and she is just kind of silly. Therefore, she provides both an easy romantic relationship and a nice method of passive-aggressive action toward Hermione, Ron's real object of desire. It becomes clear early in the relationship, however, that Lavender isn't a good partner for Ron. Another trait of anxious people, though, is that they cannot end relationships. Even when in a bad relationship, anxious people are so afraid of being alone that they cling to others. Ron therefore doesn't end things—he just waits for Lavender to become so annoyed at his lack of attention that she breaks things off.

Although his feelings seem obvious to the outside observer, Ron doesn't seem to have a grasp on them at all. He wants to be with Hermione, but he doesn't understand these cravings. Thus, this anxious conflict comes out in constant petty squabbles between Ron and Hermione, over stupid things like Hermione's cat and her surprised reaction to the news that he's been named a prefect. These fights continue for years. Finally, an implicit understanding takes place between Ron and Hermione, but only after two tragedies. Ron is accidentally poisoned in *Half-Blood Prince*, and while he's barely conscious in the hospital ward, the only word he squeaks out is, "'Er-my-nee'" (*Half-Blood Prince* 402). At the end of the book, Dumbledore's funeral pushes them over the edge, and they cling to each other in misery and grief. It seems that after six years of secret, unspoken yearning, Ron finally understands his desires and acts upon them.

Importantly, attachment theory would predict that every one of the Weasley children should have this need for attention. Bill works in a bank (a seemingly mundane job), but he refuses to conform by wearing an earring and a long ponytail. Charlie works with dangerous dragons. Percy desperately attempts to become the Minister of Magic himself, or at least be connected to the most powerful people in the wizarding world of bureaucracy. Percy is also annoyingly proud of being a prefect and Head Boy. Fred and George's attempts to be the center of attention are totally obvious. Finally, Ginny's first crush is on the most popular boy in the school, and she quickly becomes one of the most popular girls at Hogwarts. It seems the entire family shares the traits of anxious individuals. Although anxious people certainly have a rocky road toward relationship bliss, their path seems easy compared with our third and final attachment style: avoidance.

HARRY POTTER: A CASE STUDY IN AVOIDANCE

The last attachment style identified by researchers is called *avoidant*. Avoidant children are often treated as strangers by their parents, and vice versa. They don't act distressed when parents leave; often, it's more of a relief. In short, avoidant children don't attempt to make strong bonds, they act indifferently about potential romantic partners, and they consistently shut down their emotional life. Avoidant children often don't like themselves much, and they have little or no trust in others. Why should they? In essence, they have been abandoned for most of their young lives. They are pessimistic and generally have a pattern of purposeful isolation. We see all of these characteristics in abundance in our main character, Harry Potter.

Harry's home life is, in a word, pitiful. When Harry's parents are murdered when he is only a year old, Harry moves in with the

Dursleys, his aunt and uncle. However, he is never treated as a family member (more like a servant or a disobedient dog). In stark contrast to their neglect of Harry, the Dursleys pamper their own son, Dudley, to the point of absurdity. Dudley has two televisions, two bedrooms, thirty-nine birthday presents, etc. Dudley is the face of indulgence (both figuratively and literally). The direct result of this polarized treatment of the children is that Harry learns to be resentful and that others are not trustworthy. We see an example of this in the first book, during their trip to the zoo. When Harry assures the Dursleys that he'll behave, "Uncle Vernon didn't believe him. No one ever did" (*Sorcerer's Stone* 24). When it seems that things are going well, we see the first signs of Harry's chronic pessimism: "Harry felt, afterwards, that he should have known it was all too good to last" (*Sorcerer's Stone* 26). Harry simply never believes that good things will come his way, especially from his interpersonal relationships. His lack of trust and pessimism follow him like dark shadows in everything he does.

He doesn't believe Hagrid when he's told that he's a wizard. He doesn't think he'll be able to afford his required school supplies. He then thinks he'll be the worst in his classes, impossibly behind the other children. When he's awaiting Sorting, he's sure he'll end up in Hufflepuff or Slytherin. Finally, when he's actually under the Sorting Hat, he's afraid that the Hat will decide he shouldn't be in *any* of the Houses and simply kick him out of Hogwarts before he's even begun. Note, all of these examples come before Harry has even gone to his first day of school. It's clear that the Dursley home environment has taught Harry to feel worthless and that nothing good will ever happen to him.

Although Harry's first year goes extremely well (i.e., he basically saves the entire wizarding world by himself), he still has no confidence in others or in himself. During the first summer vacation after his return, he quickly believes that Ron and Hermione aren't really his friends. Later, when he has to pick his third-year school subjects, Harry assumes he'll be "lousy" at all of them, so he just picks whatever Ron picks (*Chamber of Secrets* 252). When trying to figure out how to breathe underwater for the Triwizard Tournament, Harry procrastinates until the last minute, then gives up the night before the task: "It's over, he told himself. You can't do it" (*Goblet of Fire* 488).

As he ages, Harry's pessimism takes an ugly turn to resentfulness.

This is another hallmark of avoidant people: their emotions are on a negative track, and they tend to lash out at others, pushing them away. At the beginning of *Order of the Phoenix*, Harry has spent his entire summer glowering over the fact that Ron and Hermione get to spend time together working against Voldemort, while Harry is home with the Dursleys. Harry obsesses about how he's being completely left in the dark, as their letters carefully avoid mentioning details:

> He could hardly bear to think of the pair of them having fun at the Burrow when he was stuck in Privet Drive. In fact, he was so angry at them he had thrown both their birthday presents away unopened....Hadn't he proven himself capable of handling much more than they?...The injustice of it all welled up inside him so that he wanted to yell with fury...his insides writhed with anger (*Order of the Phoenix* 8–10).

And Harry certainly does yell with fury, to anyone who will put up with his whining for more than a few minutes. Harry alternates between jealousy, laughing indignation, and guilt, but he seems incapable of taking control of his emotions or understanding the perspectives of others.

This leads Harry to the solace typical of avoidant people and the classic behavior that leads to the name avoidant: purposeful isolation. Even from the beginning, Harry avoids making new friends— for example, he tries to find a solitary compartment on the Hogwarts Express on his first day. The first time he tries out his Invisibility Cloak, he consciously does not include Ron in the adventure, and he earlier hid it when Fred and George burst into his room because "[h]e didn't feel like sharing it with anyone else yet" (*Sorcerer's Stone* 202). Before he battles with Quirrell and Voldemort, Hermione hugs him for luck, but Harry doesn't hug back; he just stands there, uncomfortable with her reaching out, both emotionally and literally. Harry could certainly use more friends and support throughout his time at Hogwarts, but he pushes away people like Colin Creevey, who clearly worships Harry and would like to get close.

Although Ron is Harry's best friend, Harry doesn't do much to maintain their relationship. When Harry's name mysteriously comes out of the Goblet of Fire, Ron believes Harry submitted it, and Harry reacts to Ron's accusations with anger and insults. The fight continues for weeks, as Harry snarls and insults Ron at every opportunity. When Ron accidentally walks in on Harry's secret conversation with Sirius, causing it to end early, Harry "knew that Ron had no idea what he'd walked in on, knew he hadn't done it on purpose, but he didn't care—at this moment he hated everything about Ron" (*Goblet of Fire* 335).

The point of attachment theory, however, is that Harry should show these avoidant characteristics in his romantic relationships. It is clear over and over again that Harry avoids romantic relationships, preferring to silently fantasize with no action. Harry has a major, *major* crush on classmate Cho Chang for years. However, all he ever does is remain passive, never acting on his feelings unless forced. The perfect opportunity to ask her out arrives with the Yule Ball, but Harry puts off asking her until the last minute. When she tells him that she's already agreed to go with someone else, Harry's reaction is relatively bland—he just kind of mutters "okay" and heads off to be by himself. He then asks the next person who happens to walk by, clearly giving up. From that point on, he never initiates anything, though he still pines for her. After their first D.A. meeting, Cho waits behind the others, crying. It is *she* who arranges for them to be alone together. It is *she* who points out the mistletoe, *she* who moves closer to Harry, *she* who tells Harry that she really likes him. Finally, they kiss, but only because (as Harry explains later), "'[S]he just kind of came at me'" (*Order of the Phoenix* 459). Harry is so stunned that he does what he always does: nothing.

Again, it is she who makes a move to progress the relationship: she approaches Harry regarding the trip to Hogsmeade on Valentine's Day. He actually asks her out, but only accidentally! When they do finally go out, Harry does nothing to make her feel comfortable or happy. She starts to cry again, and he does not comfort her. In fact, he stupidly tells her that he's going to leave to meet Hermione. She storms out, and does Harry chase her to explain? No—he only thinks to himself that Cho closely resembles a hose, considering how much water comes out of her. This is basically the end of their relationship, caused by Harry's complete inability to do anything to maintain it.

Harry's first, and relatively successful, real romantic relationship finally comes at the end of his last year at Hogwarts, with Ginny

Weasley. Importantly, although he's harbored secret desires for Ginny for several months, he has again done absolutely nothing about it. Again, it is *she* who makes the first move, running at him to kiss him after a successful Quidditch match. They are happy together for a very brief time. However, as avoidant people usually do, it is Harry who quickly ends the relationship. He tells Ginny that he won't be able to concentrate on his mission to kill Voldemort if she is there—that he must do this alone. She accepts this, but note that Harry easily agrees to be accompanied by Ron and Hermione. It is the romantic relationship that Harry cannot maintain. According to attachment theory, Harry's dismal early home life has caused him to enter a never-ending pattern of relationship misery that he cannot escape.

THE FUTURE

Things look bad for Harry. Will he ever be able to initiate and maintain a happy romantic relationship? Attachment theory would argue that this is impossible *unless* Harry can satisfy his needs for a stable parental relationship, to fulfill his deep-seated needs for nurturance and unconditional love. Is there hope for this?

Harry has had borderline parental relationships with three figures. First, Harry clearly has a loving relationship with Hagrid. However, Hagrid cannot offer the guidance that Harry needs, because he is rather childlike himself and has his own parental issues to deal with (including, most directly, his own mother's abandonment of him as a child). The next opportunity comes with Sirius Black. When Sirius and Harry finally meet and he understands that Sirius is not trying to murder him, Harry instantly bonds to Sirius as his father's best friend and as his own godfather. Clearly, Sirius could serve as a father-figure. When Harry needs advice, he thinks of Sirius: "What he really wanted...was someone like—someone like a *parent*: an adult wizard whose advice he could ask without feeling stupid, someone who cared about him.... And then the solution came to him... Sirius" (*Goblet of Fire* 22). However, this does not work out. Sirius cannot serve as a father substitute for Harry because Sirius is not grown up himself. Sirius is still the boy who lost his best friend—he acts like a child, reckless and easily angered, even daring Harry to do dangerous things just for amusement. Unfortunately, Sirius's reckless tendencies lead to his early death, leaving Harry, again, with no family to offer loving support.

Harry's last chance at a parental figure comes with his idol and distant mentor, Dumbledore. Throughout the years that Harry is at Hogwarts, Dumbledore looks after Harry, guiding him and protecting him. Whenever Harry is in trouble or his scar hurts, Ron and Hermione encourage him to seek Dumbledore. However, Harry hesitates, believing that Dumbledore either won't believe him or that Dumbledore would be disappointed in Harry for not having more control. It's clear that Harry does not want to disappoint Dumbledore, just like children avoid disappointing beloved parents. Harry has complete faith in Dumbledore's abilities and that Dumbledore can save him in any situation. Dumbledore himself realizes that he has come to see Harry as a son and admits to making mistakes in order to protect Harry. Dumbledore tells him, "'I cared about you too much....I cared more for your happiness than your knowing the truth, more for your peace of mind than my plan, more for your life than the lives that might be lost if the plan failed'" (*Order of the Phoenix* 838). Sounds just like any good parent protecting his child. Again, though, Harry's life is marked for misfortune. The death of Dumbledore seals Harry's fate: He will never have a long-term parental figure on whom he can draw support.

Attachment theory therefore predicts that Harry will never be able to resolve this missing piece of his life, and that he will never be able to maintain a healthy romantic relationship. It is not the ending we would like. Perhaps Harry will form a successful romantic relationship, perhaps with Ginny. It is possible that by observing other adult relationships (such as one between Ron and Hermione) that Harry can learn how to show love and support. It is possible that with a great partner, Harry will have a relationship that will last a relatively long time. However, it is the unfortunate prediction we must make that in the end, Harry will live his life in basic isolation. Harry must, inevitably, rely on himself for major missions and decisions in life. Harry is a great wizard. But often, greatness is bred from childhood strife and results in interpersonal loneliness and separation in adulthood. It is a reality of life that is not optimistic, that does not end with "happily ever after." But, usually happiness is only temporary, anyway. For Harry, quiet isolation, without the constant threat of murder and betrayal, may be the best we can hope for.

WIND GOODFRIEND, Ph.D., is an assistant professor of psychology at Buena Vista University. She earned her Ph.D. in social psychology in 2004 from Purdue University in Indiana. Her areas of research expertise include gender stereotypes and romantic relationships, focusing specifically on positive and negative predictors of relationship stability over time. In her final year of graduate school, Dr. Goodfriend received both the "Outstanding Teacher of the Year" award and the "Outstanding Graduate Student of the Year" award for her research.

REFERENCES

Berscheid, E. and P. Regan. *The Psychology of Interpersonal Relationships*. Upper Saddle River, NJ: Prentice Hall, 2005.

Brennan, K. A., C. L. Clark, and P. R. Shaver. "Self-Report Measurement of Adult Attachment: An Integrative Review." In J. A. Simpson and W. S. Rholes (Eds.), *Attachment Theory and Close Relationships*. New York: Guilford Press, 1998. 46–76.

C. Hazan and P. R. Shaver, "Romantic Love Conceptualized as an Attachment Process," *Journal of Personality and Social Psychology* 52 (1987): 511–524.

Rowling, J. K. *Harry Potter and the Sorcerer's Stone*. New York: Scholastic Inc., 1998.

——. *Harry Potter and the Chamber of Secrets*. New York: Scholastic Inc., 1999.

——. *Harry Potter and the Prisoner of Azkaban*. New York: Scholastic Inc., 1999.

——. *Harry Potter and the Goblet of Fire*. New York: Scholastic Inc., 2000.

——. *Harry Potter and the Order of the Phoenix*. New York: Scholastic Inc., 2003.

——. *Harry Potter and the Half-Blood Prince*. New York: Scholastic Inc., 2005.

Harry experiences an enormous amount of grief in his young life. Now, with Dumbledore's death, is it too much? Is Rowling piling on the grief just to tug at our heartstrings? Or does Harry's grief play an essential role in giving him the power to fight Voldemort? Hook suggests just that by reviewing the processes of grieving and how Harry may have naturally applied them.

MISTY HOOK, Ph.D.

What Harry and Fawkes Have in Common

The Transformative Power of Grief

THE WORLD OF Harry Potter is a very dark place indeed. It starts with the murders of Lily and James Potter and the attempted murder of one-year-old Harry. Thus, even in the first scene of *Harry Potter and the Sorcerer's Stone*, we glimpse the terrible grief that will permeate Harry throughout the series. For those familiar with the biography of author J. K. Rowling, this overarching theme of grief should come as no surprise, as she has mentioned how much the death of her own mother (at the incredibly young age of forty-five) impacted her psyche. Since her mother's death occurred just as she was writing Book One, Harry became deeply affected by loss and grief, as well.

At the end of *Harry Potter and the Half-Blood Prince*, when I was worn out from tension and emotion, I questioned the need for the magnitude of tragedy Harry has endured. Was J. K. Rowling just piling on the angst in order to spin out the tale? Does Harry really need to suffer as much as he has in order to become the person who will (most likely) vanquish Lord Voldemort? The answer is yes, he does. Lord Voldemort is an incredibly evil and talented wizard, one whom the most gifted of witches and wizards cannot destroy. How can a boy who is barely an adult be expected to defeat him? While Harry is a good wizard, his powers do not equal Voldemort's. But Harry does have some secret weapons.

As Dumbledore has repeatedly said, Harry's strengths are his humanity and his knack for both loving and being loved. Throughout the series, Harry has scoffed at these two abilities, but he would be wise to appreciate them, for they are more powerful than he knows. In order to defeat Voldemort, Harry must show resolve and the determination to do what must be done no matter the cost to himself. Thus, while Harry's humanity and capacity for love could have blossomed in the arms of loving parents and caretakers, it is only through Harry's multiple losses and his ability to be positively molded by his grief that he has discovered the toughness it will take to achieve victory over Voldemort. As such, Harry's grief is like a phoenix: it burns him up only to help him emerge a stronger, better person. It is no accident that Harry's wand contains a phoenix feather. At several points throughout the series, Fawkes the phoenix has burst into flames and grown again. So has Harry.

RESILIENCE: BUILDING THE FOUNDATION

Luckily for Harry, he has a rock-solid personal foundation upon which he can build in order to survive his terrible grief. Many people are not as fortunate. Common thought holds that children who experience major loss will have psychological problems: they will become depressed, anxious, or act out. For many children this is certainly the case, particularly for those who not only have to deal with the actual loss itself but also with poor parental care and other negative things, such as social isolation or financial difficulties (Harrington). This is especially true for boys who lose both parents unexpectedly (Dowdney et al.). Sound familiar? Wait, it gets worse. Research suggests that this tendency toward dysfunction becomes even greater when grief is not dealt with appropriately (American Academy of Pediatrics). For childhood grief to be worked through in a positive manner, experts recommend that children's feelings be respected and expressed, and they should be allowed to participate in mourning rituals (Kaufman & Kaufman). While we know very little about Harry's childhood experiences before the age of eleven, I think it's pretty safe to assume that the Dursleys do nothing positive for Harry. Instead, they are insensitive to his grief, actively degrade his parents' memory, keep Harry in relative social isolation in the cupboard under the stairs, and do not encourage him to have friends. To sum it up, Harry experiences one of the most terrible kinds of losses, is not allowed to grieve, and then is treated unkindly. If Harry has almost all of the risk factors for major psychological dysfunction, why in the world is he not only stable and functional but also, to use Dumbledore's word, exceptional? And how does he get this rock-solid personal foundation?

The answer to these questions is that, clearly, the boy is resilient. *Resilience* (the ability to recover quickly from illness, change, or misfortune) is actually much more common than people suspect and, while we don't know what exactly causes it, we do have some ideas. In Harry's case, it is most likely a combination of Lily and James's parenting ability, his own personality, and the Dursleys. Yes, you read that right, I said the Dursleys. Believe it or not, they do play a positive role in Harry's development, but I'll get to them in a minute. The base for Harry's resilience rests with the Potters. When children are born, they quickly learn that their parents (or caregivers) are either there for them or they are not. Children who know that their parents are dependable become securely attached, while those who either aren't sure or know for a fact that their parents are unreliable do not (Bowlby). Lily and James Potter must have been such good parents that even with only one year of raising Harry, he became securely attached to them. This is definitely desirable, because people who are securely attached tend to have high self-esteem, enjoy long-term intimate relationships, find social support, and are able to share their feelings with others. Harry demonstrates all of these abilities. Thus, whether Harry realizes it or not, his parents give him a legacy that is much more important and necessary to his survival than their money or even their memory.

Harry's personality also has a great deal to do with his resilience. Although there are many ways to become resilient, the traits that

Harry exhibits are hardiness, the ability to experience positive emotion, and the use of active coping strategies. While all of these serve to transform Harry's grief into strength and personal growth, the most important of the resilience factors is hardiness, because it constitutes the core of Harry's belief system. Hardiness is to believe that life has purpose, one can influence the outcome of events, and that growth can be achieved from both positive and negative experiences (Bonanno). Given the Dursleys' neglect and emotional abuse, Harry should be downtrodden and depressed, but his hardiness prevents severe psychological dysfunction. Harry believes that his life is different from that of the Dursleys, that he is not destined to be what they are: angry and (at least in their minds) average. His purpose in life at this point is to get away from Privet Drive and be different. Harry's ability to influence events also gives him a vital edge. His talent for magic (although he doesn't know that is what it is at the time) gives him the power to change the things he absolutely cannot stand, be it an imminent beating at the hands of Dudley or the potential ridicule for a horrendous outfit or haircut. All he knows is that he has the capability to impact his life. Similarly, Harry seems to realize, even at such a tender age, that he can grow from things that are either positive or negative. Most people would probably be resentful at having to live in a cupboard under the stairs or not being able to eat their fill of food, but not Harry. While he is probably not sophisticated enough to understand that these circumstances are building character, he knows enough to realize that he doesn't want to be like Dudley, the favored child. Harry can see that Dudley is spoiled, dissatisfied, and a generally horrible person, and he grasps that his own neglect and abuse, if nothing else, spare him Dudley's fate.

Harry's other resilient traits serve him equally well. Even in the cruelest of situations, Harry is able to experience positive emotion and laughter (Bonanno). This is an important strength to possess, because positive emotions can decrease distress by either quieting or undoing negative emotion. Thus, Harry's ability to laugh at Dudley's failings or humorously appreciate Uncle Vernon's red face and pulsing vein allows him to soothe himself. This, of course, will be of great assistance to him later when he needs to laugh at the heckling before a Quidditch game or, more seriously, when he deals with Snape, the Ministry of Magic, and, ultimately, Voldemort. Harry's final resilient trait, his use of active coping strategies, is of incredible value (Lin, Sandler, Ayers, Wolchik, & Luecken). In fact, as a psychologist, I wish more people would learn these skills, because they prepare you to deal with anything! In Harry's case, he expresses his emotions even when he knows they will not be welcomed (no repression for him), removes himself from harm's way when necessary (he's self-protective), doesn't hold onto his resentments (no accumulation of negative emotion), and takes pleasure where he can get it (he's optimistic and observant). In short, we all could learn a thing or two from Harry's style of coping.

Finally, as much as I hate to do it, I must insist that we appreciate the role the Dursleys play in Harry's resilience, for without them, Harry would not have developed the way that he has. Research has shown that bereaved children who can maintain a positive sense of self in the face of adversity and believe in their efficacy to cope with future stressors experience fewer psychological problems (Lin, Sandler, Ayers, Wolchik, & Luecken). Let's think for a minute about what would have happened had Dumbledore not been wise enough to leave Harry with his Muggle relatives. There are plenty in the wizarding world who gladly would have raised Harry as their own. If Harry had been brought up in the magical community, he would have been exposed to almost constant sympathy and adoration. He would not have faced any kind of adversity (can't you just hear everyone saying, "Nothing's too good for Harry Potter!") and, thus, he would not have known that he could handle stressful events. The Dursleys, as horrible as they are, give him adversity and prod and poke Harry into developing hardiness, positive emotions, and coping skills. In essence, Lily and James gave Harry his solid foundation, while the Dursleys give Harry the impetus he needs to cultivate the skills he will use to defeat Voldemort.

POSITIVE GRIEVING AS PERSONAL GROWTH

While resilience is clearly a strength of Harry's, it is not quite the sole reason he will defeat Voldemort. Although surviving the murder of his parents and living with the Dursleys certainly gives him the edge in honing his resilient skills, let's face it: being resilient is something he could have achieved without all that. Harry's capacity for resilience might not have been as powerful or well-practiced, but it would still be there. Hence, it is the rest of Harry's journey through grief that makes him such a worthy adversary against evil. I know this sounds weird, because most people believe that grief is a process or even a weakness, something to be worked through so you can return to normal. However, after losses of the magnitude that Harry experiences, there is no "normal": he has nowhere to return. So, he must do something with his grief. Additionally, some researchers and theologians believe that grief is a path toward personal growth, a way to become a stronger person (Hogan & Schmidt). People who deal positively with their grief are able to handle things that others cannot, and this is true for Harry. He uses experiences that would have broken a less resilient person and turns them into tools that he can use in his quest to kill Voldemort. As such, Harry uses the three steps of positive grieving (Gillies & Neimeyer) to transform himself into the Chosen One.

STEP 1: MAKING SENSE OF DEATH

When people you love die, your world is turned upside down. This is especially true when, as in the case of Lily and James Potter, the deaths are traumatic and/or occur at an unexpected time in the life cycle. The Potters were young, had a small child, and were good people. In short, their murders never should have happened. But they did and, in so doing, shattered Harry's "assumptive world," his beliefs about the benevolence and meaningfulness of the world as well as his own self-worth (Janoff-Bulman & McPherson). Since Harry was basically a baby when his parents died and didn't learn the truth until he was eleven, this process occurred much later than it should have. In addition, his assumptive world is different than most children his age. Children who grow up within a loving environment usually believe that the world is a nice place where bad things do not happen to good people. They also tend to have a relatively high sense of self-worth. However, because of his treatment by the Dursleys, Harry does not have these beliefs. He knows early on that the world is not necessarily a kind place and his self-worth, while not as dismal as it could be, is still low. Consequently, when he learns the truth from Hagrid about his parents' death, his world is shattered, but it doesn't disintegrate. Here again, the Dursleys' poor conduct helps him be strong.

Nevertheless, Harry still has to make sense of his parents' death. Fortunately, this is not a long process. Harry quickly discovers that his parents died protecting him. Lily in particular died so that he could live. So, making sense of that one is easy; it is the later deaths of Cedric, Sirius, and Dumbledore that are harder for Harry. While each of the deaths occurs in different ways and at the hands of different people, they all have one thing in common: they occurred because of Harry. Cedric is murdered because he is with Harry in the wrong place at the wrong time, Sirius dies because Harry is rash, and Dumbledore is killed because he spends precious time securing Harry's safety instead of defending himself. At first, making sense of these deaths is extremely difficult for Harry, and he struggles to figure out why he is worth all this destruction. However, figure it out he does. Thus, with every successive death, Harry's assumptive world keeps breaking but a little less each time. The initial shattering is tough, but from it he learns that evil does sometimes flourish, and, thereafter, he is not surprised to keep learning this lesson. Each time a death occurs he becomes a little more convinced until, with the death of Dumbledore, Harry realizes that the meaning for all of their deaths is that sometimes there are things worth dying for, and fighting evil is one of them.

STEP 2: FINDING BENEFIT IN THE EXPERIENCE

This step in the grief process can be complicated, but finding positive aspects of the loss is crucial in adapting to it (Gillies & Neimeyer). While finding the silver lining can be easy from an outside perspective (we know that Harry will gain strength from his tragedy), when you consider things from Harry's point of view, it becomes incredibly difficult. He is ripped away from his loving parents and community and put into an almost intolerable living situation only to then lose three additional people who were important to him. However, optimism is one of Harry's coping skills, so he is able to accomplish this hard task. Harry realizes early on that the attack that kills his parents also causes Voldemort to vanish for ten years. This is indeed beneficial. For Sirius, Harry reluctantly figures out that he dies doing what he wants to do, his name is cleared, and he is no longer suffering by living in a place he hates. Moreover, Sirius's actions in fighting Voldemort's Death Eaters probably save the lives of Harry and his friends. Similarly, Harry eventually accepts that Dumbledore's death also saves lives, for if the Dark Mark had not ultimately been meant for Dumbledore (both literally and figuratively), it may have heralded the death of another. Moreover, Dumbledore dies showing Harry what must be done. However, the death of Cedric is tough, as there seemingly is no benefit at all: he isn't fighting when he dies, and his death serves no purpose. It is left to Dumbledore to provide Harry its meaning. When he is addressing the students at the end of the year, Dumbledore says, "Remember, if the time should come when you have to make a choice between what is right and what is easy, remember what happened to a boy who was good, and kind, and brave, because he strayed across the path of Lord Voldemort" (*Harry Potter and the Goblet of Fire* 724). Thus, Cedric's meaningless death becomes a call to fight, and he becomes a martyr for the cause.

STEP 3: IDENTITY CHANGE

The final step of the positive grieving process is perhaps the most important one, because it builds strength. By going through the process of reconstructing the meaning of loss, you necessarily reconstruct who you are. You become different, better even. People who experience this report a deepening of social relationships, including a heightened sense of compassion, a willingness to take on new roles, existential growth, and a changed sense of self (Tedeschi, Park, & Calhoun), and we definitely see these changes in Harry. At the beginning of *Sorcerer's Stone*, Harry has the same kind of relationships with others that most kids his age have. He likes and has fun with Ron and Hermione, he both admires and fears Dumbledore, and he hates Malfoy. As his grief transforms him, however, these relationships become multifaceted and much more meaningful. Harry learns to trust and truly love Ron and Hermione. The three of them experience the bond of trauma, and it is their three-way companionship that brings Harry confidence, joy, and openness. At several times, Harry—a boy who has by necessity learned to keep things to himself—cannot wait to tell Ron and Hermione what he has found out, because he knows they will make him feel better. Thus, throughout the course of the series, Ron and Hermione become family ("in spite of the final meeting with Voldemort he knew must come . . . he felt his heart lift at the thought that there was still one last golden day of peace left to enjoy with Ron and Hermione"; *Half-Blood Prince* 652).

Similarly, Harry's relationship with Dumbledore changes from that of student to rebellious son to protégé. During his first year at Hogwarts, Harry avoids bothering Dumbledore with information. However, as their relationship deepens due to tragic events, Harry comes to trust and rely upon him. This transformation is not easy, and there are times when Harry is incredibly angry with and rude to Dumbledore, but, by the time Dumbledore dies, Harry has started relating to him as a man. This is why Dumbledore finally agrees to let Harry accompany him on his search for Voldemort's Horcrux. Dumbledore knows that Harry can be trusted to do what must be done.

While Harry's relationships with Ron, Hermione, and Dumbledore are critical to his transformation, the most telling of all of Harry's relationship changes is the one with Draco Malfoy. When the two of them first meet, they hate each other almost immediately. In addition to hating what the other believes and stands for, however, they are both jealous. Malfoy wants the fame, adoration, and love that Harry generates from others, while Harry resents Malfoy's status in the wizarding world and the fact that he has two living parents who obviously love and protect him. Both boys will stop at nothing to bring the other down. However, in Harry's final year at Hogwarts, his attitude toward Malfoy changes. Even while he is trying to figure out what he is doing, Harry notices that Malfoy is pale and less cocky. Harry hears about his breakdowns in front of Moaning Myrtle, and, when Malfoy refuses to kill Dumbledore, Harry realizes that Malfoy is trapped by evil. Thus, Harry goes from hating Malfoy and wanting him beaten at all costs to having compassion for him. Thus, the losses that Harry experiences allow a seventeen-year-old boy who has rarely been shown compassion to develop some and give it to one of his worst enemies.

However, perhaps the most significant part of Harry's identity change is his acceptance of who he is and what he is destined to do. When we first meet Harry, he is attempting to figure out what being the Boy Who Lived means to him. He is searching for how and why this happened to him. As time goes on, Harry discovers that the reason is foretold and has great significance for other people as well as himself: he is the Chosen One, the one who will end Voldemort. At first, Harry is incredibly frightened and even somewhat disbelieving of this. He tries to make it go away by focusing on the fact that Voldemort could have chosen Neville (*It shouldn't have been me*). He dismisses the two powerful weapons that Dumbledore insists he has (*I'm not good enough*). Harry then attempts to passively accept his fate by believing that the prophecy is what made him a legendary figure (*I'm destined to do this because it is foretold*). Thus, Harry does not immediately accept the meaning that everyone else assumes is a given. Instead, he comes to the same conclusion but by a different route, one born of both pain and love: "He thought of his mother, his father, and Sirius. He thought of Cedric Diggory. He thought of all the terrible deeds he knew Lord Voldemort had done. A flame seemed to leap inside of his chest, searing his throat" (*Half-Blood Prince* 512).

As the fire of grief rises in him, Harry completes his transformative journey, the one powered by unfathomable loss, trauma, and grief, and it is this that ultimately makes the prophecy come true. In a twist that not even Dumbledore anticipates ("'I never dreamed I would have such a person on my hands.... Young you might be, but you had proved you were exceptional'" [*Harry Potter and the Order of the Phoenix* 839.]), Harry's life experiences give him his purpose. In essence, Harry's meaning for his life is *because* of his grief and not in spite of it. Through that journey, Harry learns to accept and even embrace his role as the Chosen One. He becomes more confident, more independent, and more willing to do what must be done. Because of his changed identity, he breaks up with Ginny and plans to leave Hogwarts to begin his quest to destroy Voldemort. There is no doubt that he will succeed. Like a phoenix, Harry has survived the fire of grief again and again to become a new and stronger person, the one who will decimate evil. Thus, his grief has ultimately transformed him into a champion.

HARRY'S OTHER EDGE: VOLDEMORT'S GRIEF

Harry's journey through positive grieving is what will give him the tools he needs to defeat Voldemort, but there is one other edge that he has. In an ironic twist, the very thing that makes Harry a champion the transformative power of grief—is what ruins Voldemort. Both men experience incredibly similar childhoods, yet they respond to their circumstances quite differently. Like Harry, Tom Riddle suffers significant loss. His mother dies during childbirth, his father abandons him, and he is raised in a grim, loveless orphanage. Tom never has the love of parents or caregivers. He knows that the people who care for him are unreliable and, therefore, he develops insecure attachment. Characteristics of people who are insecurely attached include: an inability to develop and maintain friendships; alienation from and opposition to parents, caregivers, and other authority figures; anti-social attitudes and behaviors, aggression and violence; difficulty with genuine trust, intimacy, and affection; and a lack of empathy, compassion, and remorse (Bowlby). Sound familiar? As Tom has an insecure attachment, he never has the positive foundation that Harry has, and the resilient skills he exhibits come with a negative twist. Tom's resilience rests in his belief that he is different, more powerful than others. Through the precocious use of his magical talent, he knows that he can influence the outcome of events, but he never considers positive growth. Thus, his coping skills become cruelty, defensiveness, and domination. In addition, unlike Harry, Tom rarely, if ever, experiences positive emotion, so he does not have the ability to unravel negative emotion. It just sits there, rotting his soul away.

In events mirrored in Harry's life, Tom Riddle does not learn the true story of his parents' lives until he is older; hence his grieving process is delayed. Like Harry, Tom's assumptive world is different than those of children raised in loving environments, so he is not destroyed when he discovers his heritage. However, he still has to make sense of his parents' choices, and, through Dumbledore's stories, we hear how difficult this is for him. Tom can't believe that his mother is dead because she could do magic. He finally has to accept that she could have lived for him had she chosen to do so but that she did not, so she basically abandoned him just as his father did. To a boy who is already corrupted by a resilient yet rotting foundation, the discovery of his parents' rejection is the final straw. Instead of using his grief to mold himself into someone who will fight for what is right like Harry does, Tom does the opposite. In fact, his very name—Riddle—suggests that he has been riddled by grief, so much so that he is no longer whole. Thus, unlike Harry, Tom allows his grief to make him into an embittered, hateful man, one who seeks power and vengeance instead of love. Instead of looking for relationships that might help him heal, Tom searches for those who can help him achieve dominion. He acclimates to his changed circumstances but never adjusts; he feels his emotions but never accepts them; he destroys his beliefs but never rebuilds them. In short, he never goes through a positive grieving process to become something better.

It is no accident that both men have wands that contain feathers of a phoenix. Both men have to experience the fire of grief and become something different once reborn. Both men are highly skilled and can become great wizards. However, Tom Riddle emerges from the fire of his grief as Lord Voldemort. He becomes a powerful wizard both hated and feared but never loved, one who cannot achieve what his own philosophy espouses: purity. In contrast, Harry emerges from the fire of grief as someone tranformed, not destroyed. He has everything that Voldemort does not. He has purity of soul, purity of purpose, and even purity of lineage, as Harry's parents both had magical abilities. Harry has vision because he embraces his own humanity. Voldemort wants to destroy his humanity and everything that causes him pain. There is nothing he wants to build, thus he is limited by his shortsightedness. In contrast, just as Fawkes's tears have healing properties, Harry's tears heal him. Harry is able to see through his pain to visualize what love can achieve. He can imagine a better world and thus has hope.

However, perhaps the most important difference between the two, the undeniable edge, is that Harry was and is loved. Voldemort has no friends or people who love him. Instead, he has followers who are there because they fear him or want what they believe he can give. When the going gets tough, they do not stay loyal. Harry has many people who love him, people who would give their lives to protect his. They will be with him no matter the cost to themselves. Thus, the meaning and purpose for his life is rooted in love. For Harry, it all starts because his parents love him enough to die so that he can live. Tom Riddle doesn't have that. His father never cares about his existence, and his mother doesn't love her baby enough to survive. As a result, while Harry knows that others believe he is of worth, Voldemort constantly has to prove his importance, not only to himself but also to others. When all is said and done, Voldemort will not have anyone who will grieve his demise, while Harry's death will be mourned by many. As such, grief becomes the measuring stick by which a true hero is created or destroyed. In the end, what will matter is how the fire of grief is endured. Voldemort allows his grief to consume him, and his soul becomes so unbearable that he has to separate parts of it from his body. Thus, he emerges literally as a shell of a man. Harry uses his grief to become like Fawkes, the phoenix, reborn each time into something increasingly powerful and good. And, in the fight that is to come, that is what Harry will need in order to win.

MISTY HOOK, Ph.D., spent five years as an assistant professor of psychology, where she taught courses in family psychology, the psychology of women, and social psychology. It was in academia where she first learned how to analyze pop culture. She is now a licensed psychologist in private practice, where she sees people who do not bear any resemblance to those in the Harry Potter universe. Dr. Hook wishes she had magical ability, because it would really help in her practice. In her spare time, she enjoys being with her husband and son, with whom she one day hopes to read the Harry Potter series.

REFERENCES

American Academy of Pediatrics. Committee on Psychosocial Aspects of Child and Family Health. "The Pediatrician and Childhood Bereavement," *Pediatrics* 105 (2000): 445–447.

G. A. Bonanno, "Loss, Trauma, and Human Resilience. Have We Underestimated the Human Capacity to Thrive After Extremely Aversive Events?" *American Psychologist* 59 (2004): 20–28.

Bowlby, J. *Attachment and Loss: Vol. 3. Loss: Sadness and Depression.* London: Hogarth, 1980.

L. Dowdney, R. Wilson, B. Maughan, M. L. Allerton, P. Schofield, and D. Skuse, "Bereaved Children: Psychological Disturbance and Service Provision," *British Medical Journal* 319 (1999): 354–357.

J. Gillies and R. A. Neimeyer, "Loss, Grief, and the Search for Significance: Toward a Model of Meaning Reconstruction in Bereavement," *Journal of Constructivist Psychology* 19 (2006): 31–65.

R. Harrington, "Childhood Bereavement: Bereavement is Painful but Does Not Necessarily Make Children Ill," *British Medical Journal* 313 (1996): 822.

N. S. Hogan and L. A. Schmidt, "Testing the Grief to Personal Growth Model Using Structural Equation Modeling," *Death Studies* 26 (2002): 615–634.

Janoff-Bulman, R. and C. McPherson. "The Impact of Trauma on Meaning: From Meaningless World to Meaningful Life. In C. Brewin (Ed.), *The Transformation of Meaning in Psychological Therapies*. New York: Wiley, 1997.

K. R. Kaufman and N. D. Kaufman, "Childhood Mourning: Prospective Case Analysis of Multiple Losses," *Death Studies* 29 (2005): 237–249.

K. K. Lin, I. N. Sandler, T. S. Ayers, S. A. Wolchik, and L. J. Luecken, "Resilience in Parentally Bereaved Children and Adolescents Seeking Preventative Services," *Journal of Clinical Child and Adolescent Psychology* 33 (2004): 673–683.

Tedeschi, R. G., C. L. Park, and L. G. Calhoun. *Post-Traumatic Growth: Positive Changes in the Aftermath of Crisis*. Mahway, NJ: Lawrence Erlbaum, 1998.

Provenzano and Heyman discuss Harry's remarkable resilience: his astounding ability to shake off the neglect and abuse of the Dursleys and function normally—in fact heroically—at Hogwarts. They examine what the research tells us about resilience from such childhood trauma and show how the resilience Harry exhibits is also often found in our Muggle world.

DANIELLE M. PROVENZANO
AND RICHARD E. HEYMAN

Harry Potter and the Resilience to Adversity

THE WIZARDING WORLD celebrates Harry Potter as the miraculous "Boy Who Lived" (*Harry Potter and the Sorcerer's Stone* 1). Wizards and Muggles alike, however, should marvel at Harry, for despite the traumas, abuse, and neglect that Harry suffers as a child, he lives normally. His physical, social, academic, and behavioral functioning are average to extraordinary. Just as Muggles don't see the Leaky Cauldron because they don't look, it's easy to miss how extraordinary Harry's ordinariness is. Consider that Harry and Lord Voldemort are connected by a prophecy but not by a trajectory: both are nurturance-starved orphans, but only Lord Voldemort is unable to form loving bonds with others, and only Lord Voldemort seeks to use his magical powers to exact pain, death, and retribution. In this essay, we will examine what accounts for the miracle of Harry Potter—not the *Avada Kedavra*-defying Boy Who Lived, but the maltreatment-resilient Boy Who Lives.

THE UNFORGIVABLE DURSLEYS: EMOTIONAL MALTREATMENT AND NEGLECT

The Dursleys' treatment of Harry during his childhood and adolescence is characterized by both types of child maltreatment: *abuse* and *neglect* (see Table 1). The Dursleys' emotional maltreatment of Harry has been the most pronounced. Emotional abuse is defined as a non-physical behavior (or, most commonly, a series of behaviors) by a parent or caregiver that causes the child psychological harm or has a high potential for causing psychological harm (e.g., depression, anxiety disorder, undermined sense of self-worth). Emotional neglect involves withholding emotional nurturance, support, or bonding necessary for normal child development. The common result of caregiving characterized by these types of behavior is the transmission of the message that the child is unloved and defective (Iwaniec, Larkin, & Higgins).

Table 1. Examples of Child Maltreatment in the Harry Potter Series

NEGLECT
The Dursleys ignore Harry whenever possible (*Sorcerer's Stone*).
Harry is made to live in the cupboard under the stairs, and is sometimes locked there for a week at a time (*Sorcerer's Stone*).
There are frequent references in *Sorcerer's Stone* to Dudley hitting Harry (including Harry being Dudley's "favorite punching bag" [20]), but the Dursleys do nothing.
Harry is often described in a way that seems borderline malnourished; he frequently is punished by having meals withheld (*Sorcerer's Stone*).
Harry is imprisoned in his room "around the clock"—bars are fitted on the window and Mr. Dursley installs "a cat-flap in the bedroom door, so that a small amount of food could be pushed inside three times a day. They let Harry out to use the bathroom morning and evening" (*Harry Potter and the Chamber of Secrets* 22).
Uncle Vernon tries to banish Harry from the house after the Dementor attack, despite Harry's life being in obvious imminent danger (*Harry Potter and the Order of the Phoenix*).

EMOTIONAL ABUSE
Uncle Vernon screams that he "'WILL NOT TOLERATE MENTION OF YOUR ABNORMALITY UNDER THIS ROOF'" (*Chamber of Secrets* 2). His abnormality is mentioned again in *Harry Potter and the Prisoner of Azkaban*. Harry's "abnormality" reflects both his genetic and his cultural heritage.
The Dursleys scapegoat Harry (e.g., blame him for things either out of his control or that he did not do) (*Sorcerer's Stone* 24).
The Dursleys frequently and overtly treat Harry worse than Dudley to make Dudley feel better (*Harry Potter and the Goblet of Fire* 27).
The Dursleys "never spoke about [Harry's parents] and he was forbidden to ask questions" (*Sorcerer's Stone* 30).
Uncle Vernon threatens Harry during the Masons' dinner party: "'[Y]ou'll wish you'd never been born'" (*Chamber of Secrets* 18); he will "flay him within an inch of his life" (*Chamber of Secrets* 20).
Uncle Vernon threatens to "'*knock the stuffing out of* [Harry]'" (*Prisoner of Azkaban* 20).
Uncle Vernon tells Aunt Marge that Harry attends St. Brutus's Secure Centre for Incurably Criminal Boys (*Prisoner of Azkaban*).
PHYSICAL ABUSE
Uncle Vernon dragged Harry up the stairs (*Chamber of Secrets*).
Aunt Petunia aimed "a heavy blow at [Harry's] head with a soapy frying pan" (*Chamber of Secrets* 10).
Uncle Vernon puts "two purple hands" through the window and closes them tightly around Harry's throat (*Order of the Phoenix* 4).
Harry avoids getting too close to Uncle Vernon, as "long experience had taught him to remain out of arm's reach of his uncle whenever possible" (*Harry Potter and the Half-Blood Prince* 45), implying a history of physically abusive behavior.

Aunt Petunia and Uncle Vernon relegate Harry to the status of a second-rate member of the household, leaving him to sleep in the cupboard under the stairs and clothing him in Dudley's inappropriately-sized leftovers. While they spoil their biological son with zeal, they force Harry to survive on the bare minimum of physical sustenance and offer him no emotional support or caring. At age eleven, Harry has somewhat resigned himself to a life of being ignored or left out, demonstrated by his gleeful shock at being included in Dudley's birthday trip to the zoo (*Sorcerer's Stone*). Even on his own birthdays or at Christmas, Harry is denied any special treatment from the Dursleys, who vacillate between completely ignoring him and offering him some negligible scrap (such as old socks, a toothpick, or a single tissue) in lieu of a present. Harry's memories of growing up with the Dursleys are filled with instances of being excluded; in fact, the first memory Professor Snape can conjure during Occlumency lessons is one of Harry at five years old and "his heart…bursting with jealousy" at watching Dudley on his new bicycle (*Order of the Phoenix* 534). This obvious distinction between the doting way in which the Dursleys treat Dudley and the neglectful way in which they treat Harry conveys the message to Harry that he is somehow unworthy.

Furthermore, the Dursleys' behavior toward Harry goes beyond these passive acts of neglect and into the more active behaviors that exemplify emotional abuse. They openly acknowledge him, not as a child with needs, but as "the boy," and treat him like a bother that requires reluctant handling on their part and "like a dog that had rolled in something smelly" (*Chamber of Secrets* 5). "The Dursleys often spoke about Harry…as though he wasn't there—or rather, as though he was something very nasty that couldn't understand them, like a slug" (*Sorcerer's Stone* 22). Uncle Vernon in particular speaks to Harry in nothing but vicious and nasty snarls and relishes in his harsh discipline, sometimes confining Harry for days at a time for actions out of the child's control. In fact, the Dursleys as a whole seem to make a family pastime out of tormenting and harassing Harry, as is displayed in Harry's second memory during Occlumency lessons: "He was nine, and Ripper the bulldog was chasing him up a tree and the Dursleys were laughing below on the lawn" (*Order of the Phoenix* 534). Uncle Vernon, Aunt Petunia, and Dudley demonstrate no remorse at belittling Harry's cultural and genetic heritage (what they perceive to be freakish) and perversely take pleasure in goading him.

Less commonly described than their emotional maltreatment of Harry is the Dursleys' physical abuse. Physical abuse is defined as a caregiver's non-accidental use of physical force that causes a significant impact on the child. As can be seen in Table 1, Harry has been exposed to enough physical abuse that he consciously avoids situations that might provoke it.

DEFENSE AGAINST THE DURSLEYS' ABUSE: RESILIENCE

Even as Dumbledore chides the Dursleys for their miserable treatment of Harry, he acknowledges that Harry has emerged virtually unscathed: "'[Harry] has known nothing but neglect and often cruelty at your hands. The best that can be said is that he has at least escaped...appalling damage'" (*Half-Blood Prince* 55). To what can Harry's resilience be attributed? Although we cannot account for variables such as magical spells or charms, we can project what we know about certain factors' contribution to resilience in Muggle children and adolescents on what we know about Harry's experiences. The next section will first introduce key concepts and findings in the study of resilience and then apply these concepts to Harry.

DEFINING RISK AND PROTECTIVE FACTORS

Child maltreatment increases the likelihood of (i.e., is a *risk factor* for) negative outcomes such as behavioral problems (e.g., aggression), emotional problems (e.g., depression, anxiety), academic problems, poor peer relations, and drug/alcohol problems (Cicchetti & Toth). A risk factor is anything that we can measure that is associated with increased likelihood of negative outcomes. We say "associated with" because proof is almost always absent that risk factors *cause* negative outcomes; it could also be that the outcomes caused the risk factor (e.g., being aggressive toward peers could cause peer rejection, rather than the other way around) or that another variable is causing both (e.g., if an *aggressive gene* caused parents to hit their children and their children to hit their peers). In contrast, a *protective factor* is anything that we can measure that, in the context of risk, is associated with a reduced likelihood of negative outcomes. The concept of resilience puts together the notions of risk and protective factors.

RESILIENCE

What is resilience? Resilience requires two elements: (1) a person has experienced a noteworthy risk or a traumatic event, and (2) the person is "doing okay" (Masten & Powell). There are several implications of this definition of resilience. First, "doing okay" reflects normal functioning across the board (e.g., someone who has normal physical health but is failing in school would not be classified as exhibiting resilience [Luthar & Zelazo]). Harry is a competent, but not stellar, student: on his Ordinary Wizarding Level exams (*Half-Blood Prince*), he receives one Outstanding grade (in Defense Against the Dark Arts), five Exceeds Expectations, one Acceptable, and two failing grades. He is extraordinarily close to two friends (who are both prosocial enough to be named prefects): Hermione Granger and Ron Weasley. He has excellent general peer relations (except, for understandable reasons, with the Slytherins). He gets along well with most authority figures (with the notable exception of Professors Snape and Umbridge and members of the Ministry of Magic, who are prejudiced against him and intent on using him for their own ends). His family relationships with the maltreating Dursleys are terrible, but he forms close attachments with surrogate family members (e.g., his godfather, Sirius Black; the Weasley family). His romantic attachments are normal for a boy his age (e.g., somewhat tentative and faltering with his first girlfriend, Cho Chang, but more assured and secure with his second girlfriend, Ginny Weasley). He excels at sports (Quidditch) and was named captain in his sixth year, in recognition of both his athletic prowess and his leadership capacity. In summary, despite his youth, his extraordinary travails, the withering (and often unfair and inaccurate) publicity, and the most powerful Dark wizard in the world intent on murdering him, Harry Potter indeed can be said to be exhibiting "normal functioning across the board," and thus appears to be exhibiting resilience through age sixteen.

Second, "doing okay" reflects a *process* whereby a child adapts to his/her environment and is currently functioning normally. It is preferable not to think of a "resilient child" (i.e., a permanent quality of the child), but rather of a child whose current outcomes imply resilience (i.e., a snapshot indicates that the child is "doing okay" [Bolger & Patterson 2003]). Although a thorough assessment of Harry between ages one to eleven likely would have noted significant depression and anxiety, his capacity for normal interaction is evident from his thriving once Hogwarts cast off the yoke of his oppression under the Dursleys. In other words, once Harry is placed in a non-maltreating environment, he adapts marvelously and quickly displays normal functioning. The environment at Privet Drive, and not Harry, is dysfunctional.

Prevalence of resilience. Bolger and Patterson (2003) reported that when resilience is defined as *above average* functioning, not surprisingly, very few maltreated children qualify as resilient. However, studies that operationalized resilience as not being in the pathological range have reported one in four maltreated children demonstrate resilience (Kaufman, Cook, Arny, Jones, & Pittinsky). Thus, the Boy Who Lived beats the odds in surviving a murderous attempt by the Dark Lord; the Boy Who Lives beats the odds by not only being non-pathological, but by being average or above average in all key life areas.

Why is resilience important? What can we learn, in general, from resilient children such as Harry? All children investigated by Child Protective Services likely have some elevated risk factors for disrupted development, compared to the non-investigated population. These risk factors include the maltreatment itself (at levels that, at a minimum, warranted notification of, and investigation by, Child Protective Services) as well as elevated rates of poverty, disrupted parenting, attachment problems, corrosive family conflict, and parent-parent aggression (Heyman & Slep).

Because children are likely to have already experienced maltreatment (even at levels below the threshold for official action) by the time Child Protective Services is notified, preventing this risk is not possible. The growing focus on resilience has already influenced many aspects of society's response to child maltreatment by focusing on boosting protective factors instead of just trying to reduce risk factors (Masten & Powell).

FACTORS THAT PROMOTE RESILIENCE

The research on factors that promote resilience in high-risk environments, including maltreatment and neglect, suggests that a variety of individual, family, abuse, and community characteristics can be protective against the negative sequelae of such backgrounds. There is some evidence that a child who is temperamentally easy, outgoing, bright, and resourceful will be more stress-resistant and resilient to adversity (Clarke & Clarke). In addition, other child characteristics, such as having a positive view of the self, attributing his or her adversity to external sources, or having valued assets such as a talent or sense of humor, are associated with better outcomes in at-risk children (Wolfe; Wright & Masten). Family characteristics that confer protection against adversity include a stable home environment, parental involvement with the child's education, higher socio-economic status, higher education in the parents, and faith or religious affiliations (Wright & Masten). Abuse that is infrequent, low in intensity, and short in duration is less likely to severely impact the child than abuse that, like Harry's, is more constant, severe, and longer in duration (Iwaniec, Larkin, & Higgins). The length of the abuse is related to another factor that promotes resilience: being raised in an early environment characterized by secure and loving attachment.

The community in which a child resides can also promote resilience, especially if it consists of safe and clean neighborhoods, good public health care, and access to emergency services (Wright & Masten). In addition, effective school systems can allow high-risk children to gain social and practical support, to escape from any abuse in the family home, and to form supportive and positive relationships both with peers and with adults (Iwaniec, Larkin, & Higgins). These supportive relationships seem to play a particularly important role in buffering the child from emotional maltreatment; Doyle (1997) found that of a variety of protective factors, the most significant predictor of resilience was having one supportive figure who gave the child unconditional positive regard. We will discuss the critical importance of supportive figures later in the essay.

TEMPERAMENT/EARLY ENVIRONMENT

As noted earlier, the least is known about what protects Harry from the Dursleys through age eleven. As he does not enjoy the comforts of having close friends or much escape from maltreatment at school, the major factor that likely contributes to his functioning is what is bestowed upon him by his parents. Hardly any who knew Lily or James can resist noting the physical characteristics they transmitted to their son—James's hair and physique, Lily's piercing green eyes.

Harry also has seemed to inherit certain personality traits or characteristics, such as his father's Quidditch skills and his mother's courage. With that, it is likely that some of the positive traits Lily and James impart to Harry serve to protect him from the potentially crippling effects of the consistent emotional maltreatment he endures. It is notable that gene-environment interactions are theorized to play a role in the phenomenon of resilience, in that adverse environments more greatly affect those individuals with a genetic vulnerability than those without a heritable predisposition (Werner).

In addition to genetics, Harry also receives thirteen nurturing months from his parents, who reportedly loved and cared for him dearly. The impact of Harry's mother's love is known to have left an imprint on him in a magical sense; the remnants of that love make it painful for Quirrell/Voldemort to touch Harry and aid him in escaping death in that confrontation. Dumbledore explains, "'[T]o have been loved so deeply, even though the person who loved us is gone, will give us some protection forever'" (*Sorcerer's Stone* 299). Not only does the love Harry receives from Lily in her last moment protect him from physical harm, but the love he receives from both of his parents in infancy likely supplied him with the secure attachment and nurturance that help protect him from the later abuse he would suffer.

SCHOOL

Hogwarts certainly seems to play a significant role in bolstering Harry's resilience and fostering his success. Discovering he is a wizard and moving to Hogwarts qualifies as a "life chance" (Clarke & Clarke) that rescues him from an abusive home while simultaneously offering him a fresh academic start. Harry is relieved to learn from Hagrid that "'[e]veryone starts at the beginning at Hogwarts'" (*Sorcerer's Stone* 86), so whatever academic or peer difficulties he had while living with the Dursleys will not continue to haunt him throughout his wizarding schooling.

SUPPORTIVE RELATIONSHIPS

The literature on resilience indicates the strong role that supportive relationships can play in children whose development has been hindered or stunted by maltreatment. This support can be found within formal mentoring programs as well as within natural mentoring relationships, such as those that might spontaneously form between the child and extended family members, neighbors, teachers, employers, clergy, or coaches. DuBois and Silverthorn (2005) found that certain qualities of these natural mentoring relationships—the mentor role, emotional closeness—have differential impact on the children or adolescents in question. Harry benefits from a variety of natural mentor relationships—teachers, surrogate family members, big-brother types—and although these particular types of relationships have not been empirically compared, it is likely that these various mentors play different roles and supply different forms of support and nurturance for Harry.

Albus Dumbledore. Harry's interactions with Dumbledore could serve as an exemplar for the ideal natural mentoring relationship. Dumbledore consistently demonstrates to Harry what the Dursleys never have: that he wholeheartedly accepts Harry as a well-intentioned person. In many instances when Dumbledore might express anger or disapproval of Harry's actions—when Harry repeatedly breaks his curfew to visit the Mirror of Erised (*Sorcerer's Stone*), when Harry succumbs to his curiosity and peers into Dumbledore's Pensieve (*Goblet of Fire*), or when Harry furiously destroys objects in Dumbledore's office in a rage after Sirius's death (*Order of the Phoenix*)—Dumbledore instead empathizes with Harry and attempts to convey that Harry's wishes and desires are normal and understandable. He accepts Harry's emotions and gently guides him to make the right decisions.

Whereas the Dursleys continually drill into Harry that he is aberrant and delinquent, Dumbledore instead tries to convince Harry of the goodness within himself. It is significant that Dumbledore is the first person in whom Harry is willing to confide that the Sorting Hat wanted to place him in Slytherin, a fact that fills Harry with shame and fear that he is like Voldemort. Dumbledore does not simply dismiss these fears with empty assurance but counsels him that his choices indicate a strength of character that sets him apart from other wizards, both good and evil (*Chamber of Secrets*).

Another quality of Dumbledore's that makes him a precious mentor to Harry is his willingness to admit mistakes. After Sirius's death, he tells Harry how he is mistaken in a number of ways—in thinking that Snape could put aside his grudge and treat Harry fairly during Occlumency lessons and in placing more value on Harry's happiness than on telling him the truth about the prophecy (*Order of the Phoenix*). During this moment, he not only absolves Harry of some of the guilt of causing Sirius's death, but also models for Harry the valuable ability to acknowledge one's mistakes and view these errors as learning opportunities, which is a marker of a resilient mindset (Brooks).

Another important lesson is the practice of weighing both short-term and long-term costs and benefits of one's actions. For example, when Harry returns from having witnessed Voldemort's return in the graveyard, McGonagall and Sirius discourage Dumbledore from making Harry relive his experience and think it best to distract Harry. However, Dumbledore focuses on Harry's long-term interests and advises that Harry stay and talk about the trauma (*Goblet of Fire*). In other words, Harry might benefit in the short term from postponing his reflection on the events of the night, but, as Dumbledore tells Harry, "'Numbing the pain for a while will make it worse when you finally feel it'" (*Goblet of Fire* 695). Harry realizes once he finishes retelling his experience that he does indeed feel a sense of relief, thus internalizing Dumbledore's message that one must consider the long-term impact of one's actions.

Professor McGonagall. Minerva McGonagall serves as a natural mentor for Harry in a manner that is stylistically different from Dumbledore's but nevertheless influential in Harry's maturation and success. Whereas Dumbledore tends to be warm and gentle, McGonagall is a firmer but equally dependable figure on whom Harry can rely for more frequent direction and guidance. It is she who defiantly demonstrates great faith in Harry's ability to fulfill his career goal of becoming an Auror when Umbridge doubts him, focusing more on his aptitude than on his alleged weaknesses or criminal record (*Order of the Phoenix*). Professor McGonagall demonstrates early in her relationship with Harry that same willingness to attribute his actions to strengths rather than defects; when Harry breaks the rules by flying to catch Neville's Remembrall, Professor McGonagall overlooks this indiscretion and places him on the Quidditch team as Seeker, identifying his natural talent and admonishing that he practice hard to develop his skills (*Sorcerer's Stone*). Professor McGonagall demonstrates in this instance her ability to identify what psychologist Robert Brooks (2005) calls "islands of competence"; she channels Harry's impulsive behavior into a positive, constructive talent and an opportunity for him to experience success and pride, instead of simply punishing him for breaking rules and acting recklessly.

Hagrid. Harry's connection with Hagrid is forged when Hagrid is entrusted to retrieve baby Harry from smoldering Godric's Hollow after his parents' murder. Ten years later he is again entrusted to retrieve Harry from a shack on a rock at sea after his Hogwarts invitations go unanswered. It is Hagrid who tells Harry that he is a wizard (*Sorcerer's Stone*) and who shepherds him into the wizarding world.

Harry's relationship with Hagrid is an example of a close, confiding, natural mentoring relationship with a consistent, warm adult who acts more as a big brother than as a true adult. Harry and Hagrid confide in each other, look to each other for support or favors (sometimes secretively), bolster each other when down—all signs of a peer relationship rather than one marked by a large power differential (despite Hagrid's staff positions at Hogwarts). However, befitting a big-brotherly guide, Hagrid will gently give Harry needed feedback when he strays from his better self. For example, in *Prisoner of Azkaban*, Hagrid chides Harry (and Ron) for giving Hermione the cold shoulder: "'Gawd knows yeh've had enough ter be gettin' on with. I've seen yeh practicin' Quidditch ev'ry hour o' the day an' night—but I gotta tell yeh, I thought you two'd value your friend more'n broomsticks or rats. Tha's all'" (274).

Weasley Family. The Weasley family provides abundant natural mentoring to Harry. Mr. and Mrs. Weasley provide Harry with the supportive parenting and love that his parents' murder and the Dursleys' maltreatment denied him, and Bill and Charley are role models for Harry (albeit ones with only sporadic contact with Harry).

Molly Weasley provides the same authoritative (strict but warm) parenting to Harry as she does to her other children. She is his official surrogate mother during the Triwizard Cup competition, knits Harry a Weasley sweater each Christmas, and loves him like her own child (even to the extent of including Harry as a family member in her Boggart worst fear: dead family members [*Order of the Phoenix*]). Arthur Weasley is the kindly, gentle father-figure—the polar-opposite of purple-faced Uncle Vernon. Mr. Weasley treats Harry to Quidditch World Cup tickets (*Goblet of Fire*), is the comforting guide to the Wizengamot hearing (*Order of the Phoenix*), and is understanding and empathic when Harry overhears Mr. and Mrs. Weasley arguing about Sirius Black's connection to Harry (*Prisoner of Azkaban*). Finally, because Harry did not grow up with any knowledge of the wizarding world, Bill and Charley provide some of the few glimpses of what a positive post-Hogwarts near-future might hold for Harry. That is, Harry has wizard/witch peers and middle- to mature-aged adults in his life, but precious few young adults to emulate.

SUMMARY

From the moment of his survival through his adolescent years, wizards young and old continue to be amazed by Harry's famous defeat of Voldemort when he was only thirteen months old. The question that leaves great wizards mystified is posed by Professor McGonagall just hours after the famed incident: "'How in the name of heaven did Harry survive?'" to which Dumbledore replies: "We can only guess. . . . We may never know" (*Sorcerer's Stone* 12).

Although we can only guess, we have speculated about how Harry survives ten years of maltreatment by his adoptive family. Harry grows up in a household in which he is seen as a nuisance at best and a loathsome creature at worst. He suffers the loss of his parents at an early age and spends his childhood years trying to escape bullying at home and at school. Yet, when given the "life chance" of being placed in the supportive environment of Hogwarts, Harry emerges as a globally well-functioning adolescent. The odds are about one in four that a maltreated Muggle child will function in the "non-pathological" range; the odds are much lower of being, like Harry, average to above average in all important life domains.

Harry often downplays his personal attributes that make him resilient, even arguing, "'[A]ll that stuff was luck—I didn't know what I was doing half the time, I didn't plan any of it, I just did whatever I could think of, and I nearly always had help'" (*Order of the Phoenix* 327). However, we believe that Harry's luck was due to a Felix Felicis with four major ingredients: (1) adaptable temperament; (2) an early, loving, secure environment; (3) an academic environment well-matched to his needs; and (4) supportive natural mentors.

DANIELLE M. PROVENZANO is a graduate student in the Ph.D. program in clinical psychology at the State University of New York at Stony Brook. She is interested in couple communication and processes. All who know her comment on the striking similarity between Danielle and Hermione, except for the bushy hair and prominent teeth.

RICHARD E. HEYMAN is a research professor of psychology at the State University of New York at Stony Brook. His research focuses on family dysfunction, especially family violence. He has authored or co-authored more than sixty scholarly papers, book chapters, or books and has received more than twenty federal research grants. He initially began to read Harry Potter to stop the incessant cajoling of Danielle and her fellow graduate students. He became hooked and is especially partial to the audiobooks as read by Jim Dale.

REFERENCES

Bolger, K. E. and C. J. Patterson. "Sequelae of Child Maltreatment: Vulnerability and Resilience." In S. S. Luthar (Ed.), *Resilience and Vulnerability: Adaptation in the Context of Childhood Adversities*. New York: Cambridge University Press, 2003. 156–181.

Brooks, R. B. "The Power of Parenting." In S. Goldstein & R. B. Brooks (Eds.), *Handbook of Resilience in Children*. New York: Kluwer Academic/ Plenum Publishers, 2005. 297–314.

D. Cicchetti and S. L. Toth, "Child Maltreatment," *Annual Review of Clinical Psychology* 1 (2005): 409–438.

Clarke, A. and A. Clarke. *Early Experience and the Life Path.* London: Jessica Kingsley Publishers, 2000.

———. "The Prediction of Individual Development." In D. Messer and F. Jones (Eds.), *Psychology and Social Care.* London: Jessica Kingsley Publishers, 1999. 240–255.

C. Doyle, "Emotional Abuse of Children: Issues for Intervention," *Child Abuse Review* 6 (1997): 330–342.

D. L. DuBois and N. Silverthorn, "Characteristics of Natural Mentoring Relationships and Adolescent Adjustment: Evidence from a National Study," *Journal of Primary Prevention* 26 (2005): 69–92.

S. S. Heller, J. A. Larrieu, R. D'Imperio, and N. W Boris, "Research on Resilience to Child Maltreatment: Empirical Considerations," *Child Abuse and Neglect* 23 (1999): 321–338.

Heyman, R. E. and A. M. S. Slep (Eds.). "Special Issue: Risk Factors for Family Violence." *Aggression and Violent Behavior.* 2001.

D. Iwaniec, E. Larkin, and S. Higgins, "Research Review: Risk and Resilience in Cases of Emotional Abuse," *Child and Family Social Work* 11 (2006): 73–82.

J. Kaufman, A. Cook, L. Arny, B. A. Jones, and T. Pittinsky, "Problems Defining Resiliency: Illustrations from the Study of Maltreated Children," *Development and Psychopathology* 6 (1994): 215–229.

Luthar, S. S. and L. B. Zelazo. "Research on Resilience: An Integrative Review." In S. S. Luthar (Ed.), *Resilience and Vulnerability: Adaptation in the Context of Childhood Adversities.* New York: Cambridge University Press, 2003. 510–549.

Masten, A. S. and J. L. Powell. "A Resilience Framework for Research, Policy, and Practice." In S. S. Luthar (Ed.), *Resilience and Vulnerability: Adaptation in the Context of Childhood Adversities.* New York: Cambridge University Press, 2003. 1–25.

Werner, E. E. "What Can We Learn About Resilience from Large-Scale Longitudinal Studies?" In S. Goldstein & R. B. Brooks (Eds.), *Handbook of Resilience in Children.* New York: Kluwer Academic/Plenum Publishers, 2005. 91–105.

Wolfe, D. *Child Abuse: Implications for Child Development and Psychopathology.* Newbury Park, CA: Sage Publications, 1987.

Wright, M. O. and A. S. Masten. "Resilience Processes in Development." In S. Goldstein & R. B. Brooks (Eds.), *Handbook of Resilience in Children.* New York: Kluwer Academic/Plenum Publishers, 2005. 17–38.

IS MAGIC REAL?

Is magic real? Maybe it isn't for you or for me, but small children live in a world filled with the magical and only slowly learn to put magic aside for science and reason. How do they do this? And is nostalgia for our magical childhood part of the uncanny appeal of the Harry Potter series? For we seem to lose our sense of magic at just the time Harry begins to discover it.

KARL S. ROSENGREN, Ph.D., AND EMILY C. ROSENGREN

Discovering Magic

Harry POTTER'S DISCOVERY of the world of magic is quite different from how and when children discover magic in our relatively ordinary world. For most of Harry's childhood he is surrounded by the dreary, mundane world of the Dursley family, a family that is both oppressive and exceedingly non-magical. Even seemingly impossible events, such as the rapid growth of Harry's hair following forced haircuts, the rapid shrinking of a despised sweater, or Harry's sudden appearance on the roof of the school kitchen after being chased by Dudley and his gang, are not labeled as anything special in Harry's childhood. Instead, these events are blamed on Harry, an assumed trickster, or in the case of the sweater, attributed to some commonplace act, such as the sweater shrinking in the wash. While Harry does not fully understand these events, he does not attribute them to anything magical. It is not until Harry is ten years old that his eyes are opened to the realm of magic. In contrast, in the Muggle world, the majority of children at that age have given up belief, and perhaps hope, in magic.

Young children in our world, in contrast to young Harry, often believe in such magical things as the Tooth Fairy and Santa Claus. They also believe that the feats performed in magic shows are not merely clever trickery but involve real powers that go beyond the ordinary. In this essay we explore children's real world beliefs in magic and magical entities and how they compare to the magical world of Harry Potter.

The term *magic* is used regularly to label a wide variety of things. Magic is applied to supernatural events that only seem possible in the world of fantasy and to those natural events that stimulate a sense of wonder or amazement.

In academic settings, the term magic has been used in a slightly more specific way by researchers interested in how children and adults reason about the world. In psychology, for example, much of the current usage of the term magic can be traced to the writings of Swiss psychologist Jean Piaget (1929, 1930). Piaget is often thought of as the father of cognitive development, the branch of developmental psychology that focuses on how a child's thinking changes as the child ages and gains more experience with the world. Piaget viewed the thinking of young children as dominated by magic. He did *not* mean that children were completely captured by thoughts of the supernatural. Rather, he used the term magic to refer to a form of reasoning that was neither logical nor scientific. In particular, he thought that children under the age of seven could not relate causes and effects in any logical or reasonable manner and often treated purely coincidental events as linked in meaningful ways.

Another attribute of Piaget's view of magical thinking was the belief that one's own thoughts could bring about physical changes in the world. A nice example of this can be found in the early section of *Harry Potter and the Sorcerer's Stone*, before Harry realizes that he is quite different from the Dursleys in an important way. During a visit to the reptile exhibit at the zoo, Dudley knocks Harry out of the way as he moves in to see what a snake is doing. Harry's anger at being pushed to the floor seemingly causes the glass wall between Dudley and the boa constrictor to vanish. This incident captures an event that is quite similar to Piaget's concept of magical reasoning: a child's belief that one's anger or other strong feelings can cause certain events to occur. It differs, however, in that Harry is not fully conscious that he caused the glass to vanish. In Piaget's view, belief in the efficacy of one's thoughts involves more of a conscious belief that one's thoughts or wishes can influence physical events.

Piaget did not generally think that a child's belief in supernatural powers was connected to these kinds of thoughts; rather, Piaget viewed this type of children's reasoning as yet another example of young children linking non-causally related events as if they were linked by a distinct cause. To Piaget, this form of magical reasoning was thought to be characteristic of *all* children below the age of about seven and not reserved for a special class of non-Muggles. In Piaget's view, as children mature and gain more experience with objects and events in the ordinary world, "magical reasoning" is replaced by more powerful and effective logical and scientific reasoning. However, these supposed characteristics of the "immature mind" are often found in adults as well as children. Indeed, as Zusne and Jones (1989) and Shermer (1997) have suggested, many adults hold a wide range of strange beliefs and superstitions. One must merely watch the common practices of many professional baseball players as they perform a series of rituals prior to approaching the plate, or other athletes who refuse to wash parts of their uniforms for fear their luck will change, or people who treat inanimate objects such as cars or computers as if these objects were sentient beings, to find common examples of this phenomenon.

For the most part, psychologists have reserved the label magic for instances of faulty logic and the non-scientific beliefs held by children or individuals belonging to another culture. In other words, any form of reasoning not based on rigorous logical and scientific thinking has been labeled as magic. Because of this, some psychologists have labeled a wide range of religious beliefs as *magical thinking*. One problem with this use of the word magic is that it is used in a somewhat pejorative manner to describe the immature thinking of children or the thought processes or beliefs of adults that are different from those of the dominant culture of the psychologist. To a large extent it is as if the researchers are taking on Vernon Dursley's attitude of disdain toward Harry and other magical beings. A more productive stance, perhaps, is to label problems with cause-effect relations as just that, and to treat individuals' beliefs in magic, supernatural entities, or religious phenomena as alternative beliefs that include forms of causality that go beyond those normally attributed to the physical world. For example, religions often involve a belief in a supernatural being who has the power to make impossible events happen (e.g., making the world out of nothing). In this context, the events are labeled as miracles and not attributed to magic but to an all-powerful, supreme being. Likewise, someone might believe in magical beings, such as wizards and magicians, and that these individuals or the objects that they possess (e.g., wands, hats, etc.) contain a supernatural force that can produce amazing events; these beliefs are quite different from faulty logic in that the holder of such beliefs generally assumes that different forms of causality exist beyond the merely natural world of scientists (or the Dursleys, for that matter!). Therefore, beliefs in the efficacy of magic or the existence of a supreme being are based on a set of fundamental beliefs about what can and cannot happen in the world.

In the minds of children, it is not faulty logic but the idea that the supernatural is real that underlies a belief in what we like to refer to as magic. These beliefs, such as beliefs in the Tooth Fairy, Santa Claus, or the magic of Harry Potter, are in many ways different from purely "causal errors" because they involve relatively long-standing beliefs about how the world works. These alternative beliefs in supernatural objects and means, the prototype magic of the wizards and witches in the realm of Hogwarts, were labeled by Piaget (1930) as social magical beliefs and to be of less interest to researchers trying scientifically to understand children's thinking.

We suggest that it is perhaps best to reserve the label magic for belief in the kinds of phenomena captured by the Harry Potter series. That is, beliefs that there exist particular magical entities (people, objects, or things) that are imbued with a supernatural force, commonly labeled as magic. This force provides individuals or objects with powers or qualities that violate the everyday physical and natural laws. We treat these particular beliefs as quite distinct from those that stem from various religions, because they are different in terms of the attributed causes and origins of the supernatural powers. And given that an overwhelming majority of individuals in the United States profess to hold strong religious beliefs, it does not seem productive to label these kinds of beliefs as magical.

Eugene Subbotsky, a psychologist at the University of Lancaster, has argued that magical forms of reasoning are not replaced by scientific reasoning as children grow older; rather, magical reasoning is driven underground by social norms, to resurface in certain laboratory or real world situations. In the laboratory, Subbotsky has conducted a series of experiments that make it appear as if "real magic" occurred. In one such experiment, Subbotsky first tells a six- to nine-year-old child a story involving a magical entity. One of these entities is a magic box that can destroy objects placed inside when a magic word is uttered. At this point he will often ask the child whether such a magical box could really exist. The majority of the children respond "no." Then he produces a box, very much like the one described in the story, and demonstrates that it can magically cut a postage stamp in half when a magic word is uttered. Subbotsky then departs, seemingly to perform some other task, leaving the child alone in the room with the box. Without an adult present many of the children utter the magic word and attempt to perform the magic. The child's verbal and physical behavior, as well as responses to follow-up interviews where children express disappointment that they could not create any magic, have led Subbotsky to suggest that this form of magical reasoning is not replaced by scientific thought, but is merely driven underground.

Over the past decade we have explored children's magical beliefs and how they come to hold these beliefs. Much of this work has focused on children's belief in magic and various supernatural beings, such as Santa Claus and the Tooth Fairy, but it has also focused on children's belief in magic more generally. We have used a variety of different approaches, including interviews with children and surveys sent to parents. In these interviews children are typically shown pictures or asked to witness events. Afterwards, the children are asked questions designed to assess their underlying beliefs about what kinds of things can and cannot happen in the world. To explore children's magical experiences further, we have also talked with professional magicians.

Our work suggests that children first begin to believe in magic at about three-and-a-half years old. Prior to this age, most children do not appear to understand magic or find it very fascinating. Magicians hate to perform shows in front children under the age of three, because to the typical three-year-old nothing is really magical. Young children are confronted with new, amazing, and wonderful things on a daily basis. From rainbows, to remote controls, to new kinds of animals that change shape or color, young children are constantly encountering things that they have never seen before. So, in a way, everything is magical to the young child. At the same time, nothing is really *caused* by magic because this special category referring to a supernatural form of causality has not yet been formed. Children below the age of three do not think that magicians and wizards are the only ones capable of performing amazing feats, but assume that most if not all adults have these powers. For example, young children think that an adult (a parent, a teacher) can cause a yellow cloth to turn blue by merely pulling it through his or her fist. On the other hand, they don't think that they themselves are capable of performing this act. By the age of three and a half or four, children begin to designate events as commonplace or magical, with normal people (Muggles in Harry's world) able to perform the commonplace events and only magicians able to perform the impossible magical ones (Rosengren & Hickling, 1994, 2000).

In contrast to the rapid manner in which Harry discovers magic, children in our world seem to gradually develop a concept of magic between the ages of the three-and-a-half and five years. Before they can gain this concept, children must first acquire a certain amount of knowledge and experience with objects and events in the world. As they gain experiences, children come to realize what kinds of objects and events are typical and commonplace. These everyday, commonplace experiences form the basis for reasoning about the natural world and help children to define *natural* and *physical* forms of causality.

Before children have acquired this knowledge and experience about the physical world, children's reasoning is often quite different from that of older children and adults. Renee Baillargeon, a researcher who focuses on very young infants, has shown that while young infants seem to realize that unsupported objects fall to the ground, they think that any amount of support or contact may be enough to suspend an object above the ground. In a series of clever studies (Baillargeon), she finds that if a single finger is touching an otherwise unsupported, relatively large box, that the infants are not at all surprised that the object does not fall. In another study, researchers have found that two-year-old children are not surprised that a machine can shrink and enlarge objects such as couches and chairs (DeLoache et al.). Although a few children attribute this event to magic, the majority of children of this age attribute this event to yet another fascinating machine that they have not yet encountered, nor fully understand. Mr. Weasley's fascination with Muggle-machinery is not that different from these young children. Items that seem commonplace and not at all magical to us Muggles, such as a telephone, are fascinating to him.

By the time children in the United States reach about three-and-a-half years of age, they have acquired a relatively large number of experiences that lead them to certain kinds of expectations. Children of this age expect that if a person closes his or her hand around a small object that it will still be there when the hand is opened a moment later. If it disappears, they exhibit surprise. They clearly expect objects to continue to exist in time and space unless some sort of natural and physical means is used to destroy the object. In contrast to young infants, children of this age also expect that objects will fall to the ground if not adequately supported. By the age of three and a half, children have also gained a lot of experience with books, stories, and situations where a violation of expectations is labeled as magical. Preschool teachers and parents will also sometimes make reference to magic when presenting color-changing markers, rocks that glow under florescent light, or magnets that propel one another. These events violate the normal expectation that ink does not change color or that two objects cannot interact with one another over a distance. It is not entirely clear why adults use the term magic in these situations. It may be that teachers use the label magic to bring some mystery into the classroom as a way of making a lesson a bit more interesting. Parents may label things as magic for the same reason. In other situations, adults may use magic as a default explanation when the explanation for an event is unknown or when the adult does not have a clear understanding of the actual cause of some interesting event. Attributing these types of events to magic may actually be detrimental to the child's learning experience. If teachers want to promote inquisitive explorations they should encourage the child to search for the causes underlying particular events. By labeling an event as magical they are providing a cause, but one that is not amenable to scientific investigation. Thus, the child need look no further for an explanation. The physical world is pretty interesting by itself, thus it seems unnecessary to describe events as magical in order to capture children's attention or to promote scientific understanding.

At the same time as children are learning more and more about what can happen in the real world and what mechanisms can cause these things to happen, they are also getting information about certain events, ones that violate their normal expectations about what can happen in the world. They are exposed to magicians, Santa Claus, and, at a slightly older age, the Tooth Fairy. The majority of parents in the United States actively support beliefs in magic and supernatural entities. However, they do this selectively. Parents tend to support beliefs that are viewed as positive; for example, they generally promote beliefs in Santa Claus and fairies, but discourage beliefs in ghosts, goblins, and witches (Rosengren & Hickling). Magicians are, for the most part, treated more neutrally. Parents may take their children to magic shows, but, other than these particular events, parents in our culture do not actively encourage beliefs in this type of magic as they do with Santa Claus and the Tooth Fairy. This may be because historically magicians, like many of the characters portrayed in the Harry Potter series, such as Lord Voldemort, have a much "darker" nature. It is this "dark side" of magic that parents in the United States seem to want to avoid. This avoidance is likely linked to a general avoidance in the American culture of things that can be viewed as negative. Similarly, parents in the United States have a tendency to shelter their children from exposure to death and death-related events. There is some indication that in cultures where death is more openly talked about, such as in Mexico with its "Day of the Dead" celebration, belief in magic is more common.

To examine how children come to label certain events as magic, we brought parents and their three- to five-year-old children into watch a specially constructed televised magic show. In the show, Dean the Magician (a rather exotic-looking undergraduate student working with us) performed a number of different events, classified as commonplace, physical/natural, and magical. The commonplace events included relatively simple, rather boring events, such as blowing up a balloon or drawing a happy face on a blank piece of paper. The physical/natural ones included more interesting events that involved chemical or physical reactions such as combining two clear liquids to make a blue liquid and picking up some metal objects with a magnet. The magical events consisted of prototypical magic tricks, such as making a silk scarf disappear and making colored pictures suddenly appear on a seemingly blank page. We found that parents, when talking to their three-year-olds, often labeled our magical events as *magic* and clearly labeled our other events as *not magic*. Some even went so far as to denigrate our magician as *not a very good magician* as he performed a lot of events that were not magic.

In contrast, in this same study, parents of older children (five year olds) rarely labeled events as "magic" and often just asked the children what they thought. Although a few parents took the opportunity to explicitly label the "magic" as trickery, the majority seemed to be quite happy to let their children uncover the deception on their own. This shift in explanation type is supported by responses to surveys where parents of young children (three to four years) state that they encourage belief in magic and some supernatural creatures, but as the children grow older, the parents shift from encouragement to taking a more evasive or avoidant approach. At around age five or six, it is quite common for the parents to turn questions about magic back to the child, asking, "What do you think?" or in the case of Santa Claus, rather than explicitly saying, "No, Santa Claus does not exist," parents say such things as, "Santa exists in spirit." Across a number of studies, the majority of parents appear to shift to this avoidant or evasive approach and prefer to let children "find out for themselves" the truth about Santa Claus and the Tooth Fairy and whether there really is magic in the world.

Few, if any, children are likely to develop a richly coherent and consistent world of magic like the one that Harry must navigate. In our world, children's exposure to magical events is much less consistent and predictable than children's experiences with the natural world. Every once in a while a teacher may use the term magic in a classroom or a parent may label certain events as magic, but these occurrences are relatively rare. Parents also report rarely taking their children to magic shows (typically less than once a year). In some cases, however, specific children who are especially fascinated with the magical or fantastic may develop very coherent and detailed thinking about magic and even create quite magical fantasy realms.

These children appear to be more likely to purchase magic tricks and come to a clear understanding of the boundary between reality and fantasy at an earlier age then those children with less interest and self-directed exposure.

In contrast, one of Harry's struggles as he enters Hogwarts is to develop a coherent and consistent knowledge of magic. In many ways, as Harry first enters Hogwarts his traditional view of the world is shattered. An entirely new form of explanation and causality is thrust upon him. He comes to find that many of the things he was told all his life are untrue. He also discovers new and wildly different things from what he has always been taught by the Dursleys and his teachers in the Muggle world. In our world, children's beliefs are also changed dramatically, but in the opposite direction. When Harry enters formal schooling at Hogwarts, he discovers a wonderful world of magic. When children in our world enter formal schooling, there is a shift away from magic, as children are supposed to discover the world of science and logic. Around the time children enter formal schooling, parents shift from actively encouraging their children's magical and fantasy beliefs to becoming more evasive and avoidant, and perhaps unsure of how they should respond to their children's inquiries about the true nature of Santa Claus or the Tooth Fairy.

Researchers have not really investigated why parents first encourage magical beliefs, then shift to avoidance, or what children feel about the fact that their parents have been lying to them for a couple of years. The consequences of these parental behaviors and whether there is an optimal parental approach to the exploration of magic has not yet been examined by researchers studying the development of children's thinking. So, at present we don't really know whether it is good to encourage magical beliefs in children or what the consequences are when a child discovers that magic is not real. It does not seem that this discovery shatters children's faith in their parents; rather, it may serve to encourage children to search for magic in other places, such as in books by J. K. Rowling and others. It also may increase children's appreciation for the amazing events in the world, such as rocks or fish that glow in the dark, walking catfish, flying fish, carnivorous mushrooms, fish that change from female to male, magnets, and even rainbows. The sense of wonder caused by these events and early encouragement in magic may help spark the imagination and creativity of the next generation of inventors, scientists, and fiction writers.

KARL S. ROSENGREN, Ph.D., is a professor of psychology at the University of Illinois at Urbana-Champaign. His research examines the development of causal reasoning in children. He is co-editor of *Imagining the Impossible: Magical, Scientific, and Religious Thinking in Children*. He has been fascinated by all things magical and mysterious since growing up as a full-blooded Muggle in suburban New Jersey.

EMILY C. ROSENGREN was born in Ann Arbor, Michigan, and moved to Champaign-Urbana, Illinois, at a young age. She will be (by the time you read this book) a graduate of the University High School in Urbana and will hopefully have received an owl carrying an acceptance letter to a school of higher learning. Both her parents are developmental psychologists. At present their parenting has left no visible scars, but has led her to search out other possible careers and the possibility that she contains some non-Muggle blood. She and her sister have been the inspiration for most of her father's best work.

REFERENCES

Baillargeon, R. "A Model of Physical Reasoning in Infancy." In C. Rovee-Collier and L. P. Lipsitt (Eds.), *Advances in Infancy Research*, Vol. 9. Norwood, NJ: Ablex, 1995. 305–371.

J. DeLoache, K. Miller, and K. S. Rosengren, "The Credible Shrinking Room: Young Children's Performance with Symbolic and Nonsymbolic Tasks," *Psychological Science* 8 (1997): 308–312.

Nemeroff, C. and P. Rozin. "The Makings of the Magical Mind: The Nature and Function of Sympathetic Magical Thinking." In K. S. Rosengren, C. Johnson, and P. Harris (Eds.), *Imagining the Impossible: Magical, Scientific, and Religious Thinking in Children*. Cambridge, UK: Cambridge University Press, 2000. 1–34.

Piaget, J. *The Child's Conception of the World*. London: Kegan Paul, 1929.

——. *The Child's Conception of Physical Causality*. London: Kegan Paul, 1930.

K. S. Rosengren and A. Hickling, "Seeing is Believing: Children's Explanations of Commonplace, Magical, and Extraordinary Transformations," *Child Development* 65 (1994): 1605–1626.

Rosengren, K. S., C. Johnson, and P. Harris. *Imagining the Impossible: Magical, Scientific, and Religious Thinking in Children*. Cambridge, UK: Cambridge University Press, 2000.

Rosengren, K. S. and A. Hickling. "Metamorphosis and Magic: The Development of Children's Thinking About Possible Events and Plausible Mechanisms." In K. S. Rosengren, C. Johnson, and P. Harris (Eds.), *Imagining the Impossible: Magical, Scientific, and Religious Thinking in Children*. Cambridge, UK: Cambridge University Press, 2000. 75–98.

Shermer, M. *Why People Believe Weird Things: Pseudoscience, Superstition, and Other Confusions of Our Time*. New York: W. H. Freeman and Company, 1997.

Subbotsky, E. V. *Foundations of the Mind: Children's Understanding of Reality*. Cambridge, MA: Harvard University Press, 1993.

J. Woolley, "Thinking About Fantasy: Are Children Fundamentally Different Thinkers and Believers from Adults?" *Child Development* 66 (1997): 991–1011.

Children believe in magic, but adults outgrow such foolish notions, don't they? Nemeroff demonstrates that we Muggles often use magical-type thinking and ascribe magical-type qualities to objects of everyday life. Many of the magical concepts of Harry Potter, such as the physical connection between Harry and Voldemort through his scar and the popular reluctance to say Voldemort's name, are shown to have a clear basis in how we think. Is this perhaps why the magic of Harry Potter seems so believable?

CAROL NEMEROFF, Ph.D.

The Magical World of Muggles

INTRODUCTION

For us Muggles, the world of Harry Potter is full of surprises. Excitement lurks around every corner, both in the epic struggle between good and evil and in the more mundane details of daily life in the wizarding world. Photos and portraits smile, wave, and visit each other; pots stir themselves and dishes wash themselves; visitors show up in fireplace grates and flames. Objects levitate and are transformed; magical creatures, plants, and substances abound. Harry's world is vivid and attention-grabbing. It feels more real than the Muggle world. Coming back to the everyday world of Muggle experience feels pale and lackluster in comparison.

It is not surprising that many of us would prefer to live in Harry's world, or at least take comfort in imagining that it exists just around a corner (and through a solid wall) in London, or hidden between Platforms 9 and 10 at King's Cross Station. Apparently, it is a core part of human nature to imagine unseen, mysterious worlds lurking behind the visible, realms where the normal rules don't apply. Humans are relentlessly imaginative, creative, and symbolic thinkers, and the idea that "this is all there is" seems frankly unbearable to us.

Believing in magic is a lot of fun, of course, but we don't really *believe* in it—do we? Over the past twenty years, Paul Rozin, fellow researchers, and I have been studying everyday magical beliefs among healthy, educated adults in the U.S. Simply put, *yes, we do* believe in magic at some level—although we're not always aware of our magical beliefs. Magical thinking influences our social behaviors, how we relate to food and eating, and how we think about and try to protect ourselves from illness, among other things. At times it leads us astray. But at other times, it can be helpful and protective.

DEFINING MAGIC

But what do we mean by magic, exactly? Magic is one of those words used to mean any number of things, often seeming to have nothing at all in common with each other: the "magic" of romance; things we can't explain; things others believe that we think are naïve or false. But the stricter use of the word "magic," the core definition of it, comes from the field of anthropology and Sir James Frazer, who spent his life collecting examples of magical practices and beliefs from cultures all over the world and compiling them into a twelve-volume set of books called *The Golden Bough* (1895). Frazer identifies the key ideas that occur in his collection of examples and calls them "sympathetic magic," because they depend on the idea of a special kind of connection—a "sympathetic connection"—between things. I will describe these key ideas, illustrate them with examples from Harry Potter (mainly *Harry Potter and the Sorcerer's Stone*), and describe how they show up in our research on magical thinking in daily life.

SYMPATHETIC MAGIC

Magical Essence
The concept of *mana*, or essence, is central to sympathetic magic. Mana is the magical force or stuff that travels along the pathways determined by the other principles. It is the active stuff, the power

that those impressive-sounding spells direct, the power that makes them work. A wizard's wand shooting out green or blue sparks or bolts of lightning is mana in its purest form. Mana can be a completely impersonal force—similar to how we think about electricity. But more often, mana is specific to its source. This is why each of the magic wands in Mr. Ollivander's shop is one of a kind. Every one contains some potent magical substance at its core: a phoenix feather, a dragon's "heartstring," a unicorn hair. Each magical creature has its own individuality, its own unique mana, and this in turn makes each wand different (*Sorcerer's Stone*).

Every wizard also has a unique essence. It is *general* wizard essence, presumably, that makes one a wizard rather than a Muggle, and this is the essence the Hogwarts's admissions committee must recognize in order to send new students their letter of acceptance. But it is one's unique, personal essence that the Sorting Hat reads and recognizes when assigning new Hogwarts students to their school Houses of Gryffindor, Ravenclaw, Hufflepuff, or (ugh!) Slytherin (*Sorcerer's Stone*).

Abundant evidence suggests that the idea of personal essence is influential in the Muggle world as well as in Harry's. For instance, we respond to others as though their "stuff" lingers, not only in their physical residues such as sweat, but also in their possessions and in anything with which they come into physical contact. This shows up in the reluctance many people feel about wearing (laundered) used clothing and also in the extent to which we overvalue objects *because* of their histories of contact with celebrities. Imagine holding in your hand the pen with which J. K. Rowling wrote the first draft of the first Harry Potter book. Is it better than another identical pen that was never used by our heroine? Of course! Similarly, people pay mind-boggling sums of money to own clothing, shoes, jewelry, and all manner of objects formerly owned or even just used by Jackie O., the Beatles, Princess Diana, and so on. What is *in* these items? Their "stuff": essence of glamour, fame, success, goodness....

Across many studies (e.g., Nemeroff & Rozin; Rozin, Nemeroff, Wane, & Sherrod; Rozin, Markwith, & McCauley; Rozin, Markwith, & Ross), people show aversions to using or wearing cleaned items that have been worn or used by disliked or evil people, strangers, or even people who have been unlucky. About a third of people also *prefer* clothing or other objects that have been worn or used by good, admired, or loved people. In a study designed to clarify exactly *what* people think is *in* these objects, Rozin and I (1994) asked our research participants to imagine various people wearing a sweater and then rate how they would feel about wearing that sweater. People they imagined wearing the sweater included their best friend, their romantic partner, and a person who they felt was truly "good," as well as a person they disliked intensely and a person they felt was truly "evil," among others. We then asked them to imagine the sweater being "purified" in a series of different ways and to rate how they would feel about wearing it after each purifying action. If sterilizing the sweater worked to make the sweater neutral again but deodorizing it didn't, it would suggest a concern with germs. If just the reverse happened, it would suggest a concern with residues such as odors. If the best approach were to unravel the sweater and make a new object out of it, the "stuff" would most likely be purely symbolic. And if it were most effective to have Mother Teresa wear the sweater after an enemy or evil person wore it, this would suggest a traditional idea of mana/essence, along the lines of "vibes" or "soul-stuff."

What did we find? First, that people differed in terms of how they thought about this "stuff." While it was clearly symbolic for many people, others thought of it as a physical substance, as though evil or nastiness could be transmitted like physical grime and removed in similar ways. As one woman said about her enemy's sweater:

> Very negative. I just don't want to be around him or his objects. [Why?] Because he'd give it cooties, not that I think he has cooties—but he's just a nasty person and oozes nastiness.

Another participant said he did not want to wear his enemy's sweater because, "his stuff is in it. [Stuff?] Yeah, you know, dirt, germs, sweat—stuff!" Although this implied a physical/residue model, none of the purification strategies, such as washing or deodorizing, were effective for him. Apparently, his enemy's essence was stronger than detergent or sterilizing (although burning it to ashes worked; the remaining pile of ashes was finally neutral for him). And in a separate component of this same study, a woman said, after imagining eating ice cream out of the container right after her "good" source person had eaten from it: "No problem. I guess his germs would be okay. Good germs." She then looked startled, confused, and finally repeated, "Yes! That's really how I feel!" Good germs? Whatever was in that ice cream, in her thinking, chances are it was not actually germs. It was the essence, the personal "stuff" of her admired person. (Interestingly, she was *not* amused at the idea of her spouse eating ice cream straight from the container, which she said was disgusting....)

In addition to mana/essence, two basic principles or "laws" complete our definition of sympathetic magic. They are the *law of similarity* and the *law of contagion*. Often, the two work together to produce a (supposed) magical effect.

THE LAW OF SIMILARITY

The law of similarity can be summarized as "like equals like." Things that resemble each other are also the same at their core, sharing deeper properties as well as superficial ones. According to this law, "the image equals the object," appearance equals reality, and "like produces like." Belief in the effectiveness of the traditional voodoo doll rests on the law of similarity. In the traditional magic of Africa, one creates a physical representation of a person (the doll) and then does things to the doll in order to generate a similar effect on the person (e.g., sticking pins into the doll results in pain and loss of function in the target person). The voodoo doll does not indiscriminately affect any old person who happens to be walking by at the time the pins are stuck into it! The effect is limited to the person whose essence it shares, the person it is an image of. Why? In the law of similarity, things that are alike are assumed to remain in *sympathetic connection* with each other through their shared essence, regardless of separation or distance in time and space.

Just as a voodoo doll is an "image" of its target, pictures and even names are images or representations of their original objects, so in a magical worldview the law of similarity applies to them, too. In Harry Potter's world, the collectible photos of famous witches and wizards found in packages of Chocolate Frogs are not static. They smile, wave, and occasionally are not in their pictures at all, as they go to visit each other or take care of business. They are connected to the essence of the original. The image equals the object. When

Harry unwraps his very first Chocolate Frog and picks up the card, he is astonished when the face on the card disappears, then reappears and smiles at him. (*Sorcerer's Stone*). The portraits on the walls in Hogwarts similarly move, disappearing from their frames at times and interacting with each other and with the students directly. In fact, the portrait of the Fat Lady guards the entrance to Gryffindor Tower, only admitting students if they know the password. At one point, when Hermione follows Harry and Ron out through the portrait to argue with them, she finds herself out of luck for getting back in when the Fat Lady goes for a nighttime visit (*Sorcerer's Stone*). And to think in the Muggle world we find it disturbing when an occasional portrait seems to have eyes that follow us around the room!

Because essence calls to shared/similar essence, the law of similarity is probably also the basis for how the Hogwarts admissions letters find their way to Harry regardless of where his Uncle Vernon tries to hide him to avoid the letters. In many cultural belief systems, a person's name is not simply a label; it is a core part of him or her. A person's name is the identity tag for his or her soul essence, and knowing a person's "true name" can give one a great deal of power over the person named. It is simply a different kind of representation of a person. The famous developmental psychologist Jean Piaget referred to this type of belief about names as "nominal realism." With Harry's name on them, the envelopes find him wherever he is, tracking him to his closet under the stairs, then to a dingy hotel outside an unidentified city, and eventually all the way to "The Floor, Hut-on-the-Rock, The Sea" (*Sorcerer's Stone* 51).

Essence calls to essence in finding the right wand, too, and the mysterious and disturbing link between Harry and Voldemort, which becomes more and more evident as the series progresses, is first hinted at through this principle. When Harry finds his right wand—or rather, the wand finds Harry—Mr. Ollivander remarks how curious it is that this particular wand should be his when "its brother gave you that scar." He explains that Harry's wand contains a tail feather from a phoenix who gave only two tail feathers, and the other resides in Voldemort's wand (*Sorcerer's Stone*). Clearly, then, Harry and Voldemort have something in common, some shared nature that the wands, alike at their cores, recognize. Over the next several books, the nature and origin of this bond unfolds. We will understand more about it in a few minutes, when we learn about the law of contagion, below.

But first—why is everyone in the wizarding world so reluctant to say Voldemort's name? The logic goes like this: If the name is a representation or image of the real thing, then the name (image) equals the object, and if like calls to like, then saying Voldemort's name evokes his essence, forms a connection with him, and runs a very real risk of drawing him near.

Back in the Muggle world, my colleagues Rozin, Millman, and I (1986) wanted to see whether American college students show emotional and behavioral reactions based on the law of similarity—that is, a tendency to treat something that they *know* is an image, a replica, a mere representation of a thing, as though it were the actual thing itself. Because Rozin's area of research specialty at that time was the emotion of disgust, the first two experimental tasks involved delicious fudge shaped like dog poop, and rubber vomit (we're beginning to sound like Fred and George Weasley, aren't we?). Guess what happened when participants were asked to put either standard or poo-shaped fudge in their mouth? Even though the items were identical except for appearance, few people would taste the poo-fudge. And given a choice between putting a clean rubber sink stopper or a similarly sized clean piece of rubber vomit in their mouth, most were reluctant to try the vomit. From this we concluded that for our participants, similarity went deeper than mere appearance.

We next took photographs of well-liked people (e.g., John F. Kennedy) and intensely disliked people (e.g., Adolf Hitler) and had participants throw darts at these photos, aiming for a central point between the eyes. We also had them imagine the faces of liked and disliked people whom they knew personally, aiming darts between the imagined eyes at a dot marked on the paper. People were consistently less accurate when throwing darts at images of people they liked and more accurate when aiming at images of people they disliked. (The one exception was when they imagined the face of the researcher who had just administered the fudge and vomit conditions to them; though they claimed to like her, their dart throwing accuracy suggested otherwise....)

Would these participants actually admit to any "confusion" between the images and the actual objects/people they represented?

Probably not—but the evidence suggests it nonetheless. The use of emotional reactions to try to understand people's "beliefs" deserves a brief explanation here. It is certainly the case that emotions can be caused by thoughts. Imagine that while playing a friendly game of soccer, a ball hits you hard in the eye. Imagine that the person who did it has excellent aim and a known tendency to try to injure other players in order to win. Do you get angry? Probably so. Now imagine instead that the person who did it struggles with the accuracy of his kicks and is always friendly and pleasant to you. Now are you angry? Probably not. Emotions often follow beliefs in clear and predictable ways. They can also determine beliefs—if you were in a bad mood to begin with when you got hit in the eye with the ball, you would be more likely to assume the worst.

There are exceptions to this, however. It is generally acknowledged that emotions (feelings) and cognitions (thoughts/beliefs) involve two different "systems" that are somewhat independent of each other. My spider phobia is an excellent example of this. I have no clue where it came from. No negative event involving spiders ever happened to me. When I think of spiders, most of my thoughts are positive—they eat pests such as mosquitoes and they generally mind their own business. The extent of my fear in response to spiders is clearly linked to visual cues (size, hairiness) rather than how dangerous I know a given spider to be. A full-grown wolf spider, which is the size and hairiness of a tarantula but has no neurotoxin, upsets me far more than a black widow, which is smaller and smoother but far more dangerous. In fact, when confronted with a large, hairy spider, my mind watches my bodily reactions with some interest—and talking myself out of a fear response has no noticeable effect.

If feelings can sometimes be quite unconnected to rational thought, why do we take them as evidence of "magical *thinking*" in some studies? We look for *patterns* of emotional response, how subtle shifts in scenarios result in shifts in feelings. Because our scenarios are so carefully constructed, we know, when a research participant's feelings shift between one example and the next, exactly what caused that shift—even if the participant does not. The word "belief" can be used to mean many different things, and there are different levels of belief. Sometimes our participants believe things consciously and clearly—that is, they are able to articulate a belief and acknowledge it freely. Other times, our participants react in ways that suggest a particular underlying belief, but if we ask them outright they tell us they do *not* believe it and find it completely implausible. Their mind does not believe it—but their gut does. And sometimes they respond from a middle ground, telling us they feel "as if" a certain thing were true; they don't actually believe it—but they don't exactly disbelieve it, either. In the case of magical thinking, the core response patterns we are interested in are quite consistent across many different cultures. But the extent to which people *consciously* and *explicitly* believe is quite variable. Also, for some examples (such as the poo-shaped fudge) one can generate simpler explanations of participant's responses than "magical thinking." But none of these simpler explanations can explain the overall patterns of reaction as well as the magical principles do.

If you wish to demonstrate the magical similarity effect with your friends and family, try an idea devised by Paul Rozin: ask them to bring you a photograph, *which is a duplicate*, of a person they love very much. Verify that it is not the only one they have to ensure that their reactions can't be explained away as reluctance to lose a valued memory. Then, hand them a match and ask them to set fire to the photograph, burning it completely. Watch them carefully. Most people are unwilling to do this or at least feel *really* uncomfortable about doing it. In the one example I know in which a woman expressed *no* reluctance to burn a photograph of her romantic partner (with whom she was on good terms), when she later reported to him what she had done, it apparently caused a huge fight between them.

Why is it so hard to take this action if there isn't a measure of belief at *some* level? Again, this illustrates a very important point regarding magical thinking in modern, Western societies: people can hold magical beliefs at differing levels of awareness and acceptance, ranging all the way from an intuitive sense or vague feeling that one does *not* believe to be true (but which may direct one's behavior, nevertheless), all the way to explicit beliefs that may even be culturally taught. It all depends on the person, the situation, and the cultural context.

Rozin, Millman, and I (1986) and Rozin, Markwith, and Ross (1990) also explored "nominal realism" beliefs, in which a word or name is treated as though it carries the essence of its referent. Participants watched while two empty, clean bottles were filled with sugar from a commercially labeled box of sugar. They were then given two pre-printed labels, one with the word "sucrose," the other with the word "sodium cyanide, poison" written on it. Participants attached each of the labels to the bottle of their choice. Then, some sugar from each bottle was stirred into one of two glasses of water, and they were asked to rate their willingness to take a sip from each glass and then to actually drink some. Not only did they prefer the sugar-labeled bottle, but many were reluctant to drink from the glass containing the cyanide-labeled sugar! Their feelings puzzled them (they knew there was no "real world basis" for them) but were very real.

Those of us who study this for a living are not immune to these effects. Back when TRS-80s were cutting-edge technology in personal computers, files were deleted by typing "KILL (filename)." Not planning against the future, Paul Rozin had created a filename called CAROL (yes, after me). When we decided it wasn't needed any more, he started typing the words "KILL CAROL," and then stopped as we both stared at the screen uncomfortably. We caught ourselves and started laughing—but I have repressed the outcome of this moment and don't remember if he continued deleting or just kept the file indefinitely.

THE MAGICAL LAW OF CONTAGION

Where the law of similarity says "the image is reality"—basically, what you see is what you get—the law of contagion refers to a shared, but usually not visible, history of contact between two things. We start by identifying one object or person as a source and another as a target. The law of contagion says that physical contact between a source and a target results in the transfer of some effect or quality (essence) between them. Qualities transferred may be physical, mental, or moral, and they can be either good or bad. In exchanging qualities like this, the source and target swap essence (essence can go from source to target, or backwards from target to source, or both ways at once; other features of a spell or ritual are often performed in a specific order to direct which way it will go). By exchanging and now sharing essence, the source and target are forevermore linked in sympathetic connection—summarized as "*once in contact, always in contact*" (Mauss). Contagious contact can be direct (e.g., shaking hands or eating the source), or it can be indirect, happening through a third object (e.g., the target wears the source's sweater, source and target share food with each other).

With the law of contagion we begin to understand the mysterious link between Harry and Voldemort. At least part of the secret lies in the history of Voldemort's attempt to kill Harry with a bolt of magical energy, his personal, powerful, and evil mana. As described by Hagrid and vaguely remembered by Harry, the mark on his forehead is the result of contact with Voldemort's powerful and evil curse. This very same curse destroys Harry's mother and father and everyone else Voldemort has ever used it on. But it does not work on Harry, making him the now-famous "Boy Who Lived." Through the scar, the physical point of contact between Voldemort and baby Harry, their continued connection makes itself known repeatedly throughout the series—most obviously when it burns with searing pain whenever Voldemort is near. Once in contact, always in contact. Would Harry have been chosen by the companion wand to Voldemort's if not for this history of contact between them? Would he be able to speak to snakes? Perhaps not, although in later books we discover that their destinies would have been linked regardless. We simply don't know how much essence was exchanged during their initial contact, how much more or less alike they would have been had it never occurred. We know that they remain permanently linked through it, however.

Harry has a history of a second powerful type of contagious contact as well. At the end of Book One, Dumbledore explains that baby Harry survives Voldemort's attempt to kill him because of his mother's love. In dying to save her child, his mother's love is so pure and so powerful that it leaves its own mark, though without a scar:

> "[T]o have been loved so deeply, even though the person who loved us is gone, will give us some protection forever. It is in your very skin" (*Sorcerer's Stone* 299).

And Dumbledore really means forever. Harry's mother's love is the reason why Professor Quirrell, in the service of and physically joined with Voldemort, cannot touch Harry years later. When he tries, Harry's scar sears with needle-like pain, but Quirrell is even worse off. Forced to let go of Harry, he sees his own fingers blistering as he watches (*Sorcerer's Stone*).

Contagion effects, whether good or bad, do not easily wipe or wash off, nor do they wear off with time (once in contact, always in contact). In more of our Muggle research, Brinkman, Woodward, and I (1994) had research participants imagine silverware that had last been used by people with AIDS. They were asked how they would feel about using this silverware after it had been thoroughly cleaned. Importantly, they *were* aware that HIV is not transmitted through this type of casual contact. Even so, they were very reluctant to imagine themselves using this silverware. When we asked what *would* make them feel comfortable using it, they wanted remarkably extreme measures, including sterilizing it in a hospital gas autoclave and even melting it down into molten silver and refashioning it into new utensils! In another study using Hepatitis B as the contagious example (Nemeroff & Rozin), a participant put the issue very clearly:

> I'd feel it was contaminated in some way, not only that I could get hepatitis from it, but that it was somehow contaminated, it's just not clean. I don't really think you could get it that way.

In exploring whether the passage of time since contact made a difference, we found that ratings of the silverware stayed negative even after a year of imagined elapsed time since the people with AIDS had used it. In fact, 16 percent of our participants showed no improvement at *all* in their ratings for one year as compared with one day of elapsed time. Once in contact, always in contact.

But sometimes, having an object or person with opposite essence come into contact with a contagious item seems able to purify it by negating or canceling out the original contagion with new and opposite stuff. In the Nemeroff and Rozin (1994) sweater study, participants imagined that their best friend, romantic partner, or "good person" wore the sweater previously worn by their enemy or "evil person." For some, this improved the situation dramatically. In order for "opposite-contact" to work, the mana of the positive source has to be powerful enough to overcome the nasty mana of the original contaminating source. It is hard to imagine what it would take to make most of us willing to wear Osama bin Laden's sweater. But some years ago, Mother Teresa could often cancel out Hitler, personal enemies, and Saddam Hussein.

Knowing this, we understand better what Harry's mother did for him. Dumbledore explains that:

> "Quirrell, full of hatred, greed, and ambition, sharing his soul with Voldemort, could not touch you for this reason. It was agony to touch a person marked by something so good" (*Sorcerer's Stone* 299).

Pure goodness negates evil. Was this "opposite-contact" also the reason for Voldemort's loss of power and disappearance following his failed attempt to kill Harry? Something not only protected Harry, but also appears to have either caused the curse to backfire onto Voldemort or directly negate his mana in some other way. Did the curse ricochet off Harry's shield of mother-love back onto Voldemort? Or was it the contact with Harry, imbued as he was with the essence of pure self-sacrificing love, the complete opposite of Voldemort's essence, that undid Voldemort's power? Either way, we are pleased with the outcome....

The last aspect of magical contagion we need to understand is that *essence contains all of the important properties of its source* (summarized as, "the part equals the whole;" Mauss). That is, a lock of Voldemort's hair, a drop of his blood, or a pile of his fingernail parings contain his essence with all of its important properties intact. Similarly, the contagion from a cat whisker will be the same as the contagion from a large clump of cat fur or even direct contagious contact with the entire cat, if one can imagine such a thing. All of the "catness," or in the case of Voldemort, his evil, malice, and power, are contained in even a tiny amount of their essence. We call this the *holographic principle.*

In *Harry Potter and the Chamber of Secrets*, as they attempt to spy on the horrible plots they assume are being hatched in the Slytherin common room, Hermione, Harry, and Ron plan to use Polyjuice Potion, a particularly complicated concoction which only Hermione could have succeeded at while a second-year student! The Polyjuice Potion allows one temporarily to take on the physical appearance of another person—by adding a small amount of that person's essence to the potion and then drinking it. To do this, one has to procure an actual bit of the person one wants to change into. Hermione solves the problem of how Harry and Ron can get a few hairs from Malfoy's friends and bodyguards, Crabbe and Goyle: she spikes a couple of chocolate cakes with a Sleeping Draught and leaves them in the path of Crabbe and Goyle, knowing they will eat first and ask questions later. When Harry and Ron are reluctant, she sternly reminds them that the potion will be useless without the hairs.

For her own dose of potion, Hermione thinks she already has a hair belonging to Slytherin member Millicent Bulstrode, left on Hermione's robe when they were wrestling. "'Urgh—essence of Millicent Bulstrode,'" says Ron in disgust later on, as they add the hair to Hermione's portion of the brew. "'Bet it tastes disgusting'" (*Chamber of Secrets* 216).

Unfortunately, Hermione is wrong about the hair, which apparently belonged to Millicent's cat rather than Millicent herself. Hermione ends up with yellow eyes, a fur-covered face, pointy ears, and a tail. It may have been a good thing that Polyjuice Potion is not intended for animal transformations; presumably this is why her transformation into a cat is incomplete.

The point here is that it takes only a single hair to do the job. All the important features of essence are in any part, no matter how small the object. And this is why our Muggle research participants show little if any difference in their ratings when asked to imagine that a single HIV virus has entered their body, compared with a million live HIV viruses (Nemeroff, Brinkman, & Woodward).

CONCLUSIONS

So, why do we love Harry Potter and his wizarding world so? At least partly because the magic of Harry's world follows consistent rules that conform closely to how we think intuitively. Is it a problem to think in these ways? Not necessarily. We can think of the magical laws as an alternate type of logic, based in mental shortcuts whose purpose is to save us time and effort in making decisions in daily life (Rozin & Nemeroff). We often need to make decisions quickly and with incomplete information and, while it might be ideal to think through each decision thoroughly, following the rules of conventional logic, this isn't always practical. "Cognitive heuristics" such as "like equals like" and "once in contact, always in contact" have developed as helpful rules of thumb over the course of our evolutionary history, and although they can sometimes lead us astray, for the most part they serve us well (Kahneman, Slovic, & Tversky; Nisbett & Ross; Tversky & Kahneman). In general, it seems like a good idea to expect something that looks like a tiger to also act like a tiger (similarity), and also a good idea to avoid contact with malicious, disgusting, or otherwise negative people or substances (contagion).

How well do these heuristics do? Real world examples of "magical contagion" include germs as well as more personal essence-like traces of ourselves that we leave all over the place, both visible and invisible. In forensics we have moved far beyond simple fingerprints and can now do DNA analyses from tiny samples of residues found at crime scenes. It is hard to imagine a better example of "the part equals the whole" than DNA, in which all the information that makes up a person can be found in the nucleus of each cell. And new understandings of how DNA is "switched on" and "off" raise the possibility (*not* established and still farfetched, mind you) that personality characteristics really might be transmissible through organ transplantation and other means.

Sometimes, though, these heuristics mislead us. With HIV, people are far too worried about casual contact and not worried enough about riskier behaviors—for instance, failing to use condoms with people they love ("good germs"?). And in areas with emerging water shortage crises, such as the Southwestern U.S., magical contagion-based thinking can pose a big barrier to possible solutions. We can now ultra-purify city sewage water to a level that is cleaner than the water in many if not most lakes and rivers today, making it usable as good-quality drinking water. It even tastes great. But how do we get people to accept this recycled water? How does one get the "sewage vibes" out of it, after the real world contaminants are gone? Maybe magically based beliefs and feelings must be countered with this same mode of thinking; we are involved in ongoing research to find out.

In the meantime, we Muggles can take comfort in knowing that even if we don't have all the answers or the power to control everything we want to control, *someone* probably does in Harry's world, just around the corner and through a wall.

CAROL NEMEROFF, Ph.D., is associate professor of psychology at Arizona State University and director of the Mind-Body Health Lab. Since 1984 she has been researching the nature and impact of magical thinking in daily life. She is a tremendous fan of Harry Potter and would like to teach at Hogwarts someday.

REFERENCES

L. Comer and C. Nemeroff, "Conflations of Emotional and Physical Safety in AIDS-Risk Perception Among College Students: The 'Casual-Regular' Partner Distinction," *Journal of Applied Social Psychology* 30 (2001): 2467–2490.

Frazer, J. G. *The Golden Bough: A Study in Magic and Religion.* New York: Macmillan, 1959 (reprint of 1922 abridged edition, edited by T. H. Gaster; original work published 1890).

Kahneman, D., P. Slovic, and A. Tversky. *Judgment Under Uncertainty: Heuristics and Biases.* Cambridge, UK: Cambridge University Press, 1982.

Mauss, M. *A General Theory of Magic* (R. Brain, Trans.). New York: W. W. Norton, 1972. Original work published 1902. "Esquisse d'une theorie generale de la magie." *L'Annee Sociologique.* 1902–1903.

C. Nemeroff, "Magical Thinking About Illness Virulence: Conceptions of Germs from 'Safe' Versus 'Dangerous' Others," *Health Psychology* 14 (1995): 147–151.

C. Nemeroff, A. Brinkman, and C. Woodward, "Magical Cognitions About AIDS in a College Population," *AIDS Education and Prevention* 6 (1994): 249–265.

C. Nemeroff and P. Rozin, "The Contagion Concept in Adult Thinking in the United States: Transmission of Germs and Interpersonal Influence," *Ethos: The Journal of Psychological Anthropology* 22 (1994): 158–186.

Nemeroff, C. and P. Rozin. "The Makings of the Magical Mind." K. S. Rosengren, C. Johnson, and P. Harris (Eds.), *Imagining the Impossible: Magical, Scientific, and Religious Thinking in Children.* Cambridge, UK: Cambridge University Press. 1–34.

Nisbett, R. and L. Ross. *Human Inference: Strategies and Shortcomings of Social Judgment.* Englewood Cliffs, NJ: Prentice-Hall, 1980.

Piaget, J. *The Child's Conception of the World.* Totowa, NJ: Rowman & Allanheld (a division of Littlefield, Adams, & Co.), 1983. Original work published 1929.

P. Rozin, M. Markwith, and C. McCauley, "Sensitivity to Indirect Contact with other Persons: AIDS Aversion as a Composite of Aversion to Strangers, Infection, Moral Taint, and Misfortune," *Journal of Abnormal Psychology* 193 (1994): 495–504.

P. Rozin, M. Markwith, and C. Nemeroff, "Magical Contagion Beliefs and Fear of AIDS," *Journal of Applied Social Psychology* 22 (1992): 1081–1092.

P. Rozin, M. Markwith, and C. Nemeroff, "Operation of the Laws of Sympathetic Magic in Disgust and other Domains," *Journal of Applied Social Psychology* 50, 4 (1986): 703–712.

P. Rozin, M. Markwith, and B. Ross, "The Sympathetic Magical Law of Similarity, Nominal Realism, and the Neglect of Negatives in Response to Negative Labels," *Psychological Science* 1 (1990): 383–384.

Rozin, P. and C. J. Nemeroff. "The Laws of Sympathetic Magic: A Psychological Analysis of Similarity and Contagion." In J. Stigler, G. Herdt and R. A. Shweder (Eds.), *Cultural Psychology: Essays on Comparative Human Development.* Cambridge, UK: Cambridge University Press, 1990. 205–232.

Rozin, P. and C. Nemeroff. "Sympathetic Magical Thinking: The Contagion and Similarity 'Heuristics.'" T. Gilovich, D. Griffin, and D. Kahneman (Eds.), *Heuristics and Biases. The Psychology of Intuitive Judgment.* Cambridge, UK: Cambridge University Press, 2002. 201–216.

P. Rozin, C. Nemeroff, M. Wane, and A. Sherrod, "Operation of the Sympathetic Magical Law of Contagion in Interpersonal Attitudes Among Americans," *Bulletin of the Psychonomic Society* 27 (1989): 367–370.

Rowling, J. K. *Harry Potter and the Sorcerer's Stone.* New York: Scholastic Inc., 1997.

———. *Harry Potter and the Chamber of Secrets.* New York: Scholastic Inc., 1999.

A. Tversky and D. Kahneman, "Loss Aversion in Riskless Choice: A Reference-Dependent Model," *The Quarterly Journal of Economics* 106 (1991): 1039–1061.

Hancock and Gardner examine the nature of time as we Muggles use it versus the way the wizards in Harry Potter use it. The question is raised: Can we Muggles use the concept of time in a better, magical way rather than the normal way that rules our day?

PETER A. HANCOCK
AND MICHELLE K. GARDNER

Time and Time Again
Muggle's Watch, the Wizard's Clock[1]

JUST WHEN WE think we understand what time is, curious things happen, and we begin to realize that time is actually not at all what we considered it to be. For Harry Potter, as well, time changes and distorts along with the different challenges he meets and the different adventures he has. In recalling the terrified, pleading screams of his mother (*Prisoner of Azkaban*) and watching his godfather's fall through the ragged veil (*Harry Potter and the Order of the Phoenix*), Harry has experienced some of the subtleties of time in its many different forms. While

---

[1] A brief note on the title: the present title is a multi-layered metaphor. "Time and Time Again" refers to *time* in Muggle reality, and *time again* refers to time as it is dealt with by Harry and his friends in the wizarding world. "Muggle's watch" is not only a reference to the idea of our time as a simple, linear Newtonian-inspired dimension, but also refers to our own observations as Muggles within the Harry Potter series and our own Muggle function in reading the texts and watching the movies. "Wizard's clock" refers to the way time is treated in Harry's world. However, in British English, to *clock* is to see someone as in "I clocked him." However, it is also an informal term for the face "wipe that smile off your clock." Thus, we are watching the faces and the actions of the characters in the wizarding world.

the Muggle world continues to believe that time is a simple, linear experience, the wizarding world knows time is much more. Remember the frenzied anticipation of the Hogwarts student body leading up to the Yule Ball (*Harry Potter and the Goblet of Fire*), or the long, drawn-out boredom of sitting in the History of Magic class with Professor Binns, not knowing when and if the lecture would ever end (*Harry Potter and the Sorcerer's Stone*)? Is time then just a simple, linear experience? Certainly not. In actuality, time does very strange things at the most critical points in our lives. "For a second that contained an eternity, Harry stared into Cedric's face..." (*Goblet of Fire* 638). Was Harry's awareness of time here just another tick of the clock? Time changes with the context and nature of the things that are happening to all of us. It speeds up and slows down according to the challenges of our existence. In this essay, we examine the issue of time and the psychological foundations of this medium, which embraces all of our life's experiences. We hope to illustrate the comparable nuances of time in the Muggle world by showing how time is treated in and around Hogwarts.

ISN'T TIME JUST TIME?

In general, Muggles and wizards share a basic conceptualization of time. A watch ticks once every second. Sixty of those ticks make a minute. One minute was all the time Harry and Hermione had to rescue Buckbeak from Hagrid's pumpkin patch (*Prisoner of Azkaban*). Sixty minutes make one hour, which was the length of time Harry had to locate his "Wheezy" in the second task of the Triwizard Tournament (*Goblet of Fire* 491). There are twenty-four hours in a day and 365 days in a year. Even a true Muggle like Vernon Dursley can understand that time appears to be pretty straightforward. But just why *are* there sixty seconds in a minute and sixty minutes in an hour instead of ten or 100 (Fraser)? Why are there twenty-four hours in a day or 365 days in a year? And what year is it? Most Muggles believe it's 2007, but unfortunately more than one billion Chinese Muggles think it's 4704–4705, while many hundreds of millions of Muslims know it to be 1428, and of course to Harry it is 1997 in what will be his seventh and final year at Hogwarts (*Harry Potter Lexicon*). Of course, there are different date interpretations, but everyone knows what time is: it's, well, time!

"WHAT SORT OF TIME DO YOU CALL THIS?"[2]

More than seventeen centuries ago, the philosopher St. Augustine tried to answer the question: *What is time?* He concluded that if no one asked him, he knew very well what time was, but as soon as someone asked him to explain it, he really had no idea! (Augustine). And that's the problem: time is not straightforward at all; it might not even move forward. It may very well go in circles (Gould). It might go in spirals. There might be bubbles of it. Time can speed up, it can slow down, it might stop for a brief moment and suddenly start again, it might even run backwards, and this is only time in the Muggle world! The first step to understanding time is to realize that time itself is measured differently across the two worlds.

Before looking at ways of measuring time, we need to ask an important, albeit strange question: *What is the purpose of keeping time?* Imagine you are young Harry staring into the Mirror of Erised: do you really need to know what time is? Harry happily spends several hours with the mirror because it shows his heart's desire. Here, we can identify with Harry because when we are doing something enjoyable, time seems inconsequential. When someone interrupts our enjoyment to tell us that several hours have passed, we are surprised, since it seems like it's only been mere moments. What happened to time during such episodes? Professor Albus Dumbledore eventually warns Harry of the futility of the mirror where "'men have wasted away before it, entranced by what they have seen, or been driven mad'" (*Sorcerer's Stone* 213). But why does Harry have to worry about the time at all? Why does Professor Dumbledore not only extract Harry from this situation but also warn him against seeking out the mirror again? The answer to this question is the reason why we measure time. Like virtually all wizards and Muggles, Harry is not just an individual but also a member of a community. As such, he has responsibilities and people who rely on him to fulfill them. Social beings need a way to measure time, because as either Muggle or wizard, we need to synchronize our actions with others and with the events in our environment.

Although this is generally the case, it is not true of everyone. In

---

[2] Quote from the portrait of the Fat Lady (*Half-Blood Prince* 492).

fact, French scientist Michel Siffre, in his book *Beyond Time*, discusses his experience of living deep in a cave (outside of Hogsmeade?) far from any person-to-person (much less worldly) contact. He rapidly lost his ability to know what time it was outside the cave. He quickly started to live on his own personal schedule generated by his "internal clock." He woke up at midnight and slept at three in the afternoon, but it didn't matter to him because he didn't have to talk or meet with anyone else: he was completely on his own without even the sun and stars to keep him company. But almost no one can live like this forever, so the reason we have a common system for measuring time is because of our need to interact with other people, especially in the Muggle world.

WAYS OF MEASURING TIME

A great way to understand the difference between Muggle and wizard society is to look at the different ways time is measured in the two worlds. In early history, all Muggle time devices were rough and inaccurate. The ancient world relied on mechanisms such as sundials and clepsydrae (water clocks), which kept the approximate time. People continued to create time-keeping mechanisms that were increasingly more accurate. The accuracy of time-keeping and the accuracy of the calendar became progressively more important in the medieval world, largely because Christians needed accurate calendars to specify when certain holy days would occur, and they needed accurate clocks so monks could know when to perform their daily prayers. It is no coincidence that many of the earliest mechanical clocks were located in churches, and many early examples are still there (Humphrey & Ormrod).

As technology improved, so did the accuracy of clocks. Escapements, pendulae, and springs all helped improve their precision (Cipolla), and today we have watches that keep time to the billionth of a second. Of course, we don't need billionth-of-a-second accuracy to coordinate our Muggle social activities, but we do need this level of accuracy to coordinate our technological and computational activities. However, in this reasonable and apparently benign pursuit of improvement, we have collectively trapped ourselves into a way of thinking about time (Servan-Schrieber). The watch has become our master. Now, we all appear to be running late: we have no free time and there is too much to do and so little time in which to do it. Pre-occupation with schedules and punctuality can quickly become pathology, as John Cleese so unhappily illustrated in one of his movies (*Clockwise*). Even now, some people are so driven by punctuality that they eventually kill themselves trying to be *on time*.

Somehow, in the Muggle world, time has gone from being a useful tool to being an overpowering monster. It is now impersonal (the watch cares nothing for you), it is generic (every watch is basically the same), it is sterile (every second it records is exactly like the last one gone and the next one to come), and it is one-dimensional (it only goes forward). Not only have watches sucked much of the life out of life, but like a virulent plague they continue to spread and dominate. It is probably true to say that the watch—and the inhuman way it expresses time—is the most frequently found tool in the entire Muggle world. Think about it: every computer and most every form of technology contains some sort of time-keeping mechanism. Both the nature and reach of this monster have grown beyond our control. There are now very few places in the Muggle world where one can escape from time (Heyerdahl). Muggle time is flat, impersonal, and uncaring. The Muggle watch is there to keep everyone in line with everyone else. This watch is an object of oppression, and only the person who is actually unbound by this watch is truly free.

Occasionally, wizards use time in the same manner. For example, Harry's first detention with Professor Dolores Umbridge is at exactly 5 P.M., which of course coincides with the try-outs for Gryffindor's Quidditch team (*Order of the Phoenix*). However, the use of time-telling devices is quite different. A closer examination of wizard's clocks finds us in the Weasleys' living room looking at a grandfather clock considered "most excellent" by the brilliant Professor Albus Dumbledore (*Order of the Phoenix* 470). As the war and its associated attacks begin to escalate, Mrs. Weasley gets into the habit of carrying this clock with her from room to room (*Half-Blood Prince*). With respect to the sterile Muggle approach, this clock "was completely useless if you wanted to know the time, but otherwise very informative" (*Goble of Fire* 151). However, if you want to understand the real meaning behind the reason for time, (that is, where are the people I care about in my social world?), Mrs. Weasley's clock is ideal. Her clock displays nine golden hands, each engraved with one of the Weasley family's names: Ron, Ginny, Fred, George, Percy, Charlie, Bill, Molly, and Arthur. Not only does the clock tell you where all these people are, but also what they are doing:

> There were no numerals around the face, but descriptions of where each family member might be. "Home," "school," and "work" were there, but there was also "traveling," "lost," "hospital," "prison," and, in the position where the number twelve would be on a normal clock, "mortal peril" (*Goblet of Fire* 151).

Now, this clock does precisely what a real watch should do: it tells you where you are and what you are doing in relation to what the people you are concerned with are doing. A clock of this nature has the potential to cause more stress on the individual who views it than any watch in the Muggle world, but it is infinitely relevant and, in the final analysis, more useful.

How about a personal wizard clock that is set only to your life and schedule? Such a clock with "only one hand and no numbers at all" hangs on the wall in the Weasley's kitchen (*Harry Potter and the Chamber of Secrets* 34). The face of this clock does not tell you anything about Muggle or even wizard time. However, the information conveyed by this clock proves very helpful, because it indicates the activities that need doing as opposed to the specific time of day. "Feed the chickens, make tea." These are the activities and household chores that need to be performed. It also had one universal pronouncement to make—one we all know—"you're late"[3] (ibid 34). The measurement of time clearly varies from Number Four, Privet Drive to the Burrow. For wizards, time is personal (it is directly adjusted to you and your needs), it is specialized (different time-keeping devices have different functions), and it is multi-dimensional (it shows great variety). The wizard's clock helps put life back into the living. Harry's wizarding world beyond the confines of Privet Drive is a personal, caring place, and the interpretation of time acts in support of these characteristics.

---

[3] "You're late" is a concept that we believe both Muggles and wizards alike can agree on with little argument, but the question often becomes, late for what?

HOW CAN YOU FREE YOURSELF FROM TIME?

We have had a look at the way Muggles and wizards measure time and convey it to each other, but what of time itself?[4] One obvious way to free yourself from time is to throw away your Muggle watch. This might free you from some social obligations, but time itself continues on its merry way. Nevertheless, perhaps there is a way to free your self from time. As mentioned, albeit briefly, you can get *lost* in time depending upon your circumstances. Harry missed an Ireland goal at the Quidditch World Cup because he had turned his Omnioculars to slow in order to watch a play-by-play of the game: "'Harry, if you're not going to watch at normal speed, you're going to miss things!' shouted Hermione" (*Goblet of Fire* 107). Most of us live at a *normally perceived temporal speed*, but our perception of time can very much depend upon the nature of the particular activity or activities we are doing. Think about the time spent by each Hogwarts student under the Sorting Hat or even the month that lapsed between the time Harry bought all his first year's school supplies and when the Dursleys left him at King's Cross Station on September 1. Both of these situations seem to alter the flow of time, not just time as it was happening. It also appeared differently when Harry later reflected on such events. Like all good demonstrations of magic, here is a true illusion!

TIME IN PASSING—TIME IN MEMORY

There are a number of illusions in how we perceive time.[5] One very strange illusion is that time sometimes appears to speed up as it passes, and then that same interval seems to expand, or slow down, when we later reflect upon it (Doob). Consider, for example, Harry's combined Occlumency lessons with Professor Severus Snape, the meetings of Dumbledore's Army (D.A.), and the homework assigned in anticipation of the Ordinary Wizarding Levels (O.W.L.s) examination in *Harry Potter and the Order of the Phoenix*. With all these

---

[4] "Time also exists not by itself, but simply from the things which happen, the sense apprehends what has been done in time past, as well as what is present and what is to follow after. And we must admit that no one feels time by itself abstracted from the motion and calm rest of things" (Lucretius).

[5] "When you sit with a pretty girl for an hour it seems like a minute; but when you are on a 'hot seat' for a minute it feels like an hour. That's relativity" (Einstein).

Time-in-Passing

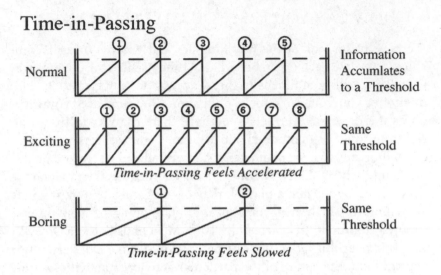

FIGURE 1: The Time-in-Passing, Time-in-Memory Illusion. The various activities such as waking up, eating breakfast, or getting dressed are *normal* information (which is represented on the top line). D.A. classes or an unauthorized trip to Hogsmeade are rated as exciting, unusual, or interesting, and the information (representing new or intense forms of stimulation) accumulates much faster than our *normal* information. Sitting in Professor Binns's History of Magic (generally viewed as boring, although the authors would welcome such an experience!), information accumulates very slowly and time seems to drag.

things happening for Harry, "January seemed to be passing alarmingly fast" (*Order of the Phoenix* 555). Clearly, time as measured by various Muggle devices in the month of January did not pass any differently than it had in previous years. Yet for Harry—who is so incredibly preoccupied with his multiple activities—the time seems to go by in a whirl, and all of a sudden it is February. How is it possible that time passed so fast?

Following such an accelerated passage of time, the Muggle mind can do strange things. Afterwards, when we were to look back on an interval such as Harry's January, time would seem to stretch out. What passed in a whirl while we were living it seems magically to have expanded: we now recall the month of January as being very long, as the events are re-calibrated in our minds. In retrospect, when he looks back in his memory, Harry's January would seem to have

Time-in-Memory

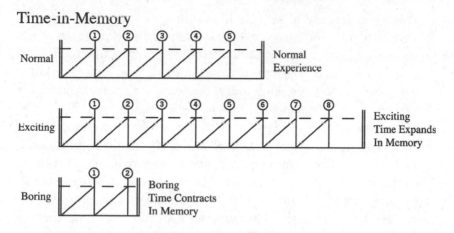

FIGURE 2: The Time-in-Passing, Time-in-Memory Illusion. Some time after these events have occurred, we go back over them in our memory. The *normal* experience remains on a normal time line and no illusion is experienced. The exciting event (Harry's month of January in *Order of the Phoenix*) fills the memory record and so seems to have occupied a longer time even though it flew past while it was happening. Finally, History of Magic occupies almost no clicks of the memory record and, even though time dragged while it was happening, upon reflection it seems to have occupied almost no time at all.

lasted almost forever. Consider the commitments Harry was able to keep in such a short span of time. This Time-in-Passing, Time-in-Memory Illusion derives from one of the ways our brain codes time. According to one temporal theory of event accumulation, the new information quickly fills up the units of our time-event record (Treisman). Consequently, time seems to pass very quickly in the month of January or even at some of the individual D.A. meetings when they are doing exciting or interesting things. Later, when Harry reflects back, his mind attempts to put a regular-time calibration template on these events, and the number of time units seems greatly expanded. Even though the experience of January seems to speed by while it is happening, in retrospect we think that it must have been a long time interval for all the accomplishments Harry achieved during that month. The opposite of this phenomenon works, as well. The hours spent sitting in detention with Professor Umbridge drag out almost interminably but seem to have passed quickly when later recalled in Harry's memory.

One great tragedy of Muggle life is this: As you grow older it is more difficult to find these novel and exciting things to do, so time-in-memory begins to speed up as time-in-passing is filled with boring or familiar events. The great dancer Agnes de Mille is reputed to have said, "I hate growing older, it seems like it's breakfast every fifteen minutes" (Hancock 150). This is the same basic illusion in time but spread over a lifespan. It might appear that this does not necessarily happen in the wizarding world, since a few individuals, such as Nicolas Flamel and his wife, lived for more than six centuries (*Sorcerer's Stone*). However, the poet Thomas Campbell suggests that the illusion we experience as we age is Nature's way to speed up time as we get older, because it shortens the appearance of time spent at the end of our life when all of our friends have passed on and left us behind. We might well wonder what Nicolas Flamel thought of this notion on his 600th birthday. Time changes for both Muggles and wizards by speeding up and slowing down according to the way we meet the challenges of our shifting existence.

TIME DISTORTION UNDER EXTREME STRESS

Since the rules of modern time-keeping are learned so well by young western Muggles, we are often insensitive to subtle changes in the flow of time. Indeed, even if we are aware of such changes, most of us quickly re-calibrate our sense of time with a quick glance at the ever-present watch on our wrist or, more likely, on the face of our cell-phone. We are more inclined to believe the displays of these mechanical monsters than our own personal perceptions. After all, arguing with everyone else's rules in the time-fixated Muggle world is always a difficult thing to do. As a result, Muggles often dismiss episodes in which time seems to be non-linear. However, there are some rare occasions in life when such time distortion is so obvious that it has a very profound effect on each of those who experience it.

Radical time distortion is often reported under extremely stressful, life-threatening circumstances. On such occasions, time either slows almost to a halt or accelerates to a complete blur. Consider the time Harry spends in the graveyard with Voldemort and the Death Eaters (*Goblet of Fire*). Harry is convinced that death is all that awaits him, and given the odds of thirty Death Eaters to one Harry, we cannot disagree with his assessment. For Harry, time changes its rate of flow at this very stressful and life-threatening moment. Remember when Harry stared into the dead eyes of Cedric Diggory (*Goblet of Fire*)? Time paused to allow Harry's full absorption of the situation. In this moment of the story, a duel forced by Voldemort locks their wands in *Priori Incantatem* (*Goblet of Fire*). Harry watches as the shadows of his parents squeeze themselves out the tip of Voldemort's wand. The time that passes as Harry and Voldemort connect wand-to-wand under a dome of thousands of gold beams is minimal but clearly stretched to allow Harry the time to escape from the situation. At the most memorable points of our lives, time becomes very different from a simple, uni-dimensional, linear flow. Why is this?

As we have already said, the content of what is happening around you has a lot to do with how you perceive time passing. However, the circumstances *out there* in the environment are often not as important as what is happening inside you. In situations of extreme stress, the brain realizes that even the simplest of mistakes might well prove fatal. Consequently, we pay careful attention to the important things going on around us. This focus of attention leaves little or no awareness for the passage of time. In a general sense, we lose contact with our various clocking mechanisms, and so when we next recover that linkage we have to reorient ourselves in time. In the same manner as the Time-in-Passing, Time-in-Memory Illusion, the threat of stress serves to pile up so many recorded events that we have filled up our register and now time seems completely distorted. This is one of the most interesting experiences in life. One funny thing (and St. Augustine would agree) is that if you have experienced this, we have no need to explain it further; you will know exactly what we mean. If you haven't experienced this, you may well wonder what we are talking about![6]

SUMMARY AND CONCLUSION

In order for us all to manage our daily existence, we have invented ways of measuring time that permit us to synchronize our actions

---

[6] Many people have experienced such stress-related time-distortion situations, such as car accidents or in combat (see Hancock & Weaver 193).

with the actions of others. However, having invented this idea of time-keeping, Muggles try even harder to make their watches more accurate. Along this path of so-called progress, somehow (and most people blame Isaac Newton, who himself was a bit of a wizard) the idea of time became mixed up with the way we chose to measure it. Increasingly, it is the numbers on the face of a watch that drive Muggles actions. This (as any wizard knows) is not the best way to approach understanding the dimension of time. Every now and then, especially when the Muggle world becomes very threatening or very exciting, some Muggles see through the illusion of time. However, most Muggles prefer to be comfortable and quickly return to the safe old way of watching the clock so that it can "tell" them the time. But, every once in a while, one of those Muggles will glimpse a vision of just how magical time can be. There's even a whisper that this realization is actually the first step on the road to becoming a wizard![7]

ACKNOWLEDGMENTS

The authors would like to first acknowledge and thank J. K. Rowling for the world she has created and allowed us all the joy of playing in. We would also like to thank Alani Davis, Gwynne Jackson, and Justin F. Morgan for their comments on and assistance with the present essay.

PETER A. HANCOCK, having achieved a score of Troll in his N.E.W.T.s, was sent into the West as a Muggle professor, where he now researches and teaches on Muggle technology, stress, and the magical nature of time at the Department of Psychology and Institute for Simulation and Training at the University of Central Florida in Orlando, Florida, where he is also currently trying to solve the mystery of golf.

---

[7] The authors feel the need to note a clear absence of the exploration of the Time-Turner device used by Hermione Granger in *Harry Potter and the Prisoner of Azkaban*. The concept of time travel and all the repercussions of such an ability represent far more information than could fit in one short essay. We do not feel we could adequately represent the complex and very important issues in such a small space and thus felt not discussing it instead of mentioning it without proper discussion was the appropriate path. We are happy to encourage others to write on this fascinating topic that we might, ourselves, be allowed to follow in the future—wherever that is.

MICHELLE K. GARDNER, if sorted, would be designated to the noble House of Ravenclaw. Although she has never read *Hogwarts, A History* (but would welcome such an opportunity), she is considered the Hermione of her generation. Michelle's research areas include all things Harry Potter with side diversions into wizards from other worlds. Commonly referred to as the woman who "loves ladybugs and all things imaginary," Michelle is the mother of a beautiful and inventive seven-year-old girl, wife of a very tolerant and loving husband, and located in the world's largest destination for theme-park entertainment. Comments on the above article are always welcome, enelya.oronar@gmail.com.

REFERENCES

Augustine. *The Confessions of St. Augustine by Bishop of Hippo Saint Augustine, Book XI. Project Gutenberg.* June 2002. <http://www.gutenberg.org/etext/3296> 400.

Campbell, T. *The River of Life.* 29 June 2006. <http://www.englishverse.com/poems/the_river_of_life>.

Cipolla, C. M. *Clocks and Culture: 1300–1700.* New York: W. W. Norton, 1967.

Clockwise. Dir. Christopher Morahan. Perf. John Cleese, Penelope Wilton, Sharon Maiden, and Alison Steadman. Anchor Bay, 1986.

Doob, L. W. *The Patterning of Time.* New Haven, CT: Yale University Press, 1971.

Fraser, J. T. *Time, the Familiar Stranger.* Redmond, WA: Tempus, 1987.

Gould, S. J. *Time's Arrow, Time's Cycle.* Cambridge, MA: Harvard University Press, 1998.

P. A. Hancock, "The Time of your Life: One Thousand Moons," *Kronoscope* 2 (2) (2002): 135–165.

P. A. Hancock and J. L. Weaver, "On Time Distortion Under Stress," *Theoretical Issues in Ergonomics Science* 6 (2005): 193–211.

Heyerdahl, T. *Fatu-Hiva.* Garden City, NY: Doubleday & Co., 1974.

"Harry Potter Lexicon." *Wizarding Through the Ages: The Complete Timeline of the Harry Potter Universe.* November 2005. <http://www.hp-lexicon.org/timeline.html>.

Humphrey, C., and W. M Ormrod (Eds.). *Time in the Medieval World.* The Boydell Press, 2001.

Rowling, J. K. *Harry Potter and the Sorcerer's Stone*. New York: Scholastic Inc., 1997.

——. *Harry Potter and the Chamber of Secrets*. New York: Scholastic Inc., 1999.

——. *Harry Potter and the Prisoner of Azkaban*. New York: Scholastic Inc., 1999.

——. *Harry Potter and the Goblet of Fire*. New York: Scholastic Inc., 2000.

——. *Harry Potter and the Order of the Phoenix*. New York: Scholastic Inc., 2003.

——. *Harry Potter and the Half-Blood Prince*. New York: Scholastic Inc., 2005.

Servan-Schreiber, J. L. *The Art of Time*. New York: Marlow & Co., 1988.

Siffre, M. *Beyond Time*. London: Chatto & Windus, 1964.

M. Treisman, "Temporal Discrimination and the Indifference Interval: Implications for a Model of the 'Internal Clock,'" *Psychological Monographs: General and Applied* 77 (13) (1963): 1–31.

THE WEIRD WORLD OF WIZARDS

What is the real difference between Harry Potter and Voldemort? Both have similar backgrounds, but one follows the course of evil while one continually struggles to do what's right. Franklin examines how social roles can lead to one path versus the other.

NANCY FRANKLIN, Ph.D.

The Social Dynamics of Power and Cooperation in the Wizarding World

IMAGINE YOU OWN an Invisibility Cloak for a day. What do you do with it? Let's make it more interesting: you can also fly, and you have a wand and access to a friend's Time-Turner. How quickly did criminal thoughts come to mind—the havoc you could wreak, the spectacular thefts you could pull off, the naked bodies you could ogle, the acts of revenge you could get away with?

Or, imagine you're a wizard who has just graduated from Hogwarts. You know something about the Cruciatus Curse, the Imperius Curse, and other tools of the Dark Arts. You've got a lot of power at your disposal. Why not use it to serve your own greedy desires? If you're more comfortable, you could stick with just the little things, like making sure your slice of pizza is bigger than the other guy's or having the only empty seat in a concert hall suddenly appear right in front of you. Even with the Ministry laws against the more damaging spells and curses, the ones that would let you have revenge or wreak havoc, there's nothing to prevent you from using your considerable talent to both commit these acts and cover your tracks. Or is there? Why *not* go for it? And (this is meant as a genuine scholarly question) why have most characters in the Harry Potter story not gone for it?

One thing that makes the characters so compelling is that, for all their amazing magical abilities, they're still stuck in the same social conundrums, feeling the same pressures and making the same social decisions, as us Muggles. They still struggle, and they live with the fact that they don't always get their way. They mostly use their power with restraint, as you and I do. In fact, social order couldn't exist unless they (and you and I) did.

To illustrate the dynamic more clearly, here's a more Muggle-oriented example: You're a burglar, and you and your partner have been caught by the police. The two of you are immediately taken to different rooms and questioned separately. Each of you has a choice: to confess and thereby implicate the other, or to keep your mouth shut. If both of you confess and implicate the other, you each get ten years in prison. If both of you keep your mouths shut, the police only have evidence for possession of a concealed weapon, which will carry one year for each of you. If one of you confesses and implicates the other, but the second person keeps quiet, the one who confesses goes free and the other goes to prison for twenty years. You can't communicate with your partner, so each of you has to make an independent decision. What do you do?

This situation, referred to by psychologists and game theorists as the Prisoner's Dilemma (Axelrod; Rachlin), can be mapped onto any situation in which social creatures, like wizards and humans, have to make decisions to cooperate or not cooperate with each other. Did you make a sufficient contribution to the house chores this week? Did you take no more than your share of the tips at work? When you don't know if the other guy is cooperating, does it make sense to cooperate (and risk getting taken advantage of) yourself? Or do you take precautions, protect yourself, and (in Prisoner's Dilemma parlance) defect? Human phenomena as seemingly irrational as the Cold War make perfect sense in light of this tough decision situation. When you don't know if the other guy is stockpiling weapons (and he or she still may be doing it surreptitiously even if the two of you signed a treaty), you risk being a sitting duck unless you, too, stockpile. This situation is non-optimal; it's a waste of money and it leads to global threat. As moral and rational beings, we like to think we can do better than that. But the fact of the matter is that defecting is sometimes rational. If the other guy defects, you've cut your losses. If he or she cooperates, your gain increases (even though your action has victimized someone else). So then, why not go for it?

People may cooperate because they're being guided by values that are more important to them than the short-term gains and losses created in the momentary Prisoner's Dilemma. You take only your fair share of the tips at work because you're a good person and a trustworthy co-worker, even though a deeper dip into the tip jar could get you that much closer to the car you've been saving for. Similarly, Hermione campaigns vociferously to end slavery for the lowly house-elves, much to the potential detriment of those they would serve (including, presumably, herself). Harry's actions are filled with this sort of selflessness. There is no reason for him to intervene on behalf of his despicable cousin when Dudley is attacked by a Dementor, other than his strong moral sense. That same moral sense has Harry rescue and then share the prize with his competitor, Cedric Diggory, whose demise seemed imminent in the Triwizard Tournament. In situations where the stakes are high and where behaving out of self-interest is awfully tempting, people can rise to the occasion and act with surprising integrity.

This kind of generosity of character can be seen in its extreme when people seem to sacrifice themselves to protect Harry's safety. We see this most clearly with his family. His mother, Lily, died protecting him. So did his godfather, Sirius. And curiously, his aunt and uncle, who make no bones about their dislike of Harry, continue their own version of altruism by allowing him to remain safe by living with them summer after summer. Although at the time of this writing, Dumbledore's reasons for ordering his own murder are mysterious, we're led to believe that it's another case of altruism, even if it means self-destruction winning out over self-interest.

Of course, people may cooperate for less noble reasons. We are, after all, social creatures, predictably influenced by social pressures. If you consistently defect, for example, you acquire a reputation, and people become less willing to trust you in the future. Thus, a tendency toward impulsive defection may gain you in the short term but may be undesirable in the long run. Your interactions with other people would devolve into perpetual defect-defect scenarios, when cooperate-cooperate would have been much more preferable. With such a structure of social rewards and punishments, people for the most part learn to cooperate, regardless of whether they are of noble character or not. The stakes are even higher in this wizarding world than they are in typical human situations, since angry defectors can perpetrate real horrors on each other (e.g., growing teeth, exploding entrails, skeletal loss, petrifaction, immediate death, etc.).

The wizarding world is as well aware of such behavioral contingencies as the human world is, and so they have formally instituted punishments to take advantage of people's motivation to avoid known negative consequences (Skinner). The no-magic-outside-school policy works so well because Hogwarts students realize they can be expelled for disobeying it. Flaring tempers are kept under control at least in part because of the points that would be deducted from the combatants' Houses. And Azkaban is a very effective external motivator for guiding behavior.

The wizarding world influences individual decisions in part because of the hierarchical power structure within society. People designated as authority figures can have tremendous influence on behavior (Milgram). Cornelius Fudge and Gilderoy Lockhart, as ridiculous as they can be, occupy positions of power that make defection against them potentially perilous. A wizard is in an even worse position squaring off against the power-hungry Dolores Umbridge. And so poor Harry, widely believed to be the Chosen One destined to ultimately face off and defeat evil incarnate, obediently spends his hours of detention scratching humiliating declarations into his hand.

Human relationships are complex, and what constitutes defection or cooperation is a matter of the beholder's interpretation. Snape will forever resent the fact that James Potter saved his life, something that another person might consider the ultimate act of generosity. After years of unambiguous bullying, though, such a major act of cooperation on James's part obligated Snape forever to the person he had come to hate. And of course, Snape's own deliberate and unprovoked killing of Dumbledore is, at the time of this writing (before the release of Book Seven), a mystery. Perhaps an unbreakable promise forced his hand, or perhaps he acted out of willful evil or calculated good. We and the wizarding community, as social creatures, are preoccupied with understanding the meaning of the act, not just the act itself. With different spins on people's actions, the motivation behind them, and thus their social and moral meaning, changes.

The central theme of the story arises from the difference in social roles played by our two main characters: good, cooperating Harry and evil, defecting Voldemort. They've made very different choices in the basic Prisoner's Dilemmas of the wizarding world, despite their deep similarity. Both have an enormous amount of power at their disposal. Both have a loyal band of willing followers (for Voldemort, the Death Eaters, and for Harry, his admiring schoolmates). Voldemort declares himself to have absolute power, while Harry seems to enjoy his role as an apprentice and prefers a democratic style with his peers. They represent the two strategic extremes in the game, though in some fundamental ways, they couldn't be more alike.

Much of the brilliance of the Harry Potter story comes from the fact that a world so completely different from ours can be painted with such depth and detail. But much of the brilliance lies in the utter familiarity of the relationships and dilemmas that the characters confront. Magic doesn't protect them from the basic stresses and pitfalls of being human. They can't utter a spell and escape the pressures and biases that come with being social creatures. And lucky for us, as we wouldn't be as thoroughly enchanted with their world if they could.

NANCY FRANKLIN, Ph.D., is an associate professor at the State University of New York at Stony Brook. She got her Ph.D. in 1989 at Stanford University, where she studied cognitive psychology. Her research is on memory, especially false memory, and she teaches courses in intro psych, cognition, and memory. She secretly has a major crush on Hagrid.

REFERENCES

Axelrod, R. M. *The Evolution of Cooperation*. New York: Basic Books, 1984.

S. Milgram, "Behavioral Study of Obedience," *Journal of Abnormal and Social Psychology* 67 (1963): 371–378.

Skinner, B. F. *About Behaviorism*. New York: Random House, 1974.

H. Rachlin, "Altruism and Selfishness," *Behavioral and Brain Sciences* 25 (2002): 239–296.

Is there a need for mental health treatment in Rowling's wizarding world? In the Western-world mental health, we have developed an elaborate classification and labeling system for diagnosing people's problems. In Harry's world, they seem quite comfortable simply labeling someone "mad." There seem to be no specific counselors to help students at Hogwarts with mental or emotional difficulties, no psychiatrists at St. Mungo's healing the mentally unstable. Could wizards learn something from us Muggles, or do they have all the support they need?

JESSICA LEIGH MURAKAMI

Mental Illness in the World of Wizardry

WHEN HARRY POTTER first learns that he is a wizard, he hears his Aunt Petunia call his mother a "'freak'" (*Harry Potter and the Sorceror's Stone* 53). Aunt Petunia then goes on to summarize her sister's short life and to insult Harry with the following statement:

> "Then she met that Potter at school and they left and got married and had you, and of course I knew you'd be just the same, just as strange, just—as—abnormal—and then, if you please, she went and got herself blown up and we got landed with you!" (*Sorcerer's Stone* 53).

In Aunt Petunia's world (made up almost entirely of her spoiled son, Dudley), her sister does not belong. Yet in the wizarding world, Harry's mother discovers a hidden talent in Potions class, finds a cocky and talented future husband, and develops the courage it will take to one day stand between Lord Voldemort and her infant son. Although her sister considers her a "freak," Lily Evans Potter becomes a heroic figure in the world of wizardry, just as Harry becomes our hero.

What does it mean to be "abnormal"? Clearly, someone ceases to be abnormal when he is surrounded with people (or wizards) just like him. Oftentimes, we describe people who are outside of the norm as "freaks," "weirdos," and "misfits," but we might also describe them as "brilliant" and "amazing" depending on how we view their abnormalities. For example, someone with an extremely high I.Q. may be described as "freakishly smart" and viewed with admiration. However, when we talk about "abnormal psychology" (a.k.a., clinical psychology), we are talking about the field of study that explores the many and varied ways that our mental health can suffer or "go wrong." More often than not, the symptoms of mental illness have a negative connotation and carry a stigma. In modern societies, the overwhelming majority of people do not want to experience the symptoms of schizophrenia, post-traumatic stress disorder, or major depressive disorder. We do not want to hear voices that aren't there, suffer from flashbacks of traumatic events, or feel like our lives are not worth living. Treatment in the form of medication or psychotherapy ("talk therapy") is often necessary to ameliorate suffering and even prevent death.

Is there a place for psychologists in the world of wizardry? What about psychiatrists? In order for there to be a place for mental health professionals in the wizarding world, there would first need to be a need for mental health treatment and for certain behaviors to be considered "abnormal" and undesirable. Mental illness is certainly prevalent in Muggle populations all over the world. In the United States, approximately one in four adults meet criteria for the diagnosis of a mental illness in a given year (Kessler, Chiu, Demler, & Walters). More than half of individuals who struggle with mental illness throughout their lives develop mental illness by the age of fourteen (Kessler, Chiu, Demler, & Walters). By year four, we would expect to see a number of Harry's classmates struggling with symptoms of anxiety and depression, especially given the increasing burden of academics, the awkwardness of adolescence, and the return of the Dark Lord!

While there does seem to be evidence of mental illness in the world of wizardry, it is not clear what role (if any) mental health professionals should play in this world. For example, it would be absurd for mental health professionals to invade another culture (or world) entirely foreign to them, using language such as "dissociative personality disorder" and "obsessive compulsive disorder," and judging the behavior of individuals within that culture by our own Western standards. All behavior occurs within a certain context, including the act of evaluating another's behavior. The wizarding world provides us with an unusual context to think about mental illness and ways to go about providing culturally sensitive treatments.

HOW DO WE DEFINE MENTAL ILLNESS?

The American Psychiatric Association (1994) defines a mental disorder as:

> A clinically significant behavioral or psychological syndrome or pattern that occurs in an individual and that is associated with present distress (e.g., a painful symptom) or disability (i.e., impairment in one or more important areas of functioning) or with a significantly increased risk of suffering death, pain, disability, or an important loss of freedom (xxxi).

Does Harry Potter meet criteria for a mental illness? He experiences distress over his monumental task of defeating the Dark Lord, suffers impairment from his quest (as evidenced by repeated offences at Hogwarts that result in detention, particularly with Professor Snape), and is at increased risk of death at the hands of Lord Voldemort. However, in the fourth revised version of the Diagnostic and Statistical Manual of Mental Disorders (DSM-IV-TR), the diagnosis of a mental disorder precludes "an expectable and culturally sanctioned response to a particular event" (American Psychiatric Association). In the school of Hogwarts, Harry's behavior is culturally sanctioned by the majority of students and professors. His actions are often described as heroic and brave, and rarely is his sanity questioned (except occasionally by Hermione).

While it does seem that unusual behaviors are more accepted in the wizarding world (i.e., Dobby banging his head against the wall), having unusual sensory experiences without known causes are troubling to both Muggles and wizards alike. In *Harry Potter and the Chamber of Secrets*, Harry asks Ron if he should tell Dumbledore about the voice he heard. "'No,' said Ron, without hesitation. 'Hearing voices no one else can hear isn't a good sign, even in the wizarding world'" (145). Later, Harry recalls Ron's words and does not tell Dumbledore about the "disembodied voice," which later turns out to be the hissing of a Basilisk. Because Harry can speak Parseltongue, he is able to understand the giant serpent's language. Without this explanation, Harry's sanity would be questioned by those told that he heard a voice, one no one else could hear, saying creepy things such as, "*Kill this time…let me rip…tear…*'" (*Chamber of Secrets* 254).

Similarly, visual hallucinations are seen as a cause for concern in the wizarding world. In *Harry Potter and the Prisoner of Azkaban*, Professor Snape confronts Harry about Malfoy seeing his floating head in Hogsmeade (Harry had been wearing his Invisibility Cloak). Snape snarls, "'It was your head, Potter. Floating in midair'" (*Prisoner of Azkaban* 283). After a careful silence, Harry remarks, "'Maybe he'd better go to Madam Pomfrey….If he's seeing things like—'" (*Prisoner of Azkaban* 283). The rest of the conversation does not go so well. Harry tries to reason with Snape, suggesting that perhaps Malfoy is experiencing hallucinations. Snape uses his own logic, snarling at Harry that if his head was in Hogsmeade, then so was the rest of him!

Obviously, this is not the way that this conversation would go in the Muggle world. If we were to see a head floating in midair, it is unlikely that there would be a rational explanation for it other than a hallucination. Yet in the wizarding world, many more explanations are possible. The examples of Harry hearing a Basilisk and wearing an Invisibility Cloak in Hogsmeade emphasize the importance of considering an individual's cultural context when determining whether a behavior or experience is unusual and problematic for the individual. It wouldn't be ethical (or accurate) to step from the Muggle world into the world of wizardry and accuse individuals of being psychotic simply because they can hear things that others can't hear or see heads floating in midair…not when there are perfectly logical explanations available in that culture. These examples also suggest that in both the Muggle and the wizarding world, a person's mental health is often questioned when there are no *acceptable* explanations for unusual phenomena reported by the individual.

THE ROLE OF CULTURE

Culture can be defined as the "human-made" part of the environment made up of both objects (e.g., paintings with moving people) and ideas (e.g., Quidditch is fun). Dimensions of culture include shared ideas, norms, material possessions, and technologies. The world of wizardry is a culture distinct from the various Muggle cultures on Earth. The most obvious difference is the use of magic. With magic it is possible to transform into a rat, store memories in a Pensieve, travel back in time to save the life of a hippograff and a falsely convicted felon, and take multiple classes at the same time. It is also possible to heal wounds with the tears of a phoenix, transform a school hallway into a swamp, and levitate objects into the air.

In the Western Muggle world, the field of psychiatry is its own culture within a culture. Mental health professionals share a common dialect ("Client A meets criteria for major depression with psychotic features and generalized anxiety disorder"), norms (i.e., the focus of therapy should be on the client and not the clinician), and physical components (i.e., the use of antidepressants, self-report measures, and waiting rooms). One of the shared assumptions in the culture of psychiatry is that mental disorders exist and can be classified into distinct categories of illness. There are currently more than 300 mental disorders listed in the DSM-IV-TR, and it is likely that there will be significantly more listed in the next version of the DSM. This is more than five times as many disorders as the number listed in the first version of the DSM, which was published in 1952 and contained approximately sixty disorders. Although the DSM is considered atheoretical (not supporting any one theory about the causes of these illnesses), based on expert opinion and empirical data of how clusters of symptoms fall together, it is also influenced by culture (e.g., homosexuality was once considered a mental illness in the DSM). Clearly, our conception of problematic behavior is influenced by our cultural environment.

One question that is often raised in the field of mental health is whether it does more harm than good to label individuals with mental disorders. This issue becomes even more salient when we talk about the benefits and disadvantages of using our classification system to label individuals from other cultures. Making a psychiatric diagnosis is helpful if it informs treatment and increases understanding between mental health treaters. It is also helpful in that it allows us to conduct research on a specific cluster of symptoms that often co-occur within the same individual. For example, we know that the majority of individuals suffering from a set of symptoms we've labeled "major depressive disorder" will respond to a form of talk therapy called cognitive therapy (Dobson). Also, diagnostic categories allow us to compare rates of mental illness across cultures. Prevalence rates of major mental disorders have been found to range from 4.3 percent in Shanghai to 26.4 percent in the United States (World Health Organization). (Such a wide range of rates of mental disorders underscore the significant contribution the environment has on a population's mental health.)

Although a potential benefit of using a diagnostic classification system is that some people may find comfort in a diagnosis if it conveys to them that what they are suffering from is at least somewhat understood, treatable, and not uncommon, oftentimes having a diagnosis of a mental disorder is stigmatizing and may increase hopelessness. When used inappropriately, making a diagnosis can also categorize people into disorders (e.g., "He's a schizophrenic" vs. "He has schizophrenia") and can be dehumanizing. Focusing on a diagnosis can also lead a mental health professional to ignore important information that does not fit with his/her conception of the illness. It is important, therefore, for mental health professionals to use the language of psychiatry minimally and in a sensitive manner. This is especially true when interacting with individuals from cultures where the language of modern day psychology is intimidating, alien, offensive... or simply meaningless. How helpful is it to diagnose Lord Voldemort with antisocial personality disorder? Or to diagnose Professor Lockheart with narcissistic personality disorder? Dobby exhibits symptoms of generalized anxiety disorder (GAD) because of his constant worrying over Harry's future, but how would Dumbledore react if we were to inform him that one of his house-elves meets criteria for GAD and might benefit from a selective serotonin reuptake inhibitor? If we didn't know that Dobby's fears were reasonable, might we also make the diagnosis of paranoid personality disorder or delusional disorder?

MADNESS IN HARRY'S WORLD

For better or worse, the terminology of abnormal psychology has made it into our everyday language. At least in the West, it is not uncommon for us to diagnose ourselves with or to refer to others as having attention deficit disorder or depression. This language is noticeably absent in Harry's world. Rather, a term that is used quite regularly is "mad." Ginny writes to Tom Riddle: "*There was another attack today and I don't know where I was. Tom, what am I going to do? I think I'm going mad...I think I'm the one attacking everyone, Tom!*" (*Chamber of Secrets* 310–311). The dissociative experiences that Ginny is writing about are similar to the extreme dissociative experiences of individuals in our culture who are diagnosed with dissociative personality disorder (DID).

Most of us have experienced mild dissociative experiences (e.g., driving to a friend's home and not remembering parts of the drive there). The level of dissociation experienced by individuals diagnosed with dissociative personality disorder (formerly known as "multiple personality disorder") is looked on with both fascination and fear in our culture. This is evident in such popular movies as *Psycho*, *Fight Club*, and *Identity*. These movies, though entertaining, are grossly inaccurate. Rather than perpetrators of violence, almost all of the individuals diagnosed with this disorder are victims of violence. The development of dissociative personality disorder can be seen as an adaptive response to traumatic experiences. In order to cope with traumatic experiences, some individuals are able to develop personalities that can cope with these experiences.

Dissociation, like other altered states of consciousness, is perceived differently depending on the culture into which you're born. For instance, Ginny interpreted her experiences as evidence that she was "going mad" since she couldn't remember chunks of time. If she had grown up in a different context, this interpretation, as well as the label that she used to describe her experiences, may have been different. In actuality, her body had been inhabited by the young Lord Voldemort through the medium of a diary...a perfectly rational explanation in the world of wizardry.

Culture affects not only how we explain behavior, but how we "treat" behaviors that we deem problematic either for the individual or for the society in which the individual lives. In the wizarding world, madness is often attributed to magic or the effects of magic. For example, Neville's parents lose touch with reality from the pain they endured from the Cruciatus Curse, an unforgivable curse that causes excruciating pain. Neville's parents live in St. Mungo's Hospital for Magical Maladies and Injuries in a "special ward for people whose brains have been addled by magic" (*Harry Potter and the Order of the Phoenix* 361). Harry, Hermione, Ginny, and Ron encounter Neville and his grandmother visiting Neville's parents and come face-to-face with the devastating effects of Dark magic. Neville's mother walks toward her son in a nightdress, her white hair "dead-looking" (*Order of the Phoenix* 514). She motions toward Neville and hands him a gum wrapper, which he takes with him. The name of the ward is "Spell Damage" and it seems that even with magic, the powerful treatment of choice in the wizarding world, these spells cannot be reversed.

Madness is also mentioned repeatedly in descriptions of Sirius Black by those who have not been in contact with him. When Madam Rosmerta asks Fudge, "'Is it true he's mad, Minister?'" Fudge answers, "'I wish I could say that he was.... I certainly believe his master's defeat unhinged him for a while. The murder of Pettigrew and all those Muggles was the action of a cornered and desperate man—cruel...pointless...'" (*Prisoner of Azkaban* 209). However, Fudge does not believe that Sirius Black is mad based on his interactions with him at Azkaban. He continues, "'You know, most of the prisoners in there sit muttering to themselves in the dark; there's no sense in them...but I was shocked at how *normal* Black seemed. He spoke quite rationally to me...'" (*Prisoner of Azkaban* 209). Surrounded by Dementors, the prisoners of Azkaban are said to go mad within weeks, "incapable of a single cheerful thought" (*Prisoner of Azkaban* 188). Yet Black, with the knowledge of his innocence and because of his ability to turn into an Animagus, is able to protect his mind from the destructive powers of the Dementors.

From the examples above, it seems that in the wizarding world, the term "madness" is used to describe individuals who have lost touch with reality. Other, less severe forms of what we would consider to be mental disorders are also mentioned. For example, in the presence of Dementors, Muggles and wizards alike experience some of the symptoms of major depressive disorder. In his first encounter with a

Dementor, Ron describes the experience as "'weird....Like I'd never be cheerful again'" (*Prisoner of Azkaban* 85). Protection from the depressing effect of Dementors requires the conjuring up of a Patronus. Professor Lupin describes the Patronus as a kind of "anti-Dementor." He explains to Harry, "'The Patronus is a kind of positive force, a projection of the very things that the Dementor feeds upon—hope, happiness, the desire to survive—but it cannot feel despair, as real humans can, so the Dementors can't hurt it...'" (*Prisoner of Azkaban* 237). The symptoms of major depression include the absence of Patronus-like qualities, namely hope, happiness, and the desire to live. In the DSM-IV, the diagnosis of depression also includes somatic symptoms (e.g., disturbances in sleeping and appetite), as well as cognitive symptoms (e.g., difficulty concentrating). In order to meet criteria for major depressive disorder, symptoms must be present for most of the day nearly every day for at least two weeks (American Psychiatric Association).

When Harry is in the presence of Dementors, he experiences a more severe reaction than most of his classmates, including flashbacks of his mother's murder at the hands of Lord Voldemort. Vivid flashbacks of traumatic events are common following traumatic experiences and may be indicative of a diagnosis of post-traumatic stress disorder (PTSD). Other symptoms of PTSD include hyper-arousal (e.g., being easily startled) and avoidance behaviors (e.g., avoiding people and events that are reminders of the trauma [American Psychiatric Association]). In the wizarding world, Dementors are able to cause emotional suffering in those who come into contact with them. They rob people of hope and happiness. In people who have experienced trauma in their lives, Dementors often have a re-traumatizing effect. Similarly, in our world, stressful life events and traumatic experiences often re-traumatize individuals, thereby precipitating the development of the symptoms of depression and PTSD (Kendler Karkowski, & Prescott).

Another character who exhibits some symptoms of what we would characterize as mental illness based on DSM-IV criteria is Lord Voldemort. As the young Tom Riddle, he displays signs of aggressive and troubling behavior at the orphanage where he is raised.

"You mean he is a bully?" asked Dumbledore.
"I think he must be," said Mrs. Cole, frowning slightly, "but it's very hard to catch him at it. There have been incidents.... Nasty things.... Billy Stubbs's rabbit... well, Tom *said* he didn't do it and I don't see how he could have done, but even so, it didn't hang itself from the rafters, did it?" (*Harry Potter and the Half-Blood Prince* 267)

Cruelty to animals is a symptom of what we refer to as conduct disorder; another symptom of conduct disorder is the use of a weapon that can cause serious physical harm to others (American Psychiatric Association). Tom Riddle's weapon is magic. When Dumbledore comes to tell him that he is a wizard and invite him to Hogwarts, Tom Riddle reacts with suspicion. "'Professor'? repeated Riddle. He looked wary. 'Is that like "doctor"? What are you here for? Did *she* get you in to have a look at me?' He was pointing at the door through which Mrs. Cole had just left" (*Half-Blood Prince* 269).

Tom Riddle believes that Dumbledore is from a mental asylum. When Dumbledore explains to Tom that "'Hogwarts... is a school for people with special abilities,'" Tom yells, "'I'm not mad!'" Dumbledore replies, "'I know that you are not mad. Hogwarts is not a school for mad people. It is a school of magic'" (*Half-Blood Prince* 270). Tom Riddle goes with Dumbledore to Hogwarts and continues to develop as a Dark wizard. What would the fate of the wizarding world have been like if Dumbledore had been from a mental health treatment facility? Is this a situation in which diagnosis may have been helpful, rather than harmful? Many children diagnosed with conduct disorder do not go on to meet criteria for antisocial personality disorder in adulthood, a disorder that is characterized by deceitfulness, aggressiveness, and a lack of remorse.

The adult Lord Voldemort would have no trouble meeting the criteria for antisocial personality disorder. Personality disorders are a class of mental disorders that are characterized by pervasive and rigid personality traits and behaviors. They are considered difficult to treat and are strongly correlated with impaired relationships in a person's life. The existence and diagnoses of personality disorders are especially controversial and carry additional stigma above and beyond being diagnosed with other mental disorders, especially among mental health professionals. It is not unusual to hear the phrase "Not another borderline!" in mental health wards, referring to patients who meet the diagnostic criteria for borderline personality disorder, which is characterized by chaotic relationships, impulsive behaviors, and mood swings. This is harmful to patients who may not receive the best care possible for their symptoms because of their diagnosis. Similar to other diagnoses such as schizophrenia, the labeling of personality disorders often conveys a sense of hopelessness, which can interfere with treatment.

CULTURALLY SENSITIVE TREATMENTS

So far, the emphasis in this essay has been on diagnostic issues in the wizarding world: Does mental illness exist in the world of wizardry? Is it appropriate or advantageous to use our diagnostic classification system in a culture very different from our own? What are some of the disorders that can be identified in Harry's world? Assuming that there are distressing symptoms of mental illness experienced by individuals in the wizarding world, what role can mental health professionals play in such a world? Let us suppose that the world of wizardry exists and we have identified similar rates of mental illness in this world compared to individuals from our Muggle world. Do we have anything to offer this world in terms of mental health treatment? Do they have anything to offer us, to heal the effects of our own Dementors?

In our culture of increasing mental healthcare needs, more attempts are being made to investigate and develop culturally sensitive treatments. The main strategy for accomplishing this has been to look at our own treatments and attempt to adapt them in some way to fit with other cultures. Perhaps after adapting some kind of Muggle intervention for use in the wizarding world, the young Tom Riddle could have been prevented from becoming the Dark Lord? Perhaps psychiatric medications could help Neville's parents gain a stronger hold on reality?

While this approach is helpful, it can also be somewhat limiting in that other, more culturally appropriate interventions tend to be understudied and overlooked. For example, for many Asian people, the idea of telling their problems to a complete stranger who is getting paid to listen to them is a bit hard to comprehend. They are more likely to seek healing through their primary care doctors or through alternative medicine. Rather than dismissing these forms of healing, more attempts should be made to understand how effective they are. Acupuncture, for instance, has been shown to be as effective as the antidepressant amitriptyline in the treatment of depression (Luo, Meng, Jia, & Zhao). Thus, the possibility exists that using such a treatment may be more helpful for Asian-Americans than implementing an adapted form of talk therapy that may not be consistent with their conceptualization of mental illness.

At Hogwarts, there are no school counselors. No one is there to counsel Cho after the death of Cedric Diggory. Instead, the students at Hogwarts turn to Madame Pomfrey to counter unfortunate spell mishaps. Harry turns to the wisdom provided by Professor Dumbledore. Meanwhile, Ron, Hermione, Neville, and Ginny provide Harry with the emotional support he needs to take on the Dark Lord. Social support is one of the key factors that protect against mental illness (Schaefer, Coyne, & Zazarus). Without his loyal friends, it is unlikely that Harry would be able to defeat Lord Voldemort and his small army of followers. They not only help him on his quest to defeat the Dark wizard, but also help him with his mental health!

In the wizarding world, magic is used in the place of medications and talk therapy, the tools of our culture. Yet there is a certain magic in all of the tools that improve mental health. Cognitive behavioral therapy has been shown to lead to changes in the brain of individuals treated for depression in a pattern distinct from those treated with antidepressants (Goldapple, Segal, Garson, Lau, Bieling, Kennedy, & Mayberg). It is amazing that talk therapy affects the brain in a different way than medication therapy, and that both treatments are equally effective for certain conditions. In both the Muggle and the wizarding world, love can also be considered a form of magic, mysterious and powerful. Dumbledore tells Harry that his ability to love is what sets him apart from Lord Voldemort, an ability that the Dark Lord is not able to comprehend. Love is also what saves Harry's life as a baby and what could potentially defeat Lord Voldemort for good.

What does magic mean to us? We often use the term to describe phenomena or events that we cannot explain. At its best, magic fills us with a sense of wonder. At its worse, it fills us with fear. Similarly, the human mind of Muggles and wizards alike is incredibly complex and can strike both of these emotions within us, especially when we perceive a person's mind to be abnormal in some way. It has been argued that cultural context is extremely important in conceptualizing, diagnosing, and treating what we consider to be "abnormal" or a form of "mental illness." In the wizarding world, there is certainly evidence of pain, perhaps the most singular indication of the need for help. In order to alleviate mental suffering in any culture, it is important first to understand the context in which the suffering is occurring and to prepare to be awed by both the similarities and differences that can exist between individuals from what are perceived to be dramatically different worlds. We must also be prepared to accept that a "freak" in one world may be a hero in another, and that "abnormal" is entirely relative and often praised.

———

JESSICA LEIGH MURAKAMI received her B.A. from the University of Pennsylvania and her M.S. in clinical psychology from the University of Oregon. She is currently a doctoral student at the University of Oregon in clinical psychology. Her main research interests are in the area of depression research, particularly related to gender and cultural differences in depression. She is also very much interested in understanding the motivations, risk, and protective factors for suicide in diverse populations. At the University of Oregon, Jessica is also pursuing her M.F.A. in creative writing (poetry). She is an avid Harry Potter fan and is convinced that Snape is innocent.

REFERENCES

American Psychiatric Association. *Diagnostic and Statistical Manual of Mental Disorders* (Fourth edition, rev.). Washington, D.C.: American Psychiatric Publishing, 2000.

D. L. Chambless, Tran, Q. Giao, and C. R. Glass, "Predictors of Response to Cognitive-Behavioral Group Therapy for Social Phobia," *Journal of Anxiety Disorders* 11(3) (1997): 221–240.

J. F. Collins and H. Lee, "Treatment Expectancy Among Psychiatric Inpatients," *Journal of Clinical Psychology* 42(4) (1986): 562–569.

K. S. Dobson, "A Meta-Analysis of the Efficacy of Cognitive Therapy for

Depression," *Journal of Consulting and Clinical Psychology*, 57(3) (1989): 414–419.

K. Goldapple, Z. Segal, C. Garson, M. Lau, P. Bieling, S. Kennedy, and H. Mayberg, "Modulation of Cortical-Limbic Pathways in Major Depression: Treatment-Specific Effects of Cognitive Behavior Therapy," *Archives of General Psychiatry* 61 (2004): 34–41.

M. E. Goossens, J. W. Vlaeyen, Al. Hidding, A. Kole-Snijders, and S. M. Evers, "Treatment Expectancy Affects the Outcome of Cognitive-Behavioral Interventions in Chronic Pain," *Clinical Journal of Pain* 21(1) (2005): 18–26.

K. S. Kendler, L. M. Karkowski, and C. A. Prescott, "Causal Relationship Between Stressful Life Events and the Onset of Major Depression," *American Journal of Psychiatry* 156 (1999): 837–851.

R. C. Kessler, W. T. Chiu, O. Demler, and E. E. Walters, "Prevalence, Severity, and Comorbidity of Twelve-Month DSM-IV Disorders in the National Comorbidity Survey Replication (NCS-R)," *Archives of General Psychiatry* 62(6) (2005): 617–27.

H. Luo, F. Meng, Y. Jia, and X. Zhao, "Clinical Research on the Therapeutic Effect of the Electro-Acupuncture Treatment in Patients with Depression," *Psychiatry Clin Neurosci* 52 (1998): S338–340.

Rowling, J. K. *Harry Potter and the Sorcerer's Stone*. New York: Scholastic Inc., 1998.

——. *Harry Potter and the Chamber of Secrets*. New York: Scholastic Inc., 1999.

——. *Harry Potter and the Prisoner of Azkaban*. New York: Scholastic Inc., 1999.

——. *Harry Potter and the Goblet of Fire*. New York: Scholastic Inc., 2000.

——. *Harry Potter and the Order of the Phoenix*. New York: Scholastic Inc., 2003.

——. *Harry Potter and the Half-Blood Prince*. New York: Scholastic Inc., 2005.

C. Schaefer, J. C. Coyne, J.C., and R. S. Zazarus, "The Health-Related Functions of Social Support," *Journal of Behavioral Medicine* 4(4) (1981): 381–406.

The WHO World Mental Health Survey Consortium (2004). "Prevalence, Severity, and Unmet Need for Treatment of Mental Disorders in the World Health Organization World Mental Health Surveys," *Journal of the American Medical Association* 291 (2004): 2581–2590.

When Dobby contemplates betraying his master, he attempts to in-jure himself in exaggerated and humorous ways. But self-injury isn't only for house-elves. Harry, Ron, Hermione, and even Voldemort injure themselves on occasion. In the Muggle world, self-injury is surprisingly common. Klonsky and Laptook review the six main reasons that people harm themselves. Given what Harry has gone through so far, one of the authors wonders (as Rowling has recently hinted): might Harry have to sacrifice himself in the end to defeat Voldemort?

E. DAVID KLONSKY, Ph.D., AND REBECCA LAPTOOK, M.A.

"Dobby Had to Iron His Hands, Sir!"

Self-Inflicted Cuts, Burns, and Bruises in Harry Potter

MENTAL HEALTH PROFESSIONALS have long known that some people purposely cut, burn, bruise, or otherwise hurt themselves. This phenomenon is known as self-injury or self-harm. Although self-injury is distinguished from suicidal behaviors, which are performed with the intent to end one's life, self-injury can still be dangerous and a sign of psychological or emotional distress. For example, people who self-injure are more likely to experience depression, anxiety, and a range of other psychiatric difficulties compared to people who do not self-injure (Klonsky, Oltmanns, & Turkheimer). Although behaviors such as skin-cutting and burning may sound rare, they are not uncommon. Would you believe that 8 percent of middle school students (Hilt et al.), 14 to 15 percent of high school students (Laye-Gindhu & Schonert-Reichl), and almost 20 percent of college students (Whitlock, Eckenrode, & Silverman) have engaged in self-injurious behavior at least once? Surprised? Well, you may also be surprised to hear that self-injurious behaviors seem to be just as common in the Harry Potter series. Don't believe us? Then read on!

This essay will discuss what we can learn about self-harm from psychological research and the Harry Potter series in order to gain a better understanding of this perplexing behavior. We will be focusing on a particularly intriguing aspect of self-injury: *Why would people choose to hurt themselves*? After all, people generally strive to avoid pain and injury as much as possible. We wear seat belts when driving, helmets when biking, thimbles when sewing, gloves when gardening, pads when playing sports, shoes while walking outside... the list of things we do to avoid pain and injury goes on and on. Mental health professionals are especially interested in figuring out why people self-injure because this knowledge would help uncover causes of and cures for this harmful behavior.

Fortunately, a growing body of research has begun to shed light on motivations for self-injury. Some of these motivations include: to calm oneself down when upset, agitated, or frustrated; to punish or express anger at oneself; to influence or manipulate others; to feel exhilarated; to halt experiences of feeling unreal or nothing at all; and to preserve one's life. In Table 1, you'll find a summary of these motivations. (Terms will be italicized in the text each time a motivation is introduced.)

It is important to note that these motivations may co-occur. In other words, just as people might eat both because they are hungry and because they enjoy the taste of food, people sometimes self-injure for more than one reason. The remainder of this essay will take a look at the various reasons why people may deliberately hurt themselves and will use the actions of our favorite (and least favorite) Harry Potter characters to illustrate these motivations.

Table 1—Common Motivations for Self-Injury

MOTIVATION	DESCRIPTION OF MOTIVATION
Affect Regulation	To cope with intense negative emotions or agitation
Self-Punishment	To punish or express anger toward oneself
Interpersonal-Influence	To manipulate or elicit desirable actions from others
Sensation Seeking	To generate exhilaration or excitement
Self-Preservation	To avoid death or suicide
Anti-Dissociation	To halt experiences of feeling unreal or nothing at all

WOULD YOU BURN OR BRUISE YOURSELF AS A PUNISHMENT FOR INAPPROPRIATE BEHAVIOR?

Dobby would! We learn in *Harry Potter and the Chamber of Secrets* that house-elves are bound to serve and not betray their masters. Dobby, however, spends much of the second book attempting to protect Harry Potter from the sinister plot devised by Dobby's master, Lucius Malfoy, who aims to unleash the Basilisk on Hogwarts students. In an effort to keep Harry away from Hogwarts, Dobby steals letters from Harry's friends, frames Harry for using magic, seals the entrance to Platform 9 ¾, and tries to scare Harry off with an enchanted Bludger. Clearly, Dobby's pattern of behavior runs counter to his master's wishes, and thus counter to house-elf tradition.

As a result, Dobby pays a heavy, self-inflicted price. He feels so ashamed and disturbed by his behavior that he repeatedly smashes his head with or against various household objects and burns his hands with an iron.

Why would anyone engage in such strange, self-punitive behavior? You might say, "Hey, that's just what house-elves do!" Hermione, of course, would scoff and start lecturing you about S.P.E.W. (Society for the Promotion of Elfish Welfare). However, a similar pattern has been observed in adolescents and adults who self-injure. Many individuals who hurt themselves report that they do so as a form of *self-punishment* (see Table 1). For example, in research studies that survey motivations for self-injury, many people endorse reasons such as: "I was angry at myself" (Favazza & Conterio) or "to atone for sins" (Laye-Gindhu & Schonert-Reichl). In light of evidence that many self-injurers feel unhappy with themselves (Klonsky, Oltmanns, & Turkheimer), some mental health professionals speculate that self-inflicted pain and physical punishment are experienced as familiar or comforting by those individuals. However, it is also true that self-punishment is just one of many possible reasons for self-harm, so let us explore other motivations.

HAVE YOU EVER FELT UPSET ENOUGH TO SCRATCH AND CLAW YOUR FACE?

Lupin has! Before the Wolfsbane Potion was available to him, Lupin would lock himself in the Shrieking Shack whenever it was his time to transform into a werewolf. Unable to attack others, werewolf-Lupin would become highly agitated and injure himself: "'I was separated from humans to bite, so I bit and scratched myself instead'" (*Harry Potter and the Prisoner of Azkaban* 353). Although we might expect a werewolf to attack humans, it is curious that werewolf-Lupin attacks himself when humans are not around. Why not growl and pound at the walls of the Shrieking Shack, looking for a way out? Why scratch and claw at his own face? In this instance, it appears that Lupin self-injures for reasons that also exist in the real world. According to the *affect regulation* model of self-harm, people often hurt themselves as a way to cope with intense negative emotions. For example, in a study of self-cutting, a majority of participants reported experiencing heightened tension before cutting and a sense of relief after cutting (Jones et al.). Another study found that feelings such as anger and anxiety decrease after cutting, whereas feelings such as peacefulness increase after cutting (Kemperman, Russ, & Shearin).

You may find it odd that we have used the behavior of a werewolf to illustrate motivations for human behavior. However, many researchers believe there is a parallel between the feelings that prompt animal and human self-injury. People and animals share many of the same genetics and biological processes. Therefore, studying self-injurious behavior in animals may help us understand self-injurious behavior in people. But do animals self-injure, or is werewolf-Lupin an exception? Well, researchers have found that between 5 and 28 percent of macaques—monkeys that share 90 to 94 percent of their genetic makeup with humans—engage in self-injurious behaviors (Tiefenbacher et al.). These monkeys sometimes bite themselves, pull their hair, and engage in head-banging. Behavioral and physiological evidence suggests that these behaviors often occur in response to tension and agitation, just as they appear to do in humans.

Lupin may not be the only Harry Potter character to exhibit this behavioral pattern. Recall that self-harm can be performed for multiple reasons. Although Dobby clearly is punishing himself when he burns and bruises himself, Dobby's self-harm also appears to be a form of affect regulation. Let's look closely at Dobby's interaction with Harry at the beginning of *Chamber of Secrets*. How does Dobby feel after speaking negatively about or attempting to betray his master? Dobby reacts by yelling, "'Bad Dobby! *Bad* Dobby!'" (*Chamber of Secrets* 14), and in a second instance makes a "choking noise" and becomes frantic (*Chamber of Secrets* 16). Clearly, Dobby becomes quite upset and agitated, and this state leads Dobby to bruise or burn himself. And how does Dobby feel after bashing himself in the head? Interestingly, after each episode of self-harm, Dobby appears to calm down and is once again able to converse normally with Harry.

Even though Dobby is not human, his tendency to feel upset, self-injure, and thereby calm down closely resembles the experience of the majority of people who self-injure. In fact, numerous studies have documented this general pattern of feeling negative emotions and agitation before hurting oneself and then feeling relief or calm afterwards. A recent and groundbreaking study sheds light on how this process might work. The study used an advanced-brain scanning technique called functional Magnetic Resonance Imaging (fMRI) to show that activating the part of the brain that responds to physical pain causes activity to reduce in another part of the brain that responds to negative emotions (Schmahl et al.). In other words, self-injury may biologically block or reduce our ability to experience unpleasant emotions.

HOW FAR WOULD YOU GO TO GET OUT OF A CLASS YOU DIDN'T LIKE?

Would you pretend to be sick, or would you actually make yourself physically ill? Apparently, Hogwarts students are willing to harm themselves to avoid classes, especially those taught by a professor they don't respect, such as Dolores Umbridge. Utilizing Fred and George's invention of Skiving Snackboxes, students willingly ingest things that make them faint, vomit, develop high fevers, or bleed profusely from their noses. The reason why Hogwarts students engage in these potentially harmful or painful behaviors appears to be similar to one of the motivations for real world self-injurious behavior. The *interpersonal-influence* model of self-harm suggests that people may hurt themselves in order to control, influence, or manipulate others in their surroundings. For example, up to 15 percent of self-injurers in one study said that they hurt themselves in order to "get control of a situation" or "try to get a reaction from someone" (Nock & Prinstein 2004). Similarly, by making themselves sick, Hogwarts students sabotage Umbridge's efforts to teach and cause her to become enraged and frustrated. Additionally, the students manipulate the situation so that they can skip classes without getting in trouble, as Umbridge is forced to let the bleeding and fainting students leave and go to the hospital wing.

It seems that Professor Umbridge has a tendency to make people want to hurt themselves, because Harry also self-injures to prove a point to her. When Harry first sits down in his detention with Umbridge in *Harry Potter and the Order of the Phoenix*, he gasps in pain as he cuts the words *I must not tell lies* into his hand using Umbridge's special pen. However, even though he continues to bleed and the words become etched deeper and deeper into his skin, Harry continues to slice open his hand. Harry then refuses Ron and Hermione's advice to tell Professor McGonagall about his inhumane punishment, even though he and his friends are convinced that she would intervene. Instead, Harry returns to detention, cuts the words over and over again into the back of his hand, and takes care not to make a noise or facial expression that would reveal the pain. Why? Harry has decided to show Umbridge that he is not weak and that he is beyond her ability to control or break.

Clearly, students are willing to harm themselves in an effort to thwart Umbridge's attempts to gain power. But students also engage in these behaviors to manipulate people in other ways. Harry, Ron, and Hermione drink the Polyjuice Potion to look like Crabbe, Goyle, and Millicent Bulstrode to dupe Draco Malfoy into revealing the identity of the heir of Slytherin in *Order of the Phoenix*. But consuming a dark, murky liquid that burns your insides, brings you gasping to your knees, and causes your skin to bubble like hot wax sounds like a painful way to get what you want! Luckily, Harry, Ron, and Hermione only have to take the potion one time. Barty Crouch, Jr., on the other hand, has to take a swig of Polyjuice Potion every hour for an entire school year in order to maintain his appearance as Mad-Eye Moody, complete with a missing leg, missing eye, and missing chunk of nose. By continuing to drink the potion and abuse his body, Crouch is able to convince everyone that he is Mad-Eye, and thus help Harry to win the Triwizard Tournament in order to deliver him to Voldemort. So, whether it's drinking a dangerous potion, cutting your own flesh, or making yourself ill, the characters in Harry Potter feel that deliberately harming themselves is a small price to pay to manipulate and influence those around them.

WHO WOULD CHOOSE TO EAT BLOOD-FLAVORED LOLLIPOPS, COCKROACH CLUSTERS, OR EXPLODING BON-BONS?

Hogwarts students would! Young witches and wizards eagerly await trips to Hogsmeade, where they can visit Honeydukes and stock up on a multitude of what Muggles would describe as disgusting and sometimes dangerous candies (*we* wouldn't want to eat something that might blow up). If you walked into any Muggle candy shop, you'd find a mouth-watering variety of conventional sweets to please the senses, from fruit-flavored gummies to chocolate peanut-clusters to strings of licorice. Now, we don't know about you, but cherry, apple, and grape-flavored jellybeans sound much more appealing than those flavored like earwax, earthworm, and dirt. So, why would anyone choose to eat such sickening flavors? Well, we believe that Harry Potter characters engage in such behavior for one of the same reasons some people self-injure in the real world: *sensation-seeking*.

Sometimes, when people engage in potentially self-injurious be-havior, they may experience a sense of excitement or exhilaration, similar to what people experience when sky-diving, bungee jumping, or performing other extreme activities. For example, some self-injur-ers say that they hurt themselves in order to "experience a 'high' that feels like a drug high" (Osuch et al.), and one study showed that just over 10 percent of participants self-injured because they "thought it would be fun" (Laye-Gindhu & Schonert-Reichl). In Harry Potter, we see that some students choose to consume things that most people would not touch with a ten-foot pole, and they do this for the novelty and excitement of the experience.

Now, eating strange and disgusting candy is one thing, but how about swallowing foods designed to make you vomit? Fred and George provide a great example of self-harm when they eagerly and repeatedly ingest their newly perfected Puking Pastilles in front of their fellow classmates in the Gryffindor common room. Earlier, we discussed how Fred and George's Skiving Snackboxes are an example of self-harm for the purposes of interpersonal influence. But here, we see how their hazardous inventions also serve the function of sensa-tion-seeking. As Fred and George take turns biting off the orange end of a chew, vomiting into a bucket, and then forcing down the purple end of a chew, their friends enthusiastically applaud them. By eating these harmful pastilles, Fred and George enjoy being the center of at-tention and hearing the applause of an adoring audience. Apparently, honing projectile vomiting skills in front of an audience and eating disgusting and potentially dangerous candies illustrates the lengths some will go to seek thrilling sensations.

CAN YOU THINK OF ANYONE WHO WOULD SEVER A PART OF HIS OWN BODY IN ORDER TO STAY ALIVE?

If you said Peter Pettigrew, you are correct! To escape being killed by Voldemort's supporters, who believe Pettigrew double-crossed the Dark Lord, Pettigrew severs his finger to fake his death. The reason for this act of self-harm may be related to a motivation discussed in the psychological literature: *self-preservation*. One reason self-injurers hurt themselves is to find an alternative to death. For example, a little less than half of the people in one self-injury study endorsed hurting themselves "to stop suicidal ideation or attempts" (Nixon et al.), and people in another study reported that self-harming "stopped me from killing myself" (Laye-Gindhu & Schonert-Reichl). The individuals in these studies appear to have been experiencing severe psychological distress and suicidal thoughts and felt that injuring themselves helped them feel better and avoid attempting suicide. Although Pettigrew and other characters in Harry Potter do not seem to be hurting themselves as an alternative to suicide, they do self-injure as a way to avoid dying. Similar to the trapped rock-climber who self-amputates an arm to save himself, Pettigrew cuts off his own finger to avoid being killed.

Interestingly, Pettigrew harms his body at least two more times to save himself. When he reads that Sirius Black has escaped from Azkaban, he knows that Sirius will hunt him down for betraying the Potters. Pettigrew realizes that Hermione's cat, Crookshanks, is working in cahoots with Sirius and fakes his own death one more time, but this time in the form of Scabbers the rat. He bites himself so that he bleeds on the bed sheet in the Gryffindor dormitory, hoping that Harry, Ron, and Hermione will think that he was killed by Crookshanks.

Pettigrew's third instance of self-injury is his most severe. He chops off his right hand and adds it to the potion that will let Voldemort rise again. By injuring himself in this way, Pettigrew shows loyalty to Voldemort. Refusing to perform this act of self-harm would mean being killed by Voldemort, or having to flee and live in danger of being tracked down and killed by Voldemort or those he betrayed. Pettigrew values his self-preservation and chooses to sever his hand.

Although Pettigrew is weak and cowardly, self-harm is also employed by the fearless and strong. Voldemort, the most fierce and powerful wizard of them all (except possibly for Dumbledore), twice harms himself for the sake of self-preservation. First, as Firenze tells Harry in *Harry Potter and the Sorcerer's Stone*, the blood of a unicorn will keep a person alive, but only to live a cursed life. Apparently, the promise of a cursed half-life doesn't bother Voldemort because he readily drinks the blood from the slain unicorn in the Forbidden Forest to stay alive. Second, Voldemort performs a horrific act of self-harm in order to ensure his continued survival: he splits his soul into seven pieces and encases the torn portions in Horcruxes. Professor

Slughorn tells a young Voldemort that splitting one's soul is against nature and an act that violates the self. However, Voldemort decides not only to split his soul once, but a shocking seven times. It is clear that Voldemort values nothing more than self-preservation.

WHAT DO YOU THINK A SIGN OF SELF-HARM COULD LOOK LIKE?

Could it be a bruise? A scratch? Or ... how about a lightning-shaped scar? It's interesting to consider that J. K. Rowling chooses to mark Harry in this way. Although Harry's scar is not self-inflicted (unless we want to argue that Rowling identifies with and chose to injure her main character), it nevertheless illustrates the principles behind one of the models of self-injurious behavior: *anti-dissociation*. Some people who self-injure describe that they sometimes feel unreal or outside of their body, feelings that can be quite scary and discomforting. The pain or shock of self-injury may help individuals to once again feel real, alive, or back inside their body. For example, in one study of self-harm, 55 percent of people indicated that they hurt themselves in order "to feel real again" (Favazza & Conterio), and in another study almost half of the people felt that they self-injured to "stop feeling numb" (Nixon et al.). In Harry Potter, we see that Harry's scar serves a parallel purpose. Harry begins school as a boy who doesn't truly understand why he is special. How could *he* survive the *Avada Kedavra* curse? How could *he* be a powerful wizard? Why does Voldemort want to kill *him*? Who is Harry Potter? Every time Harry's scar sears with burning pain, he is reminded of who he is and why he is alive, similar to how self-inflicted pain sometimes serves to help people feel real and alive again.

WHAT WOULD YOU BE WILLING TO RISK FOR THE GREATER GOOD?

So far, this essay has been devoted to examples of non-suicidal self-harm, but we feel that it's important to address the many instances in which Harry Potter characters knowingly and intentionally face potential or actual death. Why do some people choose to put themselves in a situation where they risk being killed? One reason to face death is to benefit the greater good. For example, soldiers in times of conflict understand there is a chance of injury and death on the battlefield but fight anyway. In some cases, soldiers will purposely sacrifice themselves, as in the cases of kamikaze pilots who crashed their planes into targets during World War II. In Harry Potter, we also see examples of characters deliberately placing themselves in harm's way and sacrificing themselves.

Would you knowingly enter a chamber and fight an enormous Basilisk that had a mouth full of long, razor-sharp, venomous fangs? *We* might hesitate in this particular situation, but Harry does not. Harry readily follows the tunnel in search of Ginny, drawing his wand to battle the Basilisk or whatever else gets in his way. Luckily, Harry eventually defeats the Basilisk, but not before feeling white-hot pain as one of the serpent's fangs pierces his arm. If Fawkes had not arrived to heal the wound, Harry's valiant efforts would have resulted in his death.

Harry's not the only one willing to put himself in harm's way for the greater good. As the three friends play their way across the giant chess board to reach the Sorcerer's Stone, Ron intentionally moves into a position where the queen can take him. As a result, Ron is struck hard across the head by the queen's heavy stone arm and is knocked unconscious. By putting his life in danger, Ron enables Harry to go forward and keep the Stone from Voldemort, who would use it to rise to power again.

It's one thing to place yourself in a situation where there is a risk of death, but another to face certain death. Harry's mother, Lily, does just that when she stands in front of Voldemort as he tries to kill Harry. Because Lily willingly sacrifices her life for her son, she provides Harry with a protection that Voldemort cannot penetrate. Additionally, we see another example of self-sacrifice at the end of *Harry Potter and the Half-Blood Prince*. In order to destroy one of Voldemort's Horcruxes and, hence, thwart his efforts for immortality, Dumbledore willingly drinks the emerald liquid in the stone basin where he believes the Horcrux lies. As he shakes and screams in anguish, Dumbledore continues to gulp down the potion in order to reveal the Horcrux hidden below. It is only a short time later that a weakened Dumbledore returns to Hogwarts and falls victim to Snape's Killing Curse.

Finally, you may be surprised to hear that at least one of this essay's authors (Klonsky) is concerned that Harry may have to sacrifice himself for the greater good. Some of you will undoubtedly ask: "What do you mean? Can't Harry just destroy Voldemort's Horcruxes and live happily ever after?" We hope so, but... what if Harry is a Horcrux? We learn in *Half-Blood Prince* that Voldemort probably planned to make a final Horcrux with Harry's death. We also know that something unexpected happened. Voldemort's Killing Curse did not kill Harry. Instead, the curse left a prominent scar, some of Voldemort's powers and characteristics were transferred to Harry, and Harry has access to Voldemort's thoughts and emotions. These strange occurrences have yet to be explained, unless... the piece of Voldemort's soul intended for the last Horcrux entered Harry through the scar, resides in Harry, and is the reason so many of Voldemort's characteristics, thoughts, and emotions appear to be in Harry. And if this theory is correct, *will Harry have to destroy himself to destroy Voldemort?*

A FINAL THOUGHT

Up until this point, we have explored different forms and motivations for self-harm, but we haven't talked about its consequences. Research suggests that one of the most common consequences of self-injury is scars. For example, in a study of individuals who cut themselves, 95 percent indicated that "marks are left on my skin" as a consequence of self-harm (Klonsky 2006). But the scars left by self-harm are not experienced in the same way by everyone. People report that they sometimes feel negatively, positively, or mixed about their scars. We see some parallels in Harry's feelings about his lightning-shaped scar. On the one hand, Harry's scar attracts positive attention. It marks him as the "Boy Who Lived" and the one who caused Voldemort's downfall. Harry is bombarded with handshakes and looks of awe during his first trip to the Leaky Cauldron and enjoys instant popularity in the wizarding world.

On the other hand, Harry's scar attracts unwanted attention. Harry endures people staring and gawking, and he cannot hide his scar no matter how much he tries to flatten his untidy hair. In the real world, self-injurers may have similar experiences. Scars caused by self-injury often attract quizzical or even horrified stares. Sometimes people who self-injure are put in the uncomfortable position of being asked about the cause of the scars. Additionally, just as Harry's scar reminds him of terrible memories and causes him intense pain when Voldemort is particularly angry, people who self-injure sometimes see their scars as reminders of powerful emotions and experiences from their past. We witness a fascinating moment in *Half-Blood Prince* when Harry shows Rufus Scrimgeour, the Minister of Magic, the words "I must not tell lies" that have scarred into Harry's hand as a result of Umbridge's detentions. Although this scar must remind Harry of the terrible things that happened during his fifth year at Hogwarts, in this instance Harry uses the scar to empower himself and refuse Scrimgeour's request to assist the Ministry. Whether Harry finds a way to draw power from his famous lightning-shaped scar, and whether this scar represents his salvation or downfall, remains to be seen.

Thank you for joining us on our exploration of the psychological motivations for and meanings of self-injurious behaviors. We hope that despite the evil, aggression, and self-inflicted violence that pervades Harry Potter, we might all be in for a happy ending!

E. DAVID KLONSKY, Ph.D., received his B.A. in psychology from Washington University in St. Louis and his Ph.D. in clinical psychology form the University of Virginia. He is currently an assistant professor of psychology at Stony Brook University, where he is also director of the Personality, Emotion, and Behavior Laboratory. His research examines the personality traits and emotion processes that lead to psychopathology and maladaptive behaviors. He wishes to thank his wife, Alexis, for her love, support, and numerous Harry Potter insights. David and Alexis would both like to thank J. K. Rowling for bettering the world through her books and example.

REBECCA LAPTOOK, M.A., is a graduate of SMU in Dallas. She is currently an advanced graduate student at Stony Brook University in New York earning her Ph.D. in clinical psychology. She is interested in children and adolescent psychopathology and is currently working on a large longitudinal study of temperament as a precursor for later depressive and anxiety disorders in preschool-aged children. Her research also focuses on parent-child interactions and their relations to child temperament and psychopathology. Rebecca somehow missed the entrance to Platform 9¾ and, thus, began her journey through Hogwarts only in 2004. However, she has made up for this late start by reading the series many times through, becoming possibly clinically obsessed, and always thinking of how to relate the themes in Harry Potter to her clinical work with children. Rebecca feels lucky to be surrounded by people who share her love of Harry Potter and indulge her frequent analogies to the wizarding world.

REFERENCES

A. R. Favazza and K. Conterio, "Female Habitual Self-Mutilators," *Acta Psychiatrica Scandinavica* 79 (1989): 283–289.

Hilt, L. M., M. K Nock, E. E. Lloyd-Richardson, and M. J. Prinstein. "Longitudinal Study of Non-Suicidal Self-Injury Among Young Adolescents: Test of an Interpersonal Model," *Manuscript submitted for publication*, 2006.

I. H. Jones, L. Congiu, J. Stevenson, N. Strauss, and D. Z. Frei, "A Biological Approach to Two Forms of Self-Injury," *Journal of Nervous and Mental Disease* 167 (1979): 74–78.

I. Kemperman, J. J. Russ, and E. Shearin, "Self-Injurious Behavior and Mood Regulation in Borderline Patients," *Journal of Personality Disorders* 11 (1997): 146–157.

Klonsky, E.D. "The Functions of Non-Suicidal Skin-Cutting: Extending the Evidence for Affect-Regulation." *Manuscript under editorial review*, 2006.

E. D. Klonsky, T. F. Oltmanns, and E. Turkheimer, "Deliberate Self-Harm in a Nonclinical Population. Prevalence and Psychological Correlates," *American Journal of Psychiatry* 160 (2003): 1501–1508.

A. Laye-Gindhu and K. A. Schonert-Reichl, "Nonsuicidal Self-Harm Among Community Adolescents: Understanding the 'Whats' and 'Whys' of Self-Harm," *Journal of Youth and Adolescence* 34 (2005): 447–457.

M. K Nixon, P. F. Cloutier, and S. Aggarwal, "Affect Regulation and Addictive Aspects of Repetitive Self-Injury in Hospitalized Adolescents," *Journal of the American Academy of Child and Adolescent Psychiatry* 41 (2002): 1333–1341.

M. K. Nock and M. J. Prinstein, "A Functional Approach to the Assessment of Self-Mutilative Behavior," *Journal of Consulting and Clinical Psychology* 72 (2004): 885–890.

E. A. Osuch, J. G. Noll, and F. W. Putnam, "The Motivations for Self-Injury in Psychiatric Patients," *Psychiatry* 62 (1999): 334–346.

Rowling, J. K. *Harry Potter and the Chamber of Secrets.* New York: Scholastic Inc., 1999.

——. *Harry Potter and the Prisoner of Azkaban.* New York: Scholastic Inc., 1991.

——. *Harry Potter and the Half-Blood Prince.* New York: Scholastic Inc., 2005.

C. Schmahl, M. Bohus, F. Esposito, R. Treede, F. Di Salle, et al., "Neural Correlates of Antinociception in Borderline Personality Disorder," *Archives of General Psychiatry* 63 (2006): 659–666.

S. Tiefenbacher, M. A. Novak, C. K. Lutz, and J. S. Meyer, " The Physiology and Neurochemistry of Self-Injurious Behavior: A Nonhuman Primate Model," *Frontiers in Bioscience* 10 (2005): 1–11.

J. Whitlock, J. Eckenrode, and D. Silverman, "Self-Injurious Behavior in a College Population," *Pediatrics* 117 (2006): 1939–1948.

THE WEIRD WORLD
OF MUGGLES

Is there more to Lupin than meets the eye? As a man stigmatized by society for a fate he can't control, what does Lupin teach us about Rowling's perspective on those cast out by society? And how does one explain the strange attraction we have for the werewolf, in Harry Potter and in legends throughout history? Naficy examines all this and more.

SIAMAK TUNDRA NAFICY

The Werewolf in the Wardrobe

Professor Lupin, who appears in the third book, is one of my favorite char-acters. He's a damaged person, literally and metaphorically. I think it's important for children to know that adults, too, have their problems, that they struggle. His being a werewolf is a metaphor for people's reactions to illness and disability.

—JOANNE K. ROWLING,
quoted from The Scotsman *November 2002*

THE BIG AND NOT-SO-BAD WOLF

One of the most interesting, complex, and peculiar characters in the Harry Potter universe is Professor Remus Lupin. As you may recall, Lupin (a.k.a. "Moony") is Harry's Defense Against the Dark Arts pro-fessor in Book Three, *Harry Potter and the Prisoner of Azkaban*, and he also appears in the film version of the same title. He later returns in Books Five and Six. Because Professor Lupin also happens to be a shape-shifting werewolf, he suffers to keep his condition a secret, lest others stigmatize him for it.

Often harried by his need to conceal his condition, Lupin is described in the books as sickly looking: "He looked ill and exhausted. Though quite young, his light brown hair was flecked with gray" (*Prisoner of Azkaban* 74). Perhaps it is his werewolf condition that makes him ill and exhausted—he is, after all, with perhaps a nod to menstruation, purported to go without sleep for four days a month. His affliction is engaging, but it is just the tip of the iceberg, and if one were to look below, it would seem that even an iceberg is sometimes more than just an iceberg.

It can be argued that maybe *because*, and not despite the fact that Lupin is a werewolf, his fans are legion: there is an international fan Web site, www.remus-lupin.net, devoted entirely to him. The werewolf myth itself is so popular that it is almost ubiquitous. That is, the idea of a half-man, half-beast, or of a human being who can turn into an animal, is almost universal, and pretty much every culture seems to have its beast-men—from the *kitsune* (were-fox) of Japan, to the *rakshasa* (were-tiger) of India, to the *boudas* (were-hyena) of North and sub-Saharan Africa, to the skinwalkers of the American southwest. But the werewolf arguably always was, and today certainly is, the most common shape-changer in myth and fantasy.

Perhaps one reason the werewolf is so popular a stand-in for us is because of the presence of the wolf within the werewolf. The wolf itself is a great placeholder for humans because it shares many convergent, analogous traits with us. Like us, it cooperates to get food. Like us, it dotes on its babies and takes care of its own. This is, in fact, why dogs could be so easily domesticated; our hierarchies are quite similar. Up until the twentieth century, the wolf's similar adaptable nature made it the second most widely distributed mammal in the world, after man. It is only because of us that they no longer are. And indeed, in many ways, since roughly 1.6 million years ago and the advent of *Homo erectus*—as hominins began really to enter the predatory guild—it can be argued that we have become more and more wolf-like and less and less ape-like. Apes, after all, do not share food like we do. Or like wolves do.

The wolf is also a predator. H. Clark Barrett, from the University of California at Los Angeles, has done significant and interesting work detailing children's knowledge and understanding of predators, especially predator-prey interactions. His cross-cultural findings shed light on why the behavior of dangerous predators is particularly and universally interesting to people. According to Barrett, children would have been extremely vulnerable to the dangerous animals that existed in the evolutionary past. Children pay special attention to what animals eat, categorizing easily between predator and prey, and seem to specialize in how animals are dangerous (e.g., a tiger has a deadly bite, while a boa constricts). Psychologists apply the term *prepared learning* to cognitive adaptations that allow us to learn particular bits of information faster and more permanently. Barrett has demonstrated that when it comes to animals, children are especially prepared to learn what certain species eat and what danger they pose to humans. Therefore, it should not be surprising that the world of children's fiction is rich with an inspired bestiary. From velociraptors and unicorns, to el chupacabra and the werewolf, children can easily categorize and remember the fantastic animals we adults present to them. It would be fascinating, in fact, to see what kinds of bestiaries the modern urban child could construct.

THE WOLF IN SHEPHERD'S CLOTHING

Even though many adults read the Harry Potter books, they are generally regarded as belonging in the children's, or at least young adult's, section of the bookstore. For this reason, the themes and metaphors conveyed are often discounted as being childish. But this tendency to look on creatures and characters that appear in children's literature as simplistic can be misleading, for the denizens of these stories are ultimately the creations of adult minds; that is, of adult fears, adult fantasies, and adult categories. These past years, many books, such as the one in your hand just now, have sought to deconstruct the obvious as well as the somewhat nebulous themes, metaphors, and references that appear in popular media. Perhaps because of all this, many kids today have wised up to the *real* themes, motifs, and meanings of familiar fairy tales. Talk to a savvy young adult or even a slightly precocious tween, and they will know. Go ahead. Ask them about "Little Red Riding Hood" and why we call her "little," and they will tell you, "Well, because she's too small to understand the complexity of an adult sexual relationship." Ask why she wears red, and they'll respond, "That's because red signifies the raw, it's violent—it's sex."

Enquire about what is actually in that basket of hers, and many will laugh and say, "Now, what do you think?" In fact, even the average young adult today usually understands what the "big, bad" wolf is. Or rather, what it is supposed to be—not an actual wolf at all, but the bad boy, or sometimes the bad man, who will exploit our precious, hooded innocence. What is interesting is that he can be bad, or at least naughty, while remaining sympathetic. The villainy of the Big Bad Wolf is common knowledge to kids. He's popular. He has a hold over our imaginations. But, if there were not something we liked about the Big Bad Wolf, then he would have no hold or power over us. The point is that there is often something about his villainous, predatory behavior we like—because we can identify with it. So, too, like the *wolf* of the old-fashioned fairy tale, the *werewolf* is oft seen as a rapacious and bestial creature that will sneak up on you and eat you (or worse) if you are not careful. But today, the werewolf has become a more common placeholder for the big bad man (or woman)—for he is at once man and animal, and in this way is a more obvious representation. It can be argued even that in many ways, the wolf of the fairy tale has been replaced by the werewolf of modern fantasy. As we have come to understand animals as animals and not just as playthings in a human-centered universe, we've gone from using them as iconic representations of us to using an outright amalgam of them *and* us. From Curt Siodmak's cult classic *The Wolfman* to the latest *Underworld* film, the werewolf is becoming a more common iconic representation of the hidden wild side of man. This is especially true, perhaps, of the werewolf as he appears in the Harry Potter universe. Here, the subtext of closeted danger is as subtle as the exceptionally large teeth that Grandma had—a fact that led Little Red Riding Hood to deduce that this was no Grandma at all, but actually someone or something else. Something perhaps *bad*, but at the same time something tantalizing, too.

This is nothing new, of course. Throughout history, we have attributed onto others what we viewed as undesirable in ourselves, finding scapegoats upon which we could pin our notions of fault and blame and whose sacrificial death then could bring our atonement. In this way, we put our sins upon the wolf and then put the wolf, instead of ourselves, to death—in literature, in folklore, in myth, in films, and, unfortunately too often, in real life. In his wonderful book *Of Wolves and Men*, Barry Lopez writes that the central conflict between man's "good" and "evil" natures is revealed in his twin images of the wolf as ravening and lusty killer and as nurturing and devoted mother (Lopez 226–7). The former has been the bloodthirsty and rampaging werewolf, from the beast of Gevaudan to Siodmak's *The Wolfman*; the latter the mother to children who founded nations, from Zoroaster and Romulus and Remus to Atatürk.

The legend of the werewolf or a shape-shifting man-wolf is the apotheosis of this idea—a figure who frightens us especially because he is at once a man, but also *something else*; a defector from the social contract, one who can transform himself into something that is primeval and outside convention in both form and morality. Moreover, he is a beast that can hide amongst us—a wolf in shepherd's clothing. Considering the level of voyeurism often involved in these tales of cruelty and depravity, one is struck with the clarity that these acts have really no connection with the real wolf, but more so with us. Indeed, in this way, the phenomenon of shape-shifting itself is small when juxtaposed next to the levels of violence and perversion that the creature often engages in. And it is important to keep this fact in mind, because when thinking about the werewolf, it is easy to want to impose backward such modern ideas as to how or why one becomes a werewolf—ideas that were only recently developed.

In myth, how a human being became a werewolf or even a vampire was often a mystery and varied from place to place. Often, no distinction was even made between witch, vampire, or werewolf. Sometimes a person could transform because that person was a witch, other times because he or she happened to be born on Christmas Day. The Neurians were a tribe of people said by Herodotus to inhabit Russia, and purportedly they all transformed into wolves for a few days once a year. Even the now well-known connection between shape-shifting and the appearance of a full moon, attributed to the medieval chronicler Gervase of Tilbury, was rarely associated with the werewolf until the idea was picked up by modern fiction writers in the last century. Since the development of germ theory for the etiology of disease, however, our myths have changed and become more structured. In the modern tale, vampires are made through blood transfusion. Werewolves in the modern myth, as in *Harry Potter*, become werewolves by being bitten by another werewolf. It is thus *communicable*, and this means that in order not to become a werewolf yourself, you must learn to avoid werewolves entirely, for werewolves, as we know, all have a penchant and an aptitude for biting. It is one of the hallmarks of werewolves, along with all the hair. And in this way, the character of Lupin references the theme of the stigmatized outsider. The homosexual, for example, is defined through the act of or desire for homosexual sex—and of course sex is one way in which HIV can be transmitted.

"CATCHING" WEREWOLVES

Consider the fact that, though now relegated to fantasy literature, film, role-playing games, and Halloween costumes, werewolves were seen as a stark reality in the Middle Ages. Their physical presence was not doubted. At a time before knowledge of Mendelian genetics, the idea that a person suffering from Down's syndrome—small ears, a broad forehead, a flattened nose, and prominent teeth—was the offspring of a woman and a wolf was perfectly plausible. And for this reason many people who were thought to be half-wolves or werewolves were stigmatized, ostracized, and worse; untold numbers were put to death. Why? Because we tend to fear the stigmatized, those who might contaminate us with their condition.

Now, social exclusion is a common feature of our everyday lives. Sometimes these rejections come from idiosyncratic differences among individuals, but other instances of social exclusion are due to the shared values, inclinations, and goals of groups of individuals. Through the processes of stigmatization and exclusion, specific individuals can be completely ostracized from particular social interactions simply because they happen to have a certain characteristic or be a member of a marked category or group. Social exclusion often exists for the obese (e.g., Crocker, Cornwell, & Major), homosexuals (e.g., Shears & Jensema), HIV/AIDS patients (e.g., Weitz), the mentally ill or retarded (e.g. Farina & Ring), and cancer patients (e.g., Bloom & Kessler), as well as members of numerous racial, ethnic, and religious groups (e.g., Steele & Aronson).

So, when Severus Snape takes over Lupin's class to give the children an impromptu lecture on werewolves—even though the lecture on lycanthropy is scheduled for weeks later, at the end of the class—

we can assume that he believes there is a special need to discuss it *now*. The children must be in danger. We feel this imminent danger. Here, Snape informs the students that it may be hard to distinguish werewolves from "regular people," and they need to understand that *anyone* might be a werewolf. The metaphor is especially obvious at the end of the film version of *Prisoner of Azkaban*, when Harry discovers Lupin busily packing his possessions away—closeting things up—and Harry asks if Lupin has been sacked from Hogwarts. "No," Lupin tells Harry. He's resigned from Hogwarts because someone has discovered and let slip his secret life—he's been *outed*, you see—and he tells Harry that there are a lot of parents who would not want "someone like [him]" teaching their children. And now it becomes clear: Professor Lupin is the fall guy for the stigmatized outsider. You know, the one we fear, the one we demonize—he is the homosexual, he is the immigrant, he is the AIDS victim, he is the one with a "bad" religion, and so on.

Did J. K. Rowling herself intend Lupin as such? Certainly, the quotation that begins this essay shows he is meant to represent otherwise good people stigmatized and maligned because they are different. Snape says that *anyone* can become a werewolf, should they be bitten by one. The fact that the werewolf has the power to make anyone a werewolf, simply by biting him, is quite significant and doubly frightening, for that makes this an affliction that is *contagious*. Lupin himself provides the supporting evidence: "**I was a very small boy when I received the bite**" (*Prisoner of Azkaban* 352), says Lupin, and one is now sympathetic to him, prompted to think of him as a once-innocent victim now turned into a monster.

Drawing on evolutionary psychological logic—that is, the supposition that the mind, as the body, is a product of natural selection, and that to understand the psyche of a species it is important to consider the everyday problems ancestral environments would have posed—it is interesting to explore this conflation of a marginalized "other" category with contagious disease. The "magical law of contagion," one of the laws of sympathetic magic, was first introduced by anthropologists more than 100 years ago (e.g., Mauss). This "law of contagion" holds that people, objects, and so forth that come into contact with one another can influence each other through a permanent transfer of some essential property: contagion (once contaminated, always contaminated—once in contact, always in contact) and similarity (the image is the *same* as the actual thing).

Paul Rozin and his colleagues from the University of Pennsylvania found that people often conflate exposure to contamination and essential qualities with transmission. For example, they demonstrate (Rozin et al.) that university undergraduates tended to avoid even their juice of choice if they saw a sterilized cockroach briefly immersed in the drink; they were also more reluctant to eat a piece of chocolate if it happened to be in the shape of dog feces rather than the somewhat more mundane shape of a muffin! Likewise, when offered a choice, undergraduates were much more reluctant to drink sugar water from a glass labeled "Cyanide" than they were to drink from a glass labeled "Sucrose." Further studies showed that preference for a glass of sugar water was shown even if the alternative glass was labeled in the negative ("Not cyanide, not poison") (Rozin et al). A similar magical transfer of an undesired quality from a person to an object was shown in the domain of the fear of contagion: undergraduates rated a sweater briefly worn by someone they were told had AIDS as being significantly less desirable to wear than one worn by someone they were told was healthy (Rozin et al.).

A number of other investigators have articulated evolutionary accounts of stigmatization and prejudice (e.g., Kurzban & Leary; Neuberg; Smith & Asher). The general logic follows as such: throughout much of our history, we humans existed in relatively small groups. While group living can provide us with many survival benefits, it likewise brings many costs and particular problems that are peculiar to group life, such as a greatly increased risk from contagious disease—if your roommate has a cold, chances are, you will, too. Therefore, psychological adaptations have likely evolved in response to, for example, the type of threat identified by Kurzban and Leary (the interpersonal transmission of parasites that may cause illness), causing us to avoid and fear those who may be different and therefore carry such threats.

Now, because there is a high cost in social interactions with diseased others, it would have been adaptive for individuals—and ultimately, for functional populations—quickly to identify sick individuals and to avoid interacting with them. Others (Bishop et al.) have demonstrated that individuals quickly respond to explicit linguistic labels ("HIV," "hepatitis," etc.) indexing the presence of contagion in other individuals. One possible critique of such work is that written language is relatively recent, and so perhaps of more significance is Kurzban and Leary's point that many contagious diseases are often accompanied by observable phenotypic cues: "markers, lesions, discoloration of body parts...and behavioral anomalies" (Kurzban & Leary 198). They argue that specific psychological mechanisms that attended to and precipitated avoidant reactions to these cues would have been adaptive. Therefore, in present-day populations, we should not be surprised that these cues trigger specific affective (e.g., disgust, fear), cognitive (e.g., activation of disease-connoting concepts), and nonverbal behavioral (e.g., avoidance, shunning) responses in the perceiver. As with most evolved mechanisms, these responses are likely to occur quickly, with little conscious or rational deliberation, precisely because you cannot afford to take the time to think about them.

Of course, one could argue that many such markers come from non-contagious environmental or genetic effects, such as catastrophic accidents in the former or dwarfism in the latter. Would this not have created a signal-detection problem? Perhaps. It is not very likely that the psychological disease-avoidance processes could have evolved to make fine distinctions between actual symptoms of contagious disease and the broader category of peculiar physical and behavioral features that may be unrelated to contagious disease. Because the adaptive costs of a "false positive" (incorrectly judging a healthy individual to be diseased and missing out on social interactions with such) are less than the potentially deadly consequences of a "false negative" (erroneously judging a diseased individual to be healthy and contracting a costly illness), it is likely that this disease-avoidance mechanism evolved to be biased toward false positives. In other words, the evolved disease-avoidance mechanism is likely to be sensitive and mistake a broad range of physical or behavioral features as worthy of fear and avoidance.

The fact that Lupin is a werewolf—a stigmatized, deviant other— also allows us erroneously to read in all sorts of other penchants and aptitudes that may be "deviant" from the norm. Psychologists call this the conjunction effect. The basic idea follows from probability theory. Imagine two independent conditions, A and B. Probability theory dictates that the probability of both A and B occurring cannot exceed the probability of either A or B. And yet, this is the kind of error we make quite often.

An example of this sort of error can be found in the "Linda problem" (Kahneman & Tversky 126), in which subjects were presented with personality sketches of the type illustrated below:

> Linda is thirty-one years old, single, outspoken, and very bright. She majored in philosophy. As a student, she was deeply concerned with issues of discrimination and social justice, and also participated in anti-nuclear demonstrations.

Then, in one version of the problem, subjects were asked which of the following two statements was *more* probable: (a) Linda is a bank teller, or (b) Linda is a bank teller who is active in the feminist movement. Again, based on probability theory, the first statement must be more probable. And yet the authors reported that within their sample of undergraduates, 86 percent judged the second statement to be more probable! And so, we assume all sorts of attributes and behaviors follow from the one. In a very basic and naïve universe, there are bad guys and bad animals—who are bad in almost every way—and good guys and good animals—who are good in almost every way. And it is for this reason that Lupin makes such a great metaphor—if he is a stigmatized outsider, then it is easy for us to heap upon him a wide range of other negative attributes (e.g., Is he diseased? A pedophile? etc.).

Work conducted into the extent to which a heterosexual's attitudes toward homosexuals predicts his or her prejudice (assessed with social distancing measures) against people with AIDS (Crandall, Glor, & Britt) is also of significance. The authors show that social distancing from the person with AIDS was highly correlated with HATH scores when the person with AIDS was homosexual, and only modestly correlated when the person was heterosexual. Surprisingly, the same precise pattern of correlations is found when the person was presented not as an AIDS victim, but as an amputee who had lost a leg in a motorcycle accident. The same personality construct similarly predicted social distancing from both people with contagious disease and people with a disabling condition that was clearly non-contagious. This result suggests, indirectly, a relation between concerns about disease and the desire to avoid physically disabled individuals. The werewolf metaphor, as used in Harry Potter, is just one example of how we often do the same thing when it comes to all sorts of negatively associated behaviors. We tend to correlate and assume that all deviant behaviors co-vary to some extent.

With modern germ theory, we have a better estimate of contagion risk, but it is important to remember that until only a few generations ago, how and why people became sick was largely a mystery. The kind of information state required to avoid contagion then would require strategies to recognize any possible contagion risk. If the reason why someone is sick is cryptic or a mystery, it might possibly be best to avoid him or her altogether.

MANIMALS

Let's consider at this point a story left out of the film version of *Prisoner of Azkaban*, namely the reason behind Sirius Black's dog form, Peter Pettigrew's rat morph, and Harry's own father James's stag shape. In the book, J. K. Rowling declares that the three set about to learn the art of shape-shifting in order to keep their good friend Lupin company when he was out on the prowl in his beast form. Thus, they are not just friends with Lupin the man, but Lupin the beast. This does not mean that Sirius or any of the other boys are the same as Lupin. Note that while all learn in time to assume their beast forms, they all have different ones.

We can use evolutionary theory to understand popular culture, and then use popular culture as a window into modern society. Our evolutionary past can help us to see why the werewolf is so scary and popular, and that the development of portrayals of the werewolf from terrifying monster to sympathetic victim over the last fifty years may be an example of the way all this talk of tolerance may actually be working.

And this is where we can have a warm and, yes, fuzzy ending. So yes, maybe we have evolved cognitive mechanisms that predispose us to make categories of others and then to make essentialist and sometimes misinformed judgments based on those categories. So what? Because these categories are often learned, they can be unlearned.

The answer may not be to control the baser primal urges we all have, but to be more tolerant of the tapestry of it all. As long as you are not really hurting anyone, that is—unless they really want you to (and then still, not too much). After all, we are all beasts, one way or another, and the admission of that itself can be freeing.

Documentary evidence for the life of **SIAMAK TUNDRA NAFICY** proves frustrating. Immigration records show him in these United States since 1978 and tax records exist in the files of government bureaucracy, undoubtedly, but don't set him apart from contemporaries. His interests were apparently broad and he appears to have been enrolled in an anthropology Ph.D. program at UCLA, since a thesis has been filed with the university since 1999. Further biographical information that dates from 2003 appears in the form of documents that suggest he somehow obtained access to dogs, cats, and wolves for research into inter- and intra-species communicative intelligence.

REFERENCES

G. D. Bishop, A. L. Alva, L. Cantu, L., and T. K. Rittiman, "Responses to Persons with AIDS: Fear of Contagion or Stigma?" *Journal of Applied Social Psychology* 21 (1991): 1877–1888.

J. R. Bloom and L. Kessler, "Emotional Support Following Cancer: A Test of the Stigma and Social Activity Hypotheses," *Journal of Health and Social Behavior* 35 (1994): 118–133.

C. S. Crandall, J. Glor, and T. W. Britt, "AIDS-related Stigmatization: Instrumental and Symbolic Attitudes," *Journal of Applied Social Psychology* 27 (1997): 95–123.

J. Crocker, B. Cornwell, and B. Major, "The Stigma of Overweight: Affective Consequences of Attributional Ambiguity," *Journal of Personality and Social Psychology* 64 (1993): 60–70.

A. Farina and K. Ring, "The Influence of Perceived Mental Illness on Interpersonal Relations," *Journal of Abnormal Psychology* 70 (1965): 47–51.

Fraser, L. "Harry Potter—Harry and Me" *The Scotsman* 9 Nov. 2002. <http://thescotsman.scotsman.com/s2.cfm?id=1246372002>.

D. Kahneman and A. Tversky, "On the Study of Statistical Intuitions," *Cognition* 11 (1982): 123–141.

R. Kurzban and M. R. Leary, "Evolutionary Origins of Stigmatization: The Functions of Social Exclusion," *Psychological Bulletin* 127 (2001): 187–208.

Lopez, B. H. *Of Wolves and Men.* New York: Charles Scribner's Sons, 1978. Mauss, Marcel. *A General Theory of Magic* (R. Brain, trans.). New York: W. W. Norton, 1972 (1902).

S. L. Neuberg, D. M. Smith, and T. Asher, "Why People Stigmatize: Toward a Biocultural Framework" In T. F. Heatherton, R. E. Kleck, M. R. Hebl, and J. G. Hull (Eds.), *The Social Psychology of Stigma.* New York: Guilford Press, 2000. 31–61.

Rowling, J. K. *Harry Potter and the Prisoner of Azkaban.* New York: Scholastic Inc., 1999.

P. Rozin, L. Millman, and C. Nemeroff, "Operation of the Laws of Sympathetic Magic in Disgust and Other Domains," *Journal of Personality and Social Psychology* 50 (1986): 703–712.

P. Rozin, M. Markwith, and B. Ross, "The Sympathetic Magical Law of Similarity, Nominal Realism, and Neglect of Negatives in Response to Negative Labels," *Psychological Science* 1 (1990): 383–384.

P. Rozin, M. Markwith, and C. Nemeroff, "Magical Contagion Beliefs and Dear of AIDS," *Journal of Applied Social Psychology* 22 (1992): 1081–1092.

L. Shears and C. Jensema, "Social Acceptability of Anomalous Persons," *Exceptional Children* 36 (1969): 91–96.

C. M. Steele and J. Aronson, "Stereotype Vulnerability and the Intellectual Test Performance of African-Americans," *Journal of Personality and Social Psychology* 69 (1995): 797–811.

R. Weitz, "Living with the Stigma of AIDS," *Qualitative Sociology* 13 (1990): 23–38.

Harry Potter, more than anything else, is about a struggle between good and evil. Patrick and Patrick review the psychological theories that lay behind our concept of evil. The theory of Jung is of interest here; do we all have the "shadow side" of darkness that we regularly have to struggle with, just like Harry?

CHRISTOPHER J. PATRICK, Ph.D., AND SARAH K. PATRICK

Exploring the Dark Side
Harry Potter and the Psychology of Evil

WHAT ACCOUNTS FOR the unprecedented appeal of J. K. Rowling's Harry Potter novels among readers of all ages around the world? Could it be the magical places, people, and events that populate each book—including Hogwarts School of Witchcraft and Wizardry; endearing characters such as Dumbledore, McGonagall, and Hagrid; ghosts, goblins, trolls, centaurs, dragons, unicorns, and other mythical creatures; the game of Quidditch, played at lightning speeds high above the ground on flying broomsticks; Diagon Alley, Gringotts Bank, Flourish and Blotts bookstore, Ollivander's wand shop; the Sorting Hat at Hogwarts; the Weasleys' flying car? Could it be the heroic characters of Harry, Hermione, and Ron, and the unique friendship they share? Could it be the important challenges they face together during each passing year at Hogwarts, depicted in each successive book? Or...could it be the themes of evil, darkness, destruction, and murder that permeate the novels?

Wait a minute! Darkness, evil, murder, and destruction? In the whimsical world of Harry Potter? Can this be the case? The Potter books are supposed to be entertainment for kids, right? Of course. The books are enormously popular among children of all ages. But themes of evil and death are featured prominently in many classic children's fairytales (examples include *Hansel and Gretel*, *Jack and the Beanstalk*, *Little Red Riding Hood*, and *Snow White*), and one needn't delve far into the Potter books before encountering evil of the worst kind. Early in the first book of the series, we learn that Harry's parents were deliberately killed at the hands of Lord Voldemort, an arch-evil figure who was once a wizard-in-training at Hogwarts. At the time Voldemort murdered Harry's parents, he also attempted to slay Harry, a baby of just one year at the time, but failed. The lightning-bolt scar on Harry's forehead is a remnant of this failed murder attempt.

The character of Lord Voldemort resurfaces repeatedly throughout the Potter novels, and the fight between good and evil, embodied most strongly in the characters of Harry and Voldemort, emerges as a centerpoint of the story line. This element of the Potter novels is strongly reminiscent of the struggle of good versus evil depicted in another classic work of fantasy—Tolkien's Lord of the Rings trilogy. In the Rings trilogy, the force of good is represented by the character Frodo (who is supported by the wizard Gandalf in a manner that parallels Dumbledore's mentorship of Harry) and the force of evil is embodied in the character Sauron (who, like Voldemort, was seduced over to the Dark side by the lure of power and immortality).

As in the Rings trilogy, the presence of supreme evil and the need to defeat it in the Potter books adds a compelling, universal element to the story that makes it appealing to adolescents and adults as well as younger children. But what is it about evil—and related themes of darkness, murder, and destruction—that fascinates us so much? What do we hope to learn and experience by exposing ourselves to stories of this kind? What basic truth are we seeking to understand? Some insights into these questions can be gained by considering how the theme of evil manifests itself in different ways historically and culturally, and by considering what is known psychologically about evil and the conditions that contribute to it. An important conclusion to emerge from consideration of these issues is that we are fascinated by the question of evil because all of us, as human beings, are capable of evil actions as well as good ones. As discussed below, this dual capacity for evil as well as good is something that is evidenced clearly in the character of Harry Potter.

EVIL IN HISTORY AND POPULAR CULTURE

The bestselling book of all time is the Holy Bible, which presents the foundation for Judeo-Christian belief systems in the events of the Old and New Testaments. In the Bible, the forces of good and evil are represented by the figures of God and the Devil (Lucifer). Notably, according to Old Testament writings, Lucifer was once an angel of God. Lucifer opposed God because of his own desires to attain power and self-glorification, and as a consequence was cast out of Heaven by God and banished to Hell. In parallel with this, the character of Voldemort was once a student at Hogwarts—one who showed strong potential as a wizard but who crossed over to the Dark side in search of power and immortality. Like Lucifer, Voldemort is continually seeking to pull others over to the Dark side with him to gain control over them and to do his bidding. The snake is important as a symbol of both Lucifer and Voldemort. According to the Old Testament, Lucifer approached the first humans on Earth, Adam and Eve, in the guise of a serpent and seduced them into eating from the Tree of Knowledge. Lord Voldemort is a Parselmouth who has the ability to speak with snakes in their own language. In the second book of the Potter series, Voldemort uses this ability to wield control over a giant serpent (the Basilisk) in the Chamber of Secrets and causes it to attack victims according to his will.

Parallels are also evident between certain events within the New Testament and incidents in the Potter novels. In the New Testament, the Devil attempts to seduce Jesus Christ (God's son, who is part human) into joining him by tempting Jesus with promises of power and wealth. Likewise, in the Potter novels, Voldemort tries to convince Harry to join him by threatening him with death and through promises of power and immortality. This theme of gaining power and wealth by forming an alliance with the Devil is present in many other well-known stories across the ages. In Goethe's classic story *Faust*, the protagonist sells his soul to the Devil in exchange for fame and wealth. In the *Lord of the Rings*, the lure of the One Ring exerts its evil influence on all those who possess it—including the hobbit Smeagol, who finds himself transformed into the monster Gollum, and even the hero Frodo, who is ultimately rescued from the seductive influence of the ring by his adversary Gollum.

Across the ages, the forces of evil became represented in the form of legendary monsters of various kinds, including witches, werewolves, vampires, zombies, goblins, and ghouls. In some instances, such creatures had their origins in real-life historic figures. For example, the model for the vampire Dracula in Bram Stoker's classic novel was believed to be Vlad the Impaler, a Romanian nobleman who derived pleasure from various forms of killing, including burning helpless victims alive and impaling them on wooden stakes. The character of Voldemort in the Potter books shows similarities with Dracula in that he preys upon others and seduces them into becoming like him in order to gain power and perpetuate his own life. In the first book of the series, we learn that Voldemort kills and drinks the blood of unicorns (a symbol of purity and goodness) as a means of sustaining his life.

In addition to works of fiction, monsters of various kinds have been featured in motion pictures since the earliest days of film. Max Shreck's classic silent movie, *Nosferatu*, remains one of the most chilling portrayals of vampires even to this day. Each decade, the film industry seems to find a new audience for horror movies, with some showing up in multiple sequels across the years (e.g., *Alien*, *Scream*, *Nightmare on Elm Street*). The phenomenon of horror movies is of considerable interest because such movies are created for the primary purpose of scaring people and because they have always been so wildly popular.

Figures representative of evil and darkness have also emerged in popular music. Beginning with groups such as Black Sabbath in the 1960s, rock musicians have explored themes relating to evil, black magic, and death in their music. During the 1970s, Alice Cooper brought such themes to the forefront in a series of albums featuring songs about rape, murder, suicide, and necrophilia. "Death metal" groups such as Venom, Carcass, Cannibal Corpse, and Slipknot have continued this tradition through the 1980s to present day. Probably the closest counterpart to Alice Cooper during the past decade has been the group Marilyn Manson. Reflecting their preoccupation with themes of lust and death, each member of the group bears a pseudonym consisting of the first name of a popular female sex symbol (e.g., Marilyn, Twiggy) followed by the last name of a convicted mass murderer or serial killer (e.g., Manson, Ramirez). Is it possible that the popularity of the Harry Potter novels could have something in common with the popularity of musical groups such as this?

PSYCHOLOGICAL CONCEPTS OF GOOD AND EVIL

Modern conceptions of mental illness had their origins in the idea of demonic possession. Up through medieval times and after, individuals manifesting symptoms of what would now be diagnosed as schizophrenia or other major forms of mental disorder were considered to have been possessed by devils or spirits. Accordingly, the "cure" for such conditions was sought in physical or spiritual purgation of different sorts (including draining of blood from the body) and exorcism by representatives of the Church. With the advancement of medical science and increasing understanding of the functions of the human brain, alternative ideas about mental illness gained influence in the 1800s. European physicians such as Pinel and Kraepelin distinguished among different forms of mental illness and postulated a physical (brain) basis for some of these conditions. However, through the early part of the twentieth century, quasi-religious conceptualizations persisted for some forms of mental disorder. In particular, *character disorders* marked by persistent criminal behavior, addiction, or deviant sexual activity were seen as reflecting "moral insanity"—a defect in moral capacity as opposed to a defect in reason or emotion. One specific form of character disorder, psychopathic personality (*psychopathy*), will be considered further in the second-to-last section below because of its unique relation to the question of evil.

A watershed in our understanding of human psychological processing was the emergence of Sigmund Freud's psychoanalytic theory during the first part of the twentieth century. Freud's theory began as an effort to refine the treatment of a particular form of mental disorder characterized by extreme anxiety and ritualized behaviors ("neurosis"), but it developed into a general theory of human mental phenomena. A core tenet of Freud's theory was that much of the processing that goes on within our minds is unconscious—that is, outside the range of conscious awareness. Freud viewed the contents of awareness as only the tip of the iceberg of mental processing, with the majority of the iceberg lying below the surface of conscious awareness. He pointed to phenomena such as dreams and slips of the tongue as evidence of the unconscious mind. Freud believed that the symptoms of mental illness reflected desires and conflicts that were unconscious and therefore not readily accessible or changeable. He developed the technique of psychoanalysis, involving interpretation of free associations and dreams reported by the individual, as a means for bringing such repressed material to conscious awareness.

Particularly relevant to the question of evil is Freud's conceptualization of the human mind as consisting of three distinct components: Id, Superego, and Ego. Freud viewed the Id (German for "It," or "Monster") as comprising the basic primitive, instinctual, and unconscious survival urges of the individual—in particular, urges toward sexuality and aggression. Such urges exist in all individuals because they were important for survival under primitive, "dog-eat-dog" circumstances, and thus emerged as part of our evolutionary heritage. However, to be able to live effectively with others in contemporary society, the individual must learn to control and moderate these basic urges. Left uncontrolled, such urges would result in acts of physical and sexual aggression against others as the individual moved from childhood to adulthood. According to Freud, the Superego and Ego developed to exert control over these basic instincts and moderate them in a way that allows peaceful interaction and cohabitation among individuals in society.

Thus, from the perspective of Freud, the mind of each individual in society contains a primitive, potentially evil "monster." However, the processes of socialization and development naturally promote the emergence of other components of the mind (Superego, Ego) that operate to keep this primitive component in check and to permit it to operate in ways that do not harm others. Vis-à-vis events in the Potter novels, the Id can be seen as the potential that individuals (i.e., wizards-in-training) have to go over to the Dark side—i.e., the potential for selfishness, power-seeking, and self-aggrandizement. Those who move to the Dark side are those who give in to these primitive desires and allow such desires to dictate their choices and decision-making, without regard for the welfare of others. A key point, addressed further in the final section below, is that Harry (like the character Tom Riddle, who became Lord Voldemort) has this same potential to move to the Dark side, which at times he must fight. It is this struggle between good and evil *within* Harry (as well as between Harry and Voldemort) that is so inherently fascinating to readers—because it reflects an ongoing struggle that each of us experiences within ourselves.

Carl Jung was a student of Freud's who went on to develop his own theory of the human mind during the period between the first and second World Wars. Jung's theory is valuable in thinking about why themes such as the struggle of good versus evil appear universal to human experience and arise repeatedly in various myths, legends, and stories throughout history. Two ideas of central importance in Jung's theory are: (a) the notion of the *collective unconscious*, and (b) the idea of a dialectical relationship among elements of the collective unconscious, which he termed *archetypes*.

According to Jung, the unconscious mind consists of two distinct parts—the personal unconscious and the collective unconscious. The personal unconscious consists of unique experiences of the individual that have been rendered unconscious. The collective unconscious represents the larger, more influential component of the unconscious mind that reflects our evolutionary heritage and thus is common to all humans. It consists of primitive mental representations (archetypes) that exert a motivational influence on the individual's behavior. A crucial component of Jung's theory is that each basic archetype includes an opposing archetype. For example, the archetype of the Hero reflects positive instinctual urges toward altruism and communality. The archetype of the Shadow, on the other hand, reflects urges toward aggression and ascendance over others (akin to Freud's Id). The Hero and Shadow archetypes thus oppose one another in determining the individual's behavior. The idea of a dynamic struggle between an entity or idea and its opposite, originally discussed by the German philosopher Hegel, is known as a dialectic. Another example of this is the archetypes of the Animus and Anima, which reflect competing male and female tendencies within each individual.

Jung believed that a predominant influence of any one archetype within the individual was unhealthy. According to Jung, the key to optimal, healthy functioning is a balance in the functioning of the various archetypes within the individual. Jung postulated the existence of a master archetype, the "Mandala," or magic circle, that provided a template for this dynamic balance among opposing (dialectical) tendencies within the individual. For example, from Jung's perspective, it is important that the aggressive instinctual urges of the individual (reflected in the Shadow) are capable of expression along with the prosocial urges (reflected in the Hero), because different situations call for different behavioral reactions.

With regard to the Harry Potter novels, Jung's theory helps us to understand the fascination we have with the basic question of good versus evil. Within Jung's theory, this question reflects a basic instinctual dialectic that each of us is challenged to resolve in the course of our development as individuals. According to Jung, the solution to the problem lies not in one extreme or the other, but in a dynamic balance between opposing tendencies, such that all elements of the collective unconscious are fully developed and accessible to the individual according to the demands of a given situation or challenge. Each individual carries both good and evil within him or herself, and it is the recognition of these competing tendencies and the capacity for balanced expression that determines healthy functioning.

CLASSIC PSYCHOLOGICAL RESEARCH ON EVIL

The events of the Second World War provided a major impetus for psychologists to undertake scientific investigations of the nature and bases of evildoing. In particular, the persecution and extermination of the Jewish people by Nazi Germany, its leaders (including Hitler and his commandants), and military personnel within the concentration camps were seen as the ultimate expression of evil within human society. One question of compelling interest was how people in German society could come to submit themselves so completely to authority figures as to commit acts of the utmost atrocity without opposing or even questioning orders.

One approach to addressing this question was to study personality traits within the individual that contributed to a tendency to submit oneself to the control of others. For example, a personality trait of authoritarianism was postulated, reflecting a willingness to submit to a more powerful authority figure coupled with a desire to exert power over other, less powerful individuals. Some evidence was found for differences among individuals in this trait.

Another approach to addressing this question was to examine circumstances under which individuals might challenge orders from an authority figure as opposed to obeying. Laboratory experiments of this type were conducted by Stanley Milgram and his colleagues. In these experiments, each subject participated in a learning experiment in which they served as "teachers" for another subject, who was in actuality an accomplice of the experimenter. "Teachers" (real subjects) were instructed to punish the "learner" (accomplice subject) each time a mistake was made by administering an electric shock and to increase the level of shock with each successive punishment. In some studies, the shock device was labeled such that shocks above a certain level were labeled as extremely painful or even potentially lethal. Although in some instances subjects asked the experimenter about the advisability of administering shocks of such high intensity, subjects almost never desisted when instructed by the experimenter to continue. In some studies, the "learner" was heard to cry in pain after high-intensity shocks were delivered and subsequently stopped responding altogether (implying physical incapacitation). Even under these circumstances, most subjects continued to administer shocks when instructed to do so by the experimenter.

The basic conclusion that Milgram and his colleagues drew from these studies was that the average person is naturally inclined to submit to the authority of a more powerful other even when blind obedience results in harm to others. The implication is that the average person is capable of committing extreme acts of evil when placed in the role of a subordinate. It should be noted that the Milgram obedience studies were subsequently deemed to be unethical due to the coercive nature of the instructional demands and the potential psychological harm to subjects committing such acts under these conditions. Nonetheless, the findings of this research indicate, consistent with the theories of Freud and Jung, that the average person is capable of evil acts under particular situational circumstances.

THE HUMAN EMBODIMENT OF EVIL: PSYCHOPATHS AND SERIAL KILLERS

Although psychological theorizing and research, as described above, suggest that ordinary individuals are capable of evil, it is nonetheless clear that most people never commit serious evil acts in their lives—certainly not evil acts of the sort committed by Voldemort and his followers. However, there does exist a type of individual for whom (as with Voldemort) power and self-gratification are of sole importance, with no consideration for the rights of others. Such individuals have been termed "psychopaths." A psychopath is an individual who lacks the capacity to feel guilt or concern for others (empathy) and who is incapable of love. Such individuals appear confident, sociable, and charming on the surface, but underneath this they are deceptive, exploitative, and uncaring. The classic book on psychopathy, written by Hervey Cleckley, was titled *The Mask of Sanity*, reflecting this difference between the individual's overt appearance of normalcy and his underlying personal/social maladjustment.

Most psychopaths engage in behaviors such as lying, cheating, and stealing repeatedly over long periods of time. In some cases, psychopaths can be violent. In such cases, the acts of violence they commit can be cruel, sadistic, and extreme. Predatory serial killing represents the most severe manifestation of this form of violence. Psychopathic serial murderers (typically men) prey upon helpless victims purely for reasons of self-gratification: to achieve power or control over others, or to fulfill sexual desires. One example of a psychopathic serial killer is John Wayne Gacy, who sexually assaulted and murdered more than thirty young men and buried them under his house in Chicago. Other more recent examples include the Green River Killer in Washington state, and the BTK ("bind-torture-kill") murderer in Wichita, Kansas.

The presence of sadistic serial killers such as this in our society, which illustrates the potential that humans have for extreme acts of evil, is a source of great fascination to the public at large—as evidenced by the plethora of books and films dealing with cases such as this. The kind of evil in which serial killers engage directly parallels that of Lord Voldemort in the Potter novels—it involves acts of extreme cruelty committed to achieve power and self-gratification without concern for the welfare or rights of others. At present, the causal factors that lead some individuals to become sadistic serial murderers are largely unknown. Most knowledgeable experts believe that inborn (constitutional) factors play some role in causing this type of extreme violence. However, most experts would argue that random environmental factors (e.g., early exposure to violence or deviant sexual material) also play a role in leading such individuals over to the "dark side."

CONCLUSIONS: HARRY POTTER AND THE DIALECTIC OF GOOD AND EVIL

The struggle of good against evil can be regarded as an *archetypal* theme—something fundamental to our experience of being human that is reflected across the ages in myths, legends, and stories of actual events. Freud and Jung postulated that the unconscious mind of each person includes a "dark side" that must be contended with in the course of psychological development. The presence of this dark side within each of us leads us to be fascinated with depictions of evil in the media and occurrences of evil in real life (e.g., cases of serial killers).

In the Harry Potter novels, Harry is presented as a figure of good in opposition to the evil figure of Voldemort. At the same time, however, Harry recognizes striking similarities between himself and Voldemort: both are half-bloods with obvious physical resemblances, both are orphans raised by Muggles, both are Parselmouths, etc. Harry maintains a physical connection with Voldemort in the form of his lightning scar, which aches intensely at times when he is close to things relating to Voldemort. At the time of his housing assignment by the Sorting Hat, Harry fights against the possibility of his being assigned to Slytherin (the House to which Tom Riddle, a.k.a. Voldemort, belonged), even though he is told this may be his destiny. When battling directly with Voldemort, Harry fights against using the deathly curses that he knows will draw him over to the Dark side. These and other incidents in the Potter books show us clearly that Harry is engaged in an ongoing battle with forces inside himself as well as without. We as readers find this fascinating because we recognize that the battle within is something all of us, in some sense, are fighting.

CHRISTOPHER J. PATRICK, Ph.D., is Hathaway Professor of Psychology and Director of Clinical Training at the University of Minnesota, where his teaching and research interests focus on emotional and cognitive aspects of crime, violence, antisocial personality, and psychopathic behavior. He is a recipient of early scientific career awards from the American Psychological Association and the Society for Psychophysiological Research. His extracurricular pursuits include fiction reading and writing, cooking, softball, ocean surfing, and guitar playing.

SARAH K. PATRICK has always enjoyed reading and books of all kinds, including Harry Potter. Besides reading, Sarah also loves oil painting, acting, playing guitar, surfing, and, most of all, listening to her music (some of which is mentioned in this essay).

Lyubansky examines the question of racial prejudice in the world of Harry Potter. Rowling portrays a race-blind society at Hogwarts but pursues the issue of race through proxy: the hatred of the pure-bloods for the "Mudbloods" and the slavery of the house-elves. But, Lyubansky argues, the issues of race and prejudice are not so easily categorized.

MIKHAIL LYUBANSKY, Ph.D.

Harry Potter and the Word That Shall Not Be Named

"RACE" IN THE twenty-first century is ubiquitous. It influences our understanding of history and current events, school achievement and athletic success, and both interpersonal relationships and group dynamics. Yet, in many contexts and social circles, race is so emotionally threatening that for many White people it has simply become "the word that shall not be named." Moreover, even those willing to name it struggle to find shared meaning in a word that means many different things to different people. But what if there were a magical parallel universe where these racial themes could be safely explored under the guise of wizards and Muggles and elves? At its best, by taking advantage of our suspension of disbelief, fiction can penetrate our psychological defenses and reach our core beliefs. J. K. Rowling understands this. She uses the Harry Potter series not only to entertain, but to provide readers with a real world moral framework that explicitly encompasses race-related issues. This essay will examine contemporary assumptions about race in the Harry Potter universe using two different levels of analysis. The first part will examine the series' underlying racial ideology of color-blindness, while the second will examine the nature of racism and the psychological impact of enslavement, as portrayed by the characters.

THE RACIAL UTOPIA

At first glance, the Harry Potter universe seems to have little racial tension. There are a handful of non-White characters, including fellow Gryffindors Lee Jordan, Dean Thomas, Angelina Johnson, and Parvati Patil, as well as Harry's first romantic interest, Cho Chang. Yet Rowling treats race with far less attention than she does the Weasleys' hair color. Even though she provides the non-White characters with racial identifiers (e.g., Angelina Johnson is described as "a tall black girl with long, braided hair" [*Harry Potter and the Order of the Phoenix* 224] and Dean Thomas as "a Black boy even taller than Ron" [*Harry Potter and the Sorceror's Stone* 122]),[1] neither race nor racial status are ever mentioned by any of the characters.

Indeed, the racial identifiers seem to exist only as a vehicle for Rowling to show how race has no real meaning in her magical universe. Perhaps she wants to show the reader a racial utopia, even as she is depicting parallel forms of racism directed against Muggles, half-bloods, and elves. If so, it is worth pointing out that in the real world, there is little agreement about what a racial utopia would look like, with multiculturalists and social conservatives (who are predominantly White) usually having contrasting visions. The racial utopia of the Harry Potter series falls squarely within the neo-conser-

---

[1] In contrast to the non-White characters, none of the White characters are racially identified. Part of the reason lies in the privilege of Whiteness: "As the unmarked category against which difference is constructed, whiteness never has to speak its name, never has to acknowledge its role as an organizing principle in social and cultural relations" (Lipsitz 1). But like Lord Voldemort's name, the omission of "The Race That Shall Not Be Named" (Woods 2) signifies more than merely the absence of necessity. Naming "Whiteness" brings to mind various racial discrepancies that affect every aspect of our lives and brings awareness to racial privilege, a process that tends to make White people feel uncomfortable (Kivel), even though there is no similar discomfort in using racial identifiers to refer to people of color. To experience this discomfort, I invite you to try Thandeka's "Race Game," in which the African-American theologian and journalist challenges White people, for one week, to racially identify other Whites whenever making reference to them (e.g., "my White friend Ron").

vative racial ideology (Omi & Winant). According to this ideology, race is assumed to be socially constructed and racial justice is pursued via a color-blind society in which everyone pursues the American/British dream by "lifting themselves up by the bootstraps" (i.e., a "just world" that rewards good choices and a strong work ethic). "'It is our choices, Harry, that show what we truly are, far more than our [biological or God-given] abilities,'" says Dumbledore (*Harry Potter and the Chamber of Secrets* 333), who later reminds Fudge, the Minister of Magic, that what people grow to be is much more important than what they were when they were born (*Goblet of Fire* 708). Accordingly, for neo-conservatives, the belief that race (a biological or God-given characteristic) does not matter is typically grounded in one or both of two seemingly contradictory but actually compatible beliefs—that "we" are all the same (i.e., "humans" or "Americans" or "Muggles") or that each one of us is a unique person.

The color-blind ideal is so eminently reasonable that it can seem almost objectionable even to question it. After all, who wouldn't want to be perceived as a unique being, while at the same time have his/her humanity recognized? Yet, critics of a color-blind ideology (and there are many) reject it for several reasons. To begin with, they point out that a color-blind ideal, at best, does nothing to curtail the institutional and interpersonal racism that are still experienced by people of color on a daily basis and, at worst, actually works to maintain the racial hierarchy by pretending and acting as though it doesn't exist (think the Ministry of Magic during its denial of Voldemort's return).[2] In addition, critics of racial color-blindness argue that racial status is associated with cultural experiences (e.g., music preferences, experiences of discrimination) that shape a person's identity or sense of self. This perspective is well-captured by Dr. Lisa Delpit, executive director of the Center for Urban Education & Innovation:

---

[2] This is the stance taken by most social scientists interested in race, as well as the official position of the American Sociological Association, whose 2002 statement on race posits that "Refusing to acknowledge the fact of racial classification, feelings, and actions, and refusing to measure their consequences will not eliminate racial inequalities. At best, it will preserve the status quo."

"I don't see color, I only see children." What message does this state-ment send? That there is something wrong with black or brown, that it should not be noticed? I would like to suggest that if one does not see color, then one does not really see children. Children made "invis-ible" in this manner become hard-pressed to see themselves worthy of notice.

To be sure, there is no evidence in the books that any of the non-White characters suffer from poor self-esteem or any other negative state, but there is no evidence to the contrary, either. One of the privi-leges of Whiteness is to deny the impact of race on people's lives, and this privilege is readily apparent in the Harry Potter series. The truth is that, because the stories are almost exclusively told through the eyes of White characters who don't notice race, we really don't (can't!) know anything about the reality of the non-White characters. To see racism, critics of color-blindness argue, it is first necessary to see race.[3]

Yet, even within the neo-conservative ideology, Rowling's portrayal of race is problematic in that non-White characters barely seem to exist and none occupy positions of authority. This is evidenced by the fact that Cho Chang is the only non-White character who is de-veloped to any degree, as well as by the fact that not a single adult character in any of the books is a person of color—not even in the otherwise progressive Hogwarts. Their absence is conspicuous, espe-cially given that Rowling has worked for Amnesty International and clearly intended to create a multicultural society in which cultural differences, while generally unnoticed, are celebrated when the oc-casion permits (e.g., Seamus Finnigan's shamrock-covered tent and other decorations at the Quidditch World Cup). No doubt, Rowling intended to comment on race by focusing on blood status and elf rights. Her treatment of these topics provides ample opportunity to examine both contemporary and historical race relations, and it is to these racial metaphors that I now turn.

---

[3] This statement is a reasonable summary of the multicultural racial ideology—that race, al-though socially constructed, should be recognized (seen) in order to validate the experiences (both positive and negative) and cultural differences (e.g., food, music, dialect) that members of racial minority groups may share.

THE COLOR OF BLOOD

The tendency of some wizards to place a premium on pure blood (that is, on pure breeding) and treating half-bloods and Muggles as second-class citizens is an obvious parallel to our own society's history of oppression of Blacks and obsession about interracial sex and marriage. A number of characters, including Draco and Lucius Malfoy, explicitly espouse the superiority of pure blood, but this racist[4] attitude may be best personified by the portrait of Sirius's mother:

> "Filth! Scum! By-products of dirt and vileness! Half-breeds, mutants, freaks, begone from this place! How dare you befoul the house of my fathers.... Yoooou!" she howled, her eyes popping at the sight of the man [Sirius]. "Blood traitor, abomination, shame of my flesh!" (Order of the Phoenix 78).

Contained in this epithet are a number of important ideas: (1) that half-bloods (i.e., those of both Muggle and wizard parentage) are subhuman and undesirable, and that (2) their very presence threatens the purity and cleanliness of both their surroundings and their selves.[5] Thus, her disgust extends to her son, who befriends and invites the half-blood members of the Order into his house, and by so doing contaminates not only the house but himself. This view is remarkably similar to the beliefs held by supporters of anti-miscegenation laws in the United States, who thought that interracial unions would contaminate and dilute the pure White blood and lead to moral degeneracy and ultimately the country's downfall. While the last U.S. anti-miscegenation law was finally struck down in 1967 (Loving v. Virginia), interracial marriage continues to be controversial for many people.[6] It is certainly a sign of progress that the contemporary argument against such unions is more likely to be framed as

---

[4] Racism refers to the belief that race accounts for differences in human character or ability and that a particular race is superior to others. The emphasis on lineage and blood status suggests that Muggles and wizards can be treated as racial groups.

[5] University of Pennsylvania psychologist Paul Rozin likes to illustrate the permanence of the idea of contamination by asking people first to imagine a fly landing in their drink and then consider the possibility of finishing the drink after the fly is removed.

[6] A 2001 study carried out by the New York Times and published in the book How Race is Lived in America found that 29 percent of Whites and 15 percent of Blacks disapproved of Black-White marriages.

an issue of compatibility than as blood contamination, but no doubt there are still more than a few people who, when it comes to Black-White marriage, have the same reaction as Sirius's mother.[7]

Rowling makes a strong link between the evil of Voldemort and the Death Eaters and the belief in pure-blood superiority. Throughout her books, all examples of prejudice and discrimination against half-bloods or Muggles are perpetrated by either the Slytherins or Voldemort's supporters, while each "good" character, without exception, not only explicitly denounces prejudice against half-bloods but behaves accordingly. Thus, Dumbledore hires Hagrid to teach at Hogwarts, despite the fact that he is a half-giant, and when Rita Skeeter reveals his half-blood status, Dumbledore, along with Harry, Ron, and Hermione, convinces him that blood status is irrelevant. Similarly, the Weasleys, Sirius, and all members of the Order clearly reject the notion of half-blood inferiority—despite the scorn and disgust such a stance engenders from the pure-blood racists among them.

Not only is there a clean division between the evil racists and the good egalitarians in the first six Harry Potter books, but the tendency to be racist or non-racist seems impervious to change. For all the emphasis on choices, we have yet to see any racist character choose to denounce racism—though Draco seems at least to have the potential to do so. To this point, however, he has proven to be closed to any information that contradicts his deeply held conviction of pure-blood superiority. This is consistent with cognitive dissonance theory, which holds that people experience emotional discomfort when their attitudes are challenged and tend to try to eliminate this discomfort by discounting the challenging information, rather than engaging in the more difficult task of changing their belief system to accommodate it. Thus, when Draco's belief in pure-blood superiority is challenged by Hermione's obvious intelligence, he finds reasons to invalidate her accomplishments (e.g., she sucks up to the teachers or she studies so much because she is too ugly to have friends).

This is not to say that there would be no hope for Draco in the real

---

[7] One of the practical problems of racial purity that Rowling does not take up is the issue of deciding who qualifies as a "pure-blood." The term "half-blood" suggests that one parent is a Muggle, but it's not clear how a person with three "pure-blood" grandparents would be classified. The United States historically solved this problem (and simultaneously discouraged miscegenation) by adopting the "one-drop rule," which held that a person with even one drop of Black blood would be considered Black.

world. Racial identity models (e.g., Cross, Helms) suggest that emotional, personal experiences regarding race may create enough cognitive dissonance to inspire real attitude change. Perhaps Dumbledore's unflinching faith in him in *Harry Potter and the Half-Blood Prince* may inspire Draco to re-examine his beliefs.

In addition, psychologists have identified a number of factors associated with creating group-level attitude change (including racial attitudes). If the teachers at Hogwarts want to facilitate more open-mindedness and less prejudice in their students, they could draw on contact theory, but they'd have to proceed carefully. According to contact theory[8] ethnic and racial group prejudice can be reduced or even eliminated by bringing group members (in this case, half-bloods and pure-bloods) into cross-group contact with each other, but only as long as the nature of the contact meets a prescribed set of conditions. These conditions include ensuring that status is not dependent on blood lineage, having ample opportunity to get to know members of the other group, not behaving according to the other group's stereotypes, requiring cooperation, and having support from the relevant authority.

It is not coincidental that the problem of intolerance of half-bloods seems limited to the Slytherin House, despite the likely presence of both pure-bloods and half-bloods in all four Houses.[9] In Gryffindor, for example, the students seem completely disinterested in blood lineage, perhaps because all of the above conditions are met. In contrast, none of the necessary conditions are met in the Slytherin House, where the hostile environment toward half-bloods makes them reluctant even to disclose their status. It is noteworthy that even Snape, the head of Slytherin, does not readily disclose his half-blood status, much less do anything to promote tolerance or open-mindedness in his students.

The research on contact theory suggests that prejudice against half-bloods in Slytherin would be most easily eliminated if House membership were re-sorted each year, as this would facilitate equal status and acquaintanceship and require cross-group cooperation. Of course, given Hogwarts's history and tradition, this intervention is

---

[8] The original foundation for contact theory is Sherif's classic 1954 study on intergroup conflict and cooperation (i.e., the Robber's Cave experiment). The study is available online (http://psychclassics.yorku.ca//Sherif/index.htm).

[9] At the very least, we can be reasonably sure that half-bloods are well represented in each House, as we are told by Hagrid that "'Most wizards these days are half-blood anyway. If we hadn't married Muggles we'd've died out'" (*Chamber of Secrets* 116).

not likely to be adopted. Even so, prejudice against half-bloods could be considerably lessened through the creation of a safe, equal-status environment in the Slytherin House. This would require Snape to model tolerance and acceptance and take an assertive stance against intolerance of any kind, including inappropriate jokes and teasing. While this is not likely to dissuade the hard-core racists, it will effectively move their belief system outside the mainstream and, consequently, outside of most people's comfort zones.

It is worth noting that the obsession with blood and lineage is not limited to wizards. Even in the Harry Potter universe, select Muggles are shown to be as racist as any Death Eater. Consider the not-so-subtle undertone of eugenics[10] espoused by Vernon Dursley's sister, Marge, who, in reference to Harry, comments:

> "This one's got a mean, runty look about him. You get that with dogs.
> I had Colonel Fubster drown one last year. Ratty little thing it was.
> Weak. Underbred" (*Harry Potter and the Prisoner of Azkaban* 27).

Much like the Malfoys, Marge Dursley seems invested in "pure-blood," and like them, she seems to endorse the protection of racial purity via both selective breeding and targeted killing. Such attitudes are so abhorrent that it is tempting to dismiss them as fictional evil that could not exist in our world. But they are, in fact, an allegory for the anti-Semitism and racial ideology of Hitler and the Nazis.[11, 12]

The racism of the Nazis and the Death Eaters is easy to identify and poses few moral questions. Contemporary racism, however, is more complicated. To be sure, some racism is still perpetrated by

---

[10] Eugenics is the study of hereditary improvement of the human race by controlled selective breeding.

[11] In a July 2000 interview with the CBC, Rowling said, "In the second book, *Chamber of Secrets*, in fact he [Voldemort] is exactly what I've said before. He takes what he perceives to be a defect in himself, in other words the non-purity of his blood, and he projects it onto others. It's like Hitler and the Aryan ideal, to which he [Hitler] did not conform at all, himself. And so Voldemort is doing this also. He takes his own inferiority, and turns it back on other people and attempts to exterminate in them what he hates in himself."

[12] Describing even a few of the parallels between WWII and Harry Potter is beyond the scope of this essay, but I draw on these parallels to make the following fearless prediction (warning: possible spoiler): The Death Eaters (i.e., the Nazis) will be defeated in Book Seven when Voldemort (i.e., Hitler) decides to betray the Giants (i.e., the Soviet Union), who despite Hagrid's efforts are still aligned with Voldemort at the conclusion of *Half-Blood Prince*. Forced to defend themselves against Voldemort, the Giants join forces with Dumbledore's supporters and the Ministry of Magic (i.e., the Allies) and manage to pull out a hard-fought victory, despite significant losses.

avowed racists (e.g., White supremacists) who strive to promote a racist agenda by intentionally hurting, humiliating, or intimidating non-Whites.[13] But today's racism is often much more subtle, and, unfortunately, it is not only perpetrated by those who are evil or who want to hurt others. Good people, even those with the best egalitarian intentions, can and do perpetuate acts of racism, sometimes without even being aware of having done so (Gaertner & Dovidio).[14] Harry's and Ron's indifference to elf rights and S.P.E.W.[15] is a good example. Although Harry frees Dobby and neither of them engages in explicitly racist behavior, their lack of support for S.P.E.W. can be interpreted as an implicit endorsement of elf inferiority, especially given their propensity for actively confronting perceived injustice.

Unintentional and aversive racism[16] may seem hard to study, but

---

[13] Many race scholars and anti-racism activists argue that racism (as opposed to prejudice), by definition, can only be perpetrated in the context of considerable institutional power. According to this definition, people of color in both the United States and Europe can be prejudiced and can commit hate crimes, but they cannot be racist.

[14] Fyodor Dostoyevsky captured this tendency in his 1864 *Notes from the Underground*, observing that "Every man has reminiscences which he would not tell to everyone but only his friends. He has other matters in his mind which he would not reveal even to his friends, but only to himself, and that in secret. But there are other things which a man is afraid to tell even to himself, and every decent man has a number of such things stored away in his mind. The more decent he is, the greater the number of such things in his mind."

[15] This issue is examined in more depth in the next section.

[16] In my five years of teaching an upper-level undergraduate course on race, this notion of unintentional racism is the one that White students consistently find to be the most challenging to acknowledge—even in others. This is most likely because, like Harry and Ron, these students tend to associate racism exclusively with evil and sadism, rather than with ignorance and conditioning. As a result, they consider racism to be something that they, as well-meaning individuals, would never (could never!) perpetrate, which makes the idea of unintentional racism extremely threatening to their self-concept. This was evident, for example, when we watched and discussed the 2006 Academy Award-winning film *Crash*. In the film, Officer Tom Hansen (played by Ryan Phillippe), a junior member of the police department, seems to have made a conscious choice not to be a racist. He is shown standing up against racial injustice in multiple scenes, even with more senior members of the department, and he goes out of his way to make sure that he treats African-Americans with compassion, even under very stressful conditions. Tragically, in a later scene in his squad car, he misinterprets the intention of his passenger (a Black hitchhiker he picked up on a deserted road) and shoots him dead when he reaches into his pocket. When I discuss this scene in class, White students (even those who identify with a progressive, multicultural racial ideology) tend to believe that race was not a relevant factor. They acknowledge that Officer Hansen acted out of fear and argue that it was the situation that scared Hansen, not the passenger sitting beside him. "If it were a White man sitting next to him," they say, "he would have shot him, too, because his reaction was rational under the circumstances, even if it turned out to be misguided." I suggest that Officer Hansen's reaction is not at all rational. He didn't point his gun and say, "Okay, let's see your hands nice and slow;" he didn't shoot at the hand that was reaching for the pocket. He shot to kill. "A reflexive act," the students say. "He didn't mean to do it." I agree. He didn't. He acted out of a deep, primal fear, a racial fear that would *not* have been present with a White passenger. This makes it a racist act, albeit one that most White students and adults are not willing (able?) to acknowledge.

psychologists interested in social cognition and group relations have designed a variety of methods to do just that. Perhaps the best known of these is the Implicit Association Test (IAT)[17] an online test measuring implicit attitudes and stereotypes that was developed by Brian Nosek, Mahzarin Banaji, and Anthony Greenwald in 1998. An implicit stereotype, according to the IAT FAQ, is "a stereotype that is powerful enough to operate without conscious control." For example, if you think that John Walters is more likely to be the name of a famous person than Jane Walters, you might be indirectly expressing a stereotype that associates the category of male (rather than female) with fame-deserving achievement—despite the fact that there is a famous female with this last name (Barbara Walters). This was the finding of one of the first experimental studies of implicit stereotypes, and this tendency was found to be uncorrelated with explicit expressions of sexism or stereotypes (Banaji & Greenwald).

In the race IAT, users are first asked to put positive and negative words, such as "failure," "glorious," "terrific," and "nasty" into categories of "good" and "bad" by clicking the appropriate key on the keyboard as the words flash on the screen. Then, they are asked to do the same with images of Black and White faces. By having users respond to the prompts as quickly as possible, the test aims to side-step both lack of awareness and cognitive control—the brief, but significant, time lapse we need to give an "acceptable" answer rather than a truly honest one. Consistent with previous studies of implicit attitudes, studies using the race IAT reveal that White respondents tend to show implicit bias against Blacks.

So, what would happen if there was a blood-status IAT and all the Hogwarts students were required to take it? Consistent with their explicit attitudes, Draco and many other Slytherins would show anti-half-blood bias, but what about Harry, Ron, and Hermione? Research with the IAT reveals that implicit racial bias among White respondents is present as early as age six, with ten year olds showing the same magnitude of pro-White bias as adults (Baron & Banaji). These findings suggest that Ron, having been socialized in a wizard society in which there is open racism against half-bloods, probably holds some

---

[17] The race IAT (as well as age, sex, and other versions) and associated data can be found at https://implicit.harvard.edu/.

implicit negative stereotypes of half-bloods, although his friendship with Hermione probably mitigates the bias (remember that implicit stereotypes are not correlated with explicit attitudes). The results are harder to predict for Harry and Hermione, both of whom are raised by Muggles and have Muggles in their lineage. However, some IAT studies (e.g., Margie, Killen, Sinno, & McGlothlin) suggest that although they would show no bias regarding potential friendships, they would be more likely to associate transgressors with pure-bloods. There is little doubt, of course, that everyone at Hogwarts would show an implicit anti-elf bias, but this topic requires considerable elaboration.

THE TROUBLE WITH ELVES

Poor Hermione. Unlike practically everyone else, she considers the treatment of elves to be morally problematic. "'You know house-elves get a *very* raw deal!'" said Hermione indignantly. "'It's slavery, that's what it is!...Why doesn't anyone *do* something about it?'" (*Goblet of Fire* 125). Ron's response seems representative of almost everyone in the book: "'Well, the elves are happy, aren't they? You heard old Winky back at the [Quidditch] match... "House elves is not supposed to have fun"...That's what she likes, being bossed around...'" (*Goblet of Fire* 125).

Hermione protests, but Ron seems right. When Barty Crouch threatens Winky with clothes (the only path to freedom), she prostrates herself at his feet, shrieking, "'No, master! Not clothes, not clothes!'" (*Goblet of Fire* 138)—hardly the reaction we would expect from someone unhappy with his/her circumstances.

Hermione, of course, is undeterred. After researching the history of elf enslavement (it goes back centuries), she decides to form S.P.E.W. (Society for the Promotion of Elfish Welfare), with the initial intention of obtaining fair wages and working conditions and the long-term goal of getting elf representation in the Department for the Regulation and Control of Magical Creatures (*Goblet of Fire*). Both Harry and Ron join, but they do so reluctantly and clearly only as a favor to Hermione. Neither they, nor any of their classmates, are actually interested in acting on behalf of elf rights. Ron again seems to speak for everyone when he says, "'Hermione—open your ears....They. Like. It. They *like* being enslaved!'" (*Goblet of Fire* 224).

In the real world, there has never, to my knowledge, been a group of people who liked being enslaved, although slaveholders in the United States certainly made that argument.[18] It is therefore somewhat troubling that Rowling creates a race of sentient beings that does, in fact, seem to enjoy enslavement and prefer it to freedom. That said, the attitude of the elves creates an interesting moral dilemma. Should we respect and honor the wishes/desires of the "oppressed" group (Ron's position)—even if our own moral sensibilities are offended by their "enslavement"—or should the value of universal freedom (Hermione's argument) trump the value of free will?

It is tempting to dismiss Hermione's argument, especially considering that neither Harry nor Ron nor any of the adults at Hogwarts or in the Order of the Phoenix seem interested in taking up the cause. Harry and the Order, after all, are supposed to represent what is good and just. Surely, we are intended to let them guide our moral judgments, especially since Rowling had previously trained us that there is little moral ambiguity in her characters (i.e., all the good characters are open-minded toward half-bloods, while all the evil characters are prejudiced). Taken together, it is not unreasonable to conclude that Hermione's campaign for elf rights is misguided idealism, a not uncommon adolescent malady.

Moreover, there is something to be said for free will. Most of us have had the experience of doing something nice for someone else and enjoying both the process of this selfless act and its consequence. It's not so hard to imagine a group of beings whose meaning in life was based on just this kind of selfless helping. If they really like it (and there is no evidence that anyone but Dobby is unhappy in their "servitude"), then it would not only be unwarranted to set them free, but immoral and unkind, as well.

And yet, I believe that it is Hermione's position that is more morally acceptable. For one, it is Albus Dumbledore, not Harry, who serves as the moral compass of the wizarding world. Harry wants to do the right thing, and he never lacks the courage to follow through, but

---

[18] The absurdity of this belief is evident in Louisiana physician Dr. Samuel Cartwright's 1851 proposal of a psychiatric diagnosis (*drapetomania*) to explain the *pathological* tendency of Black slaves to flee captivity. In a paper published in the *New Orleans Medical and Surgical Journal*, Cartwright argued that *drapetomania* was both treatable and preventable and prescribed whipping and amputation of the toes as the most effective treatments.

he sometimes lacks the experience and wisdom to know what the right thing is—as when he tries to rescue Sirius. Here, too, he lacks the requisite wisdom. Dumbledore's explanation to Harry concerning Kreacher's complicity in Sirius's death is instructive:

> "Kreacher is what he has been made by wizards, Harry…Sirius did not hate Kreacher.…He regarded him as a servant unworthy of much interest or notice. Indifference and neglect often do much more damage than outright dislike.…We wizards have mistreated and abused our fellows for too long, and we are now reaping our reward" (*Order of the Phoenix* 832–834).

To be sure, Dumbledore seems to be arguing more for treating the elves compassionately than for setting them free, but he is also drawing a parallel between indifference and neglect and mistreatment and abuse, which certainly suggests that he would be much more sympathetic to the goals of S.P.E.W. than to Harry's and Ron's professed indifference.

Psychological and historical research also supports the goals of S.P.E.W., as there is evidence that prolonged enslavement (and even second-class status) can lead to the victimized group's internalization of the oppressors' belief system. This is evident in the writings of Black civil-rights leaders such as Malcolm X[19] as well as in the numerous studies that have documented the tendency of members of oppressed groups to endorse negative stereotypes of their own group. If contemporary experiments demonstrate the presence of internalized racism under relatively egalitarian (and legally equal) conditions, it is possible to imagine that the much more severe oppression of enslavement could, after several centuries, produce the type of reliance on the masters and the unwillingness to make free choices that the house-elves espouse. If true, and Dumbledore's commentary on Kreacher seems to imply as much, then the house-elves' preference for enslavement is a product of oppression rather than an exercise of free will. Hermione may indeed be idealistic, and she underestimates how challenging the transition to freedom would be for both elves and wizards, but her position on elf rights (and even her methods of achieving change) is morally just and scientifically valid.

---

[19] I am referring to the part of his autobiography in which he comments on his life prior to his imprisonment and subsequent conversion to Islam.

Notably, a lack of prejudice against Muggles or half-bloods does not seem associated with a greater likelihood of supporting elf rights. This is evident in *Order of the Phoenix*, in which even Sirius Black, whose rejection of his family's obsession with pure blood caused him to run away at age sixteen and his family to disown him and burn his name off the family tapestry, was unable to see the elves as anything other than servants. Ditto the Weasleys, despite Sirius's observation that they are the prototypical blood traitors. In fact, of all the positive characters, Ron seems to be the least interested in elf rights and the least sensitive to their plight. For example, when Hermione accuses him of making up his Divination homework, Ron (who is guilty as charged) pretends to be outraged. "'How dare you!'" said Ron.... "'We've been working like house-elves here!'" (*Goblet of Fire* 223). Although it may be tempting to dismiss the comment as a meaningless joke, humor can often provide important insight into people's belief systems. Hermione rightfully raises her eyebrow at the comment, as it suggests that Ron is unaware that comparing an evening of schoolwork to a lifetime of slavery could be considered offensive.

Unfortunately, this happens in our world, too. Although many individuals do see human rights as important across a variety of different identity groups, it is also true that advocates for racial equality do not always act as allies for the LGBT and disability communities, and vice versa. The bottom line is that Harry and Ron mean well and clearly have the courage to act consistently in accordance with their convictions, but their views about certain types of oppression are nonetheless narrow-minded. Like most of us, young and old, they still have some learning and growing to do.

MIKHAIL LYUBANSKY, Ph.D., is a lecturer in the department of psychology at the University of Illinois-Urbana-Champaign, where he teaches psychology of race and ethnicity and theories of psychotherapy. His research interests focus on conditions associated with changes in social identity and beliefs about race, ethnicity, and nationalism, especially in immigrant and minority populations. He recently co-authored a book on the Russian-Jewish diaspora (*Building a Diaspora: Russian Jews in Israel, Germany, and* *the United States).* He admires Hermione for her progressive social justice orientation, but his favorite character is Snape, and according to three different online quizzes, he would be sorted into Hufflepuff House.

REFERENCES

"Statement of the American Sociological Association on The Importance of Collecting Data and Doing Social Scientific Research on Race." 9 August 2002. *American Sociological Association.* <http://asa.internetgravity.com/galleries/default-file/asa_race_statement.pdf>.

M. Banaji and A. Greenwald, "Implicit Gender Stereotyping in Judgments of Fame," *Journal of Personality and Social Psychology* 68 (1995): 181–198.

A. Baron and M. Banaji, "The Development of Implicit Attitudes," *Psychological Science* 17 (2006): 53–58.

Crash. Dir. Paul Haggis. Perf. Sandra Bullock, Don Cheadle, Matt Dillon, Jennifer Esposito, William Fichtner, Brendan Fraser, Terrence Dashon Howard, Ludacris, Michael Pena, Ryan Phillippe, Larenz Tate, Shaun Toub. Lions Gate Films, 2004.

Gaertner, S. and J. Dovidio. "The Aversive Form of Racism." In J. F. Dovidio and S. L. Gaertner (Eds.), *Prejudice, Discrimination, and Racism.* Orlando: Academic Press, 1986. 61–89.

Kivel, Paul. *Uprooting Racism: How White People Can Work for Racial Justice.* Gabriola Island, BC: New Society Publishers, 1996.

Lipsitz, George. *The Possessive Investment in Whiteness: How White People Profit From Identity Politics.* Philadelphia: Temple University Press, 1998.

N. Margie, M. Killen, S. Sinno, and H. McGlothlin, "Minority Children's Intergroup Attitudes About Peer Relationships," *British Journal of Developmental Psychology* 23 (2005): 251–269.

Omi, Michael and Howard Winant. *Racial Formation in the United States: From the 1960s to the 1980s.* New York: Routledge, 1986/1989.

Rowling, J. K. *Harry Potter and the Sorcerer's Stone.* New York: Scholastic Inc., 1998.

———. *Harry Potter and the Chamber of Secrets.* New York: Scholastic Inc., 1999.

———. *Harry Potter and the Prisoner of Azkaban.* New York: Scholastic Inc., 1999.

———. *Harry Potter and the Goblet of Fire.* New York: Scholastic Inc., 2000.

———. *Harry Potter and the Order of the Phoenix.* New York: Scholastic Inc., 2003.

———. *Harry Potter and the Half-Blood Prince*. New York: Scholastic Inc., 2005.

Thandeka. *Learning to be White: Money, Race, and God in America*. New York: Continuum Publishing Inc., 2000.

Rakison and Simard consider the emerging perspectives of evolutionary psychology and how the Harry Potter books use them in various ways. Evolutionary psychology looks at the human mind and how we seem to retain, across generations, ways of thinking from our ancestors. If this evolutionary theory holds true in the series, the authors predict some interesting developments in the next novel. However, they leave us with the question: If evolution of the mind continues, could we evolve to some of the magical arts of Harry Potter?

DAVID H. RAKISON
AND CAROLINE SIMARD, BSc., DMV

Evolution, Development, and the Magic of Harry Potter

W E LIKE TO think of ourselves as unique, as different from everyone around us. Although this is true on a genetic level—identical twins being the exception—we also share many traits and behaviors with the rest of humankind. Many of you reading this tend to find the same individuals attractive, have similar taste preferences and dislikes (we doubt any of you like the smell of rotting eggs or sour milk), and would do more to help your family members than non-kin. In all likelihood, you experience some fear of spiders or snakes, will have asserted your dominance over others with verbal or physical aggression, and will have formed friendships with members of the same sex. The same can also be said for the characters of the Harry Potter books: Ron is far from enamored with spiders, Malfoy is constantly putting down his friends and foes with nasty jibes, and Harry and Ron are loyal and trusting friends. So, although we are different in many ways from the people around us, we have a great deal in common in the way we think about the world and the way that we act.

According to the emerging perspective of evolutionary psychology, these characteristics are common among humans because our ancestors faced specific obstacles or challenges known as *adaptive problems*. Over many generations, heritable characteristics that solved these adaptive problems better than rival designs—characteristics leading to greater survival or reproduction—were passed on in greater numbers and eventually became features in the universal or species-typical design of humans. These specialized mechanisms—or *adaptations*—often arise because of a *mutation* or copying error in the genetic code. Many mutations do not confer any benefit or advantage to their owner; indeed, many are deleterious, harming the smooth functioning of existing adaptations. However, those that do bestow a reproductive or survival advantage—such as a preference for calorie-rich fatty foods (think of the Ben and Jerry's ice cream in your freezer)—will spread through the population. Evolutionary psychology applies the principles of evolutionary biology to the human mind: just as the heart is thought of as an evolved mechanism for pumping blood, so, according to evolutionary psychology, the brain consists of mechanisms for dealing with the problems that were faced by our ancestors over thousands or millions of years. Some of these adaptive problems are still with us today.

According to evolutionary psychologists, many of these adaptations emerge or become activated only in adulthood. Just as women's breasts do not become capable of lactation until puberty, evolved psychological mechanisms involved in mate selection and mate competition do not come "on line" until puberty. Other mechanisms must be present in babies and children either to help them survive or because they are a precursor for those that are needed in later life. The discovery, study, and elucidation of adaptations that are present in the first years of life are the aims of evolutionary developmental psychologists (Ellis & Bjorklund).

You are probably wondering what this has to do with Harry Potter and the writings of J. K. Rowling. The answer is, surprisingly, quite a lot. As you shall see, J. K. Rowling is either a closet developmental evolutionary psychologist—which we think unlikely—or humans' evolved psychological mechanisms are so ingrained in the mind that they cannot help but be unconsciously expressed in literature (and presumably movies, songs, adverts, and other forms of media). In other words, we suggest that our evolved psychological preferences are such an integral part of how we think and act that authors cannot help but express them when they write fiction. In this essay, we contemplate several examples of evolved adaptations that are expressed in the Harry Potter series as a means of demonstrating this notion. We also use evolutionary psychology to make some predictions about Harry and his chums' futures: Will their friendship last? Who will Hermione marry? And, more importantly, will there ever come a time when they no longer eat Bertie Bott's Beans?

> *"I—don't—like—spiders."*
>
> —RON WEASLEY
> (*Harry Potter and the Chamber of Secrets* 154)

Without a doubt, dying young is the worst thing that you can do for your genes: if you are unable to survive until at least puberty, then you cannot reproduce. This means that there would be considerable *selection pressure* for the emergence of adaptations that help infants and children to avoid or live through potentially dangerous situations. The writings of J. K. Rowling are replete with instances where Harry, Hermione, and Ron encounter a creature that wants to attack, eat, maim, or kill them (or worse). But no species of animal play a more prominent role in the Harry Potter series than snakes and spiders. Snakes appear in almost every book in one form or another and are generally introduced as a threat or during a time of danger. Lord Voldemort resembles a snake, speaks Parseltongue (as does Harry), and is a member of Slytherin, whose House mascot is a snake. In *Chamber of Secrets*, Harry confronts an enormous snake-like creature called a Basilisk, which is a legendary reptile considered to be the king of serpents. *Harry Potter and the Goblet of Fire* opens with Voldemort, Peter Pettigrew, and a large snake in Tom Riddle's ancestral home. And in *Harry Potter and the Order of the Phoenix*, Arthur Weasley is attacked by Nagini, Voldemort's pet snake. Likewise, spiders make a scary and threatening appearance in *Chamber of Secrets*, when Harry and Ron are introduced to Aragog, a blind spider the size of a small elephant, whose minions chase the two boys in a manner suggesting that they might fancy them as a tasty snack. Ron also highlights his fear of arachnids during *Harry Potter and the Prisoner of Azkaban*, when he wakes from a nightmare claiming that spiders want him to tap-dance (though why they would want such a thing mere scientists cannot explain). Even Professor Dumbeldore refers to spiders' menace in *Harry Potter and the Half-Blood Prince* when he says, "'I take my hat off to you—or I would, if I were not afraid of showering you in spiders'" (77).

We suggest that J. K. Rowling's decision to repeatedly use snakes and spiders as threatening creatures is an implicit consequence of her (and all humans') evolved snake-and-spider detection and avoidance mechanisms. Among the most recurring animal threats to humans over evolutionary history—much of which was spent on the savannah plains in Africa (Orians)—are thought to have been snakes and spiders, and this is probably why they are today among the most common object-related phobias in adults (Nesse). A psychological mechanism to detect and avoid such creatures is of paramount importance. It is not adaptive to learn which ones are dangerous by waiting until you are attacked. If you are dead, it is too late to learn. If infants and young children possess such a mechanism, how would it work? It is unlikely that babies are born with an apprehension of either snakes or spiders, because they rarely exhibit fear prior to seven months of age. Instead, they most likely possess a mental template—like a simplified image—of snake and spider shapes, which allows them to learn a fear response more quickly when they see another's negative emotional response to them.

Support for this view has recently emerged from a variety of sources. For example, there is evidence that five-month-old babies, who are unlikely to have any experience with spiders, will track a spider-like image longer than scrambled versions of the same image (Rakison & Derringer). By ten months of age they also group spiders and snakes together in a category of "dangerous animal"—despite the fact that they do not look alike—and as different from non-threatening animals such as frogs and guinea pigs (Rakison). These behaviors, the first of which matches the behavior found in young babies' tracking of face-like stimuli (Johnson & Morton), can only be explained by the presence of an innate perceptual template in humans. What about learning that these animals are potentially threatening? Obviously, it is not ethical to teach babies to be afraid of spiders or snakes; however, the available evidence suggests that a perceptual template "prepares" adult human and non-human primates to learn this information more quickly than other kinds of information. For instance, Cook and Mineka found that young, lab-raised rhesus monkeys would more rapidly learn to associate snakes with a fearful response—as emitted by another monkey—than learn to associate flowers with a fearful response. Indeed, human adults discover fear-relevant stimuli—snakes and spiders—against a background of non-fear relevant stimuli—such as flowers and mushrooms—faster than fear-irrelevant stimuli hidden amongst fear-relevant stimuli (Öhman, Flykt, & Esteves). In other words, they see dangerous things faster than they see harmless things.

Our claim, then, is that it is not surprising that Rowling uses spiders and snakes so often as threatening creatures in the Harry Potter series. She, like her readers, possesses an innate psychological mechanism that is specifically sensitive to snakes and spiders, and their presence effectively triggers a response we have evolved to learn: that of fear.

> *"Vacant expressions, tatty second-hand books,*
> *you must be the Weasleys."*
>
> —Lucius Malfoy
> (*Harry Potter and the Chamber of Secrets*)

Unless you have recently enjoyed a sojourn at Azkaban, in all likelihood you like to think that you are a friendly, moral, and generally decent person. And you probably are. But there were doubtless times in your life as a child—and more recently as an adult—when you were not so pleasant to others. Males, for example, often engage in physical and verbal aggression with other males; females, in contrast, often engage in verbal aggression, though not typically physical aggression, toward other females. And when each sex engages in verbal aggression they do so in markedly different ways. It is unlikely that these behaviors are taught to boys and girls, because few parents—the Dursleys and Malfoys excluded—encourage aggression toward others. Rather, an evolutionary psychology perspective views them as the result of an evolved mechanism that, when displayed in an appropriate context, determines status and dominance within a group, helps a child to gain the resources of others (toys or Invisibility Cloaks, for instance), defends against attack, and deters rivals from future aggression.

In short, these behaviors increase an individual's likelihood of survival and reproduction: children (and then adults) who displayed these behaviors were more likely to have higher status and resources and therefore be more attractive to potential friends (and later mates). If, by chance, you do not accept the importance of dominance and status striving among humans, note that it takes between one and five minutes for individuals in a group of three people to accurately evaluate their status within that group, and they can do so without speaking a single word (Kalma). Also note that competition plays a major role in the everyday life of the students at Hogwarts, whether they are trying out for or playing Quidditch, contesting the Triwizard Tournament, or attempting to impress a professor by knowing how to make Veritaserum Potion. Indeed, the battle between the Death Eaters and the Order of the Phoenix is a classic form of status striving, in which dominance is achieved both by conquering foes and by fulfilling dangerous acts (think of Draco's ultimate task in Book Six of the series).

The Harry Potter series abounds with acts of dominance and status striving that follow closely the predictions of an evolutionary perspective. We shall focus here on male acts of aggression for two reasons. First, with the exception of Hermione, males play the main characters in the Harry Potter series (think of Harry, Ron, Draco, Neville, Snape, Dumbledore, Voldemort), and as a consequence there is significantly more male-on-male action than female-on-female action to be found. Second, according to evolutionary theory, males are more likely to engage in dominance striving than females because male reproduction is more varied than that of females, and dominance and status can greatly increase a male's reproductive potential (Buss). In other words, a female can, at most, produce fifteen to twenty children in one lifetime, but a male, albeit a busy male, can produce thousands of children in one lifetime. Ghengis Khan, for example, who fathered several hundred children, is believed by geneticists to have 30 million descendants living in the world today. Thus, high status is more important to males than females, and females find it a highly desirable trait in males (Buss). Think, for instance, of how consistently appealing Harry is to the girls of Hogwarts or how Hermione tells Harry in *Goblet of Fire* that girls only like Viktor Krum because he's famous.

So, how do males establish status and dominance? Most commonly, they use size, strength, intelligence, resources, and acts of bravery, and examples of these acts are common in J. K. Rowling's works. Harry and Draco are more than happy to draw wands on each other, as they do in the duel during *Chamber of Secrets*, spontaneously in *Goblet of Fire*, and when Draco paralyzes an invisible Harry on the Hogwarts Express in *Half-Blood Prince*. Adults are not exempt from this behavior: recall, for example, that Arthur Weasley and Lucius Malfoy engage in some fisticuffs in Flourish and Blotts in *Chamber of Secrets*. Interestingly, when males use verbal aggression against other males they tend to point out to others that their rival lacks the traits that are crucial for status and dominance. (Females, in contrast, generally derogate other females by referring to their sexual promiscuity and unattractive features of their physical appearance [Buss].) Draco Malfoy, for example, comments to Neville Longbottom that "'if brains were gold you'd be poorer than Weasley,'" and that "'then there's the Weasleys, who've got no money'" (*Harry Potter and the Sorcerer's Stone* 223). Neville also remarks that "'there's no need to tell me I'm not brave enough to be in Gryffindor, Malfoy's already done that'" (218). These classic examples of *male derogation* are perhaps not surprising given that Draco has never been on the best of terms with Harry, Ron, or Neville; however, there are also times when the boys of Hogwarts derogate those within their own group. In *Chamber of Secrets* Draco tells Goyle (who is actually Harry under the influence of the Polyjuice Potion) that "'if you were any slower, you'd be going backward'" (224). And it is not just children who engage in this kind of verbal aggression. Lucius Malfoy notes in *Chamber of Secrets* that Arthur Weasley is a poorly paid disgrace to the wizarding world, while during the Quidditch World Cup in *Goblet of Fire* he asks Arthur, "'What did you have to sell to get seats in the Top Box?'" (101).

Somewhat surprisingly, Harry (and Dumbledore, and to some extent Ron) are the only ones not susceptible to what Rowling might have called the *Dominance Charm*. Despite our best efforts, we could find no evidence that Harry resorts to this kind of characteristically male derogation toward his adversaries or his associates. During *Prisoner of Azkaban* as well as the denouement of *Half-Blood Prince*, Harry calls Professor Snape a coward, but this is the exception that fails to disprove the rule. Harry does refer to others as "gits," "slime," "vile," "cruel," and other generally negative terms, but he does not refer to their lack of intelligence, bravery, or resources. Why should Harry be presented in a different light than the other males? Again, we suggest that Rowling (along with everyone else) is sensitive—albeit implicitly—to the fact that typical males say not-so-nice things about other males, and that they do so by impugning their status, dominance, intelligence, physical prowess, resources, and courage. But Harry—and his mentor Dumbledore—are not typical males: they are, to put it frankly, nicer than any of the other boys or men in the Harry Potter series and above the sort of mean behaviors in which other males engage. To present either of these characters in such a light would bring them down to the level of, say, Lucius or Draco Malfoy, and then where would we be?

Thus, the way that status striving, or lack thereof, is presented in the Harry Potter series indicates the awareness—albeit an unconscious one—on the part of the author of the behaviors that human males use to establish dominance and status. The villains in the book display both the more positive version of these behaviors—physical aggression—as well as their more negative version—verbal aggression. In contrast, the heroes use only the former. Harry and Dumbledore demonstrate their status by their actions, their cleverness, their bravery, and their loyalty—and they do not need to stoop to more underhanded behaviors to do so.

"Only Muggles talk of 'mind reading.'"

—Professor Snape
(*Order of the Phoenix* 530)

Avid readers of the Harry Potter books will be well aware that characters within the series often seem to know the content of other people's thoughts or feel that their thoughts are somehow exposed to others; in other words, mind-reading is a common occurrence in the world of Harry Potter. In *Chamber of Secrets*, for example, Dumbledore gives Harry a searching look that makes him feel "as though he were being X-rayed" (144), and in *Sorcerer's Stone* Lord Voldemort (conjoined with Quirrell) is aware that the Stone is in Harry's pocket. A character's belief that his or her mind is being examined is not the result of paranoia. Instead, Rowling writes about a form of magic called Legilimency, which allows an individual to study the content of other's minds, as well as its magical defense, called Occlumency. According to Snape, Legilimency is "the ability to extract feelings and memories from another person's mind" (*Order of the Phoenix* 530), and the Dark Lord is highly accomplished at its use. As a consequence, in *Order of the Phoenix* Harry is given lessons by Snape in Occlumency to protect himself from Voldemort's mental probing. Harry is not the only one who receives private tutorials on the subject, however; in *Half-Blood Prince*, the reader discovers that Bellatrix Lestrange has been teaching Draco Malfoy to defend himself using Occlumency, which he successfully does against Snape.

At this point you are perhaps thinking that evolutionary psychology surely cannot explain this seemingly mythical ability, and that J. K. Rowling just invented the whole notion of Legilimency. Somewhat surprisingly, however, humans are impressive mind readers. All of us have a "theory of mind" (Wellman 18) that allows us to make inferences about the thoughts, feelings, and desires of others. We infer whether someone finds us attractive or likes us, whether they will be true to their word, and whether they believe they are above us in a dominance hierarchy. These insights are based in part on what people say, in part from their past behavior, and in part from their body language; but above all it is our understanding of our own desires, beliefs, and feelings that allows us to interpret and predict the actions and behaviors of others.

It is now well established that children's mind-reading ability— that is, their theory of mind—emerges around three to four years of age. It is at this age that children start to understand that other people will act in accord with their own beliefs rather than the child's beliefs. Evidence to support this view comes from the classic *false-belief* task (Gopnik & Astington). In this task, if a two-and-a-half-year-old and a four-year-old are shown, for example, a wand box and asked what is inside it, they will say, "a wand." If they are then shown that it is full of Bertie Bott's Beans and asked what someone else outside of the room will say is in the box, the younger child will respond, "Bertie Bott's Beans," but the older child will respond, "A wand." Thus, by three to four years of age children have a naïve understanding of psychology and can infer the mental states underpinning people's actions and what they may do in the future. Over time, this theory of mind becomes more sophisticated as children begin to understand that appearance and reality are not necessarily the same thing (e.g., a sponge may look like a stone, but it is in fact a sponge).

According to evolutionary developmental psychologists, this theory of mind mechanism evolved to help individuals tackle the adaptive problems that occurred because of group living (anthropologists maintain that humans' ancestors lived in groups of fifty to 150 people). If one is able to make predictions about people's future behaviors it is possible to infer who may form a coalition with you, who may attack you, and who may become your mate (we mean that in an American, not a British, sense) (Buss). Perhaps, above all, a theory of mind allows you to evaluate who may cheat you within friendships and romantic relationships. Humans are among only a handful of species that form coalitions with non-kin in the form of cooperative alliances—Ron, Harry, and Hermione provide an excellent example of such an alliance. These kinds of relationships are typified by personal sacrifices whereby members of the group aid other members of the group in times of need; each member of the trio at Hogwarts has risked his or her life for one or both of the others. But what if one individual reneges on their friendship in times of need? Or to put it another way, what if someone possessed an adaptation for "cheating" on a friendship and reaped the benefits of it without paying the costs? Imagine, for example, if Ron decides not to help save Harry because the risks are too high for his own safety. A theory of mind mechanism allows humans—and perhaps only humans—to predict whether others will hold up to their end of the bargain within relationships (Buss). It allows us to assess who is likely to lie and cheat and who is likely to stick around when the going gets tough (Cosmides & Tooby). Of course, our powers of mind reading are not infallible. As we await the seventh and final volume in the Harry Potter series, we, and the characters of the Harry Potter books, do not know whether Snape is working for the Death Eaters or the Order of the Phoenix. Why are our mind-reading abilities so limited? Because we, like Snape, are skilled at employing a version of Occlumency. Just as we have a theory of mind mechanism to give us insight into other's thoughts and emotions, so we are able to shield some of our own intentions from others. If we did not have such powers, then our thoughts would be an open book to everyone around us.

Once again, then, we suggest that Rowling's inclusion of Legilimency and Occlumency in the Harry Potter books is the expression of an evolved theory of mind mechanism that she, and all humans, possess. Sensitivity to others' feelings and thoughts is not only for those in realm of the wizarding world. It is part of adaptive mechanism into the psychology of others that is possessed by wizards and Muggles alike.

CONCLUDING THOUGHTS

In this essay we proposed that J. K. Rowling's Harry Potter series is unwittingly inspired in a number of areas by psychological mechanisms that have evolved over the course of millions of years of human evolution. In some ways this is hardly surprising. The contents of the books are the creation of Rowling's mind, and its output cannot help but be influenced by these mechanisms. And, of course, she is not alone in this regard. Look at any fiction book on your bookshelf and you will see the same connections: a struggle for power, courtship between two potential lovers, family relationships, alliances among non-kin. These themes have been constants among humans throughout evolutionary history, and it is therefore not surprising that they appear in all forms of media (e.g., the TV show *Lost*, the book *The Da Vinci Code*, movies such as *Star Wars* and *Schindler's List*) (see also Carroll).

We have, of course, only touched the surface when it comes to applying an evolutionary psychology perspective to the Harry Potter series of books. Most notably, as the students of Hogwarts reach puberty, as they have in the last volumes in the series, so a multitude of applications of evolutionary psychology will open up to the knowledgeable reader. After all, at the heart of evolution is reproduction, and so many, if not all, adaptations are directly or indirectly devoted to this aspect of humans. We leave it to you to apply the tenets of evolutionary psychology where you see fit. And if you are wondering how, just remember that you already have many of the answers in your own mind: you possess the same adaptive mechanisms as everyone else, including those of the author of the Harry Potter books. Consider the questions we posed at the beginning of the essay: Whom will Hermione marry? Do you believe that Ron has the traits that women typically find attractive in a man? Will Harry, Hermione, and Ron remain friends? Do you envisage a struggle for dominance leading to conflict among them? We leave it for you to decide.

We cannot finish without discussing whether magic might be an evolved psychological mechanism. There is no doubt that those who possess wizarding genes would have a distinct survival and reproductive advantage over those who do not. Imagine the time you could devote to other activities if you did not have to wash dishes (think of Mrs. Weasley in *Chamber of Secrets*) or the advantage you would have over sexual competitors if you could appear anywhere at will using Apparition. The possibilities are endless. If we assume that the ability to perform magic is a psychological adaptation—for how else would it have evolved?—then it is somewhat surprising that a greater proportion of the population in the Harry Potter books are not capable of using it. If using magic provided an individual with such a distinct advantage over others, then surely the gene would spread quickly through the population. There are a number of possible reasons why this has not happened. But the answer that we favor is the idea that everyone in the world of Harry Potter—Muggles included—possesses some of the genes for magic, though perhaps not in sufficient numbers or the proper combinations to be able to use it. Admittedly, this notion is speculative. Yet at the same time it is a heart-warming idea to think that if there are by chance wizards out there somewhere in the world, then we all might have a little magic in us.

ACKNOWLEDGMENTS

The authors wish to thank David Buss for helpful and constructive feedback on this essay.

DAVID H. RAKISON is an associate professor of psychology at Carnegie Mellon University. His research focuses on the development of cognition and perception in infancy as well as evolutionary developmental psychology. He has edited two books, *Early Category and Concept Development: Making Sense of the Blooming Buzzing Confusion* and *Building Object Categories in Developmental Time*.

CAROLINE SIMARD, BSc., DMV, is an expert in the care of magical and not-so-magical creatures. She currently resides in Pittsburgh and her passions are her three cats, her dog, her husband (in that order), and the Harry Potter books.

REFERENCES

Buss, D. M. *Evolutionary Psychology: The New Science of the Mind.* Second edition. New York: Allyn and Bacon, 2004.

————. *The Evolution of Desire: Strategies of Human Mating.* New York: Basic Books, 1994.

Carroll, J. *Evolution and Literary Theory.* Columbia: University of Missouri Press, 1995.

M. Cook and S. Mineka, "Selective Associations in the Observational Conditioning of Fear in Rhesus Monkeys," *Journal of Experimental Psychology: Animal Behavior Processes* 16 (1990): 372–389.

L. Cosmides and J. Tooby, "Cognitive Adaptations for Social Exchange," In J. Barkow, L. Cosmides, and J. Tooby (Eds.), *The Adapted Mind.* New York: Oxford University Press, 1992. 163–228.

Ellis, B. J., and D. F. Bjorklund (Eds.). *Origins of the Social Mind: Evolutionary Psychology and Child Development.* New York: Guilford, 2005.

A. Gopnik and J. W. Astington, "Children's Understanding of Representational Change and Its Relation to the Understanding of False Belief and the Appearance-Reality Distinction," *Child Development* 59 (1988): 26–37.

Harry Potter and the Chamber of Secrets. Dir. Chris Columbus. Perf. Daniel Radcliffe, Rupert Grint, and Emma Watson. Warner Bros., 2002.

Johnson, M. H. and J. Morton. *Biology and Cognitive Development: The Case of Face Recognition.* Oxford, England: Blackwell, 1991.

A. Kalma, "Hierarchisation and Dominance Assessment at First Glance," *European Journal of Social Psychology* 21 (1990): 165–181.

R. M. Nesse, "Evolutionary Explanations of Emotions," *Human Nature* 1 (1990): 261–289.

A. Öhman, A. Flykt, and F. Esteves, "Emotion Drives Attention: Detecting the Snake in the Grass," *Journal of Experimental Psychology: General* 130 (2001): 466–478.

G. Orians, "Habitat Selection; General Theory and Applications to Human Behavior," In J. S. Lockard (Ed.), *The Evolution of Human Social Behavior.* Chicago: Elsevier, 1980. 49–66.

D. H. Rakison and J. Derringer, "Do Infants Possess an Evolved Spider-Detection Mechanism?" *Manuscript in preparation,* 2006.

Rakison, D. H. "Mechanisms for Predator Detection and Response in Infancy." In Lobue, V., and D. H. Rakison. *Adaptive Mechanisms in Early Development.* Paper presented at the Society for Research in Child Development Biennial Conference, Atlanta. April 2005.

Rowling, J. K. *Harry Potter and the Sorcerer's Stone.* New York: Scholastic Inc., 1998.

———. *Harry Potter and the Chamber of Secrets.* New York: Scholastic Inc., 1999.

———. *Harry Potter and the Prisoner of Azkaban.* New York: Scholastic Inc., 1999.

———. *Harry Potter and the Goblet of Fire.* New York: Scholastic Inc., 2000.

———. *Harry Potter and the Order of the Phoenix.* New York: Scholastic Inc., 2003.

———. *Harry Potter and the Half-Blood Prince.* New York: Scholastic Inc., 2005.

Wellman, H. *The Child's Theory of Mind.* Cambridge, MA: MIT Press, 1990.

LEARNING
FROM HARRY

In this essay I describe some of the different methods I've used in my psychology practice to help adults, adolescents, and children and how these could be used to help Harry himself with the challenges he now faces. In particular, I've found Harry Potter characters a useful tool in helping some people overcome their issues, and I show how you might use him, too.

NEIL MULHOLLAND, Ph.D.

Using Psychological Treatment with Harry

I AM A TREMENDOUS Harry Potter fan. As a reader, I revel in vicariously experiencing his triumphs and disasters and in imagining the adventures that this amazing young hero bravely jumps into while searching for his destiny. As a professional psychotherapist, though, it is even more intriguing to me to wonder how Harry's travails mirror our own, and how the way in which Harry deals with his challenges, his enemies, and his own self-doubt has implications for those of us who are trying to overcome our own personal Voldemorts, Dementors, and painful scars.

If you are like most people, you have never experienced counseling or psychotherapy from a professional. However, if you have been fortunate in your life, you may have come across an older relative, a caring parent, a teacher, or a friend who believed in you and helped guide you on your way. You may even, like Harry, have had serendipitous "magical moments" when you met a stranger who, by what seemed pure coincidence, was able to help you in a crucial moment of life with just the right idea or gesture. At those times in life when such a person is not available, though, a trained counselor can employ proven psychotherapeutic techniques to help his clients bring about their own magical moments of growth and understanding. Although Harry Potter never officially received therapy, he had such a trusting and supportive relationship with Dumbledore that you might say Dumbledore was Harry's best psychotherapist!

Of course, when reading the Harry Potter novels, we can see many instances of bravery and heroic deeds. But when are the rest of us called upon to face a dragon, battle Dark Lords, or catch a Snitch? How could the path of scary pitfalls Harry must travel possibly apply to our own life's journey? I contend that by following Harry's example and incorporating his wizardry (bravery and wisdom) into tried-and-true therapy techniques, we, too, could perform "magic" of our own on our thinking and on our lives.

Abusive foster parents and Death Eaters notwithstanding, a large part of Harry's bravery is simply his ability to be open and initially trusting of those he encounters. We may be more accustomed to thinking of bravery as the physical accomplishment of heroic deeds, but trusting other people carries risk, and choosing to take that risk can sometimes be even scarier than facing the Basilisk. The courage that Harry displays in this area is often needed for a psychotherapy client to be open to talking about and facing his or her own "Dark forces" (i.e., problems). A great benefit of the therapeutic relationship is that the laws and ethics of confidentiality (i.e., knowing that the counselor will not reveal the client's feelings and secrets) make the therapist's office a safe place for the client to practice this bravery and this trust before bringing it out into the world and into other relationships.

Another common psychotherapeutic issue worth noting and comparing with Harry's story is that when a person is "ready" to change (because he or she can't bear it any more and is highly motivated to turn things around), change happens more easily. We can see that when Harry is told his destiny and the challenges it will bring, he doesn't hesitate but jumps right in; he's ready. Somehow, deep inside he *knows,* as we all do when we find ourselves in those certain moments of clarity and truth.

When these two factors (trust in and openness with the psychotherapist and the client's readiness to change) are strong, then the collective wisdom of the psychotherapist and the client come together, as if by magic, and together they can often find amazing solutions to what once seemed impossible challenges. By exploring the underlying issues or Dark forces of the client's beliefs, a problem can be seen more clearly and a plan can be developed toward overcoming it rather than avoiding it in fear, as Harry often sees others do with Voldemort. So, let's take a look at some models of psychotherapy that could be best suited to Harry's story and where we can draw comparisons from Harry's many predicaments to those of our own challenges and goals for change. These are:

1. Narrative Therapy
2. Cognitive Behavior Therapy (CBT)
3. Eye Movement Desensitization and Reprocessing (EMDR)
4. Mindfulness Training/Acceptance and Commitment Therapy

NARRATIVE THEORY

Just as Rowling's novels are the story of Harry Potter's life, each of us have stories of our own lives. You may notice that as we repeat these recollections of our own experiences several times to others, a story about them begins; we start to repeat our tale in a similar way each time we tell it. We also find that a family story can develop about us, as others in our family recount *their* recollections about us. How we put these memories of our experiences about ourselves, and how others have seen it and then tell it, becomes our narrative of how we see ourselves. Narrative therapy encourages us to look at these stories we tell of our lives, with an emphasis on the meaning we give to them. If we are struggling with a problem, are we consumed by the problem itself, or is it the story we're focused on, with all of its drama and its twists and turns? Are there perhaps other stories (memories of our experiences) where we triumphed over similar problems that we are forgetting? Can we call into consciousness our stories of strength and courage instead of focusing on the current fear or anxiety or anger story that we are telling? All of these stories of "who we are" would be explored by the narrative therapist.

To look at this in Harry's terms, a good time for us to seek help from a narrative psychotherapist is when the Dark force of a problem is threatening to defeat us. Many people wait and struggle with a problem for a long time before seeking professional help. They have probably talked to several friends or family members at length about the problem, and so they often come to psychotherapy with the story of their life saturated in the problem (i.e., people have often thought about or talked about their problems so much that their life story is centered or consumed by their problem story).

Like all of us, Harry's story is not just about one main problem or challenge that he faces on the way to his destiny to fight and win against the Dark force of Voldemort and his followers. Other stories or sub-plots of his life story are also worth noting, and exploring them may be useful to him. Let's look at some of Harry's possibilities: he suffered from the abuse and neglect of his aunt, uncle, and cousin. His ability to endure this for so many years, as he grew up, would be seen by many as a story of sadness and unfairness. Yet, in spite of all this hardship as he grew up, Harry appears to remain positive and carry on with a reasonably normal life—so it seems that Harry chose to see his story as one of strength, endurance, and patience. This is one of the goals of narrative therapy—to explore the positive skills and experiences of a client to see how these memories of strengths and triumphs might be used to help overcome the problem story. Narrative therapy encourages people to look at the other stories or plots of their own life's experiences, as well as their skills and accomplishments. Often these previously overlooked stories of strength can help clients realize their strengths and the wisdom that has been gained by their hard-earned life lessons. There is then a particular focus on those positive skills and realizations of the client that might be useful to tackle the current problem or to reach the desired goal. In Harry's case, we could explore how his natural talent as a great Quidditch player and his ability to be a Seeker, to dodge the Bludgers, and to quickly notice and zoom in on the Snitch were skills that often saved him just in time, and we could help him determine how these talents could help him overcome future obstacles.

Perhaps one of the reasons Harry endures so successfully is that he intuitively focuses less on all of the fearful dangers (problems) that he faces and more on how he has always eventually been able to "magically" defend against them, to dodge them, to beat them back, to face them with bravery and not let them defeat him. We all have stories to tell of such feats in our lives; perhaps they are not quite as mystical and unusual and dangerous as Harry's, but they are certainly heroic in their own way.

Once the client and the narrative psychotherapist have collaborated on a new plan for the client to tackle or dodge his problem (by remembering and using past stories of proven strengths), they can do what Harry did so well when he had problems: get support and help from others. A narrative therapist will encourage clients to look at who in their circle of family and friends can they look to and ask to be on their cheering team to support them in their "fight" against the problem and to help in their solution for change. It is important to note that the purpose of a cheering team is to help support the client with his solution plan rather than simply listening to the same old moaning or complaining about the problem and offering sympathy.

Fortunately, Harry has many people on his cheering team: he has the support of Hagrid, Sirius, and Professor McGonagall. He has his two best friends, Ron and Hermione, who stand by him in the face of fear, danger, and ridicule. He has all those close positive mentors at Hogwarts, his Gryffindor Housemates, and his Quidditch teammates to take his mind off the negatives. He also had the Weasley family to support him and show him how positive family life can be. But no mention of Harry's cheering team would be complete without mentioning the most influential support person of all: Dumbledore. Harry knows he can always count on Dumbledore; he has complete trust in him. When things are looking grim, Dumbledore is always there to listen and encourage Harry, without telling him what he should do—and that is the same kind of magic I try to create with my clients, whenever I can. A psychotherapist/magician who shows trust and encouragement can work wonders in a client's life, as Dumbledore does for Harry as he spurs him to grow and to develop his bravery. Harry's life is proof that it is often our support team of friends and family that get us through the hardest times. With a team like that, maybe you or I could face similar dangers!

So, we can see that Harry, even without the benefit of official narrative therapy, is able to use many of its elements. His cheering team (especially Dumbledore) helps Harry focus on his strengths, remember his successes, and move forward positively toward solutions instead of remaining stuck in his problems. Harry's whole life has been a story of overcoming adversity and staying strong in the face of danger; whenever he encounters a new enemy, he can call on the memories of his previous deeds to remind himself that he is a strong, resourceful hero.

COGNITIVE BEHAVIOR THERAPY (CBT)

This particular approach has been the hot-shot superstar of psycho-therapies for the last ten to twenty years in the Western world, and it could be very useful for someone like Harry Potter. In fact, it could be argued that Harry intuitively incorporates many CBT strategies into his life already.

CBT focuses on the "Cognitive Triangle" (that almost sounds like a new magic spell, doesn't it?). Imagine a triangle: at one point are our *thoughts* or *beliefs* about a particular problem, at the second point lie our *feelings* about that particular problem, and at the third point are the *actions* or *behaviors* that we engage as a response to the prob-lem. All three pieces of the triangle interact with each other within us, to varying degrees; our thoughts influence our feelings, which then influence our actions (or inaction)—which then, in turn, influ-ence our next thought, and the cycle begins again. One of the three aspects is usually dominant in any given moment (e. g., when we are "exploding" in anger or are "knocked out" by sad feelings, our thinking is usually lost). The cognitive psychotherapist would help us identify the thoughts or beliefs (deeply held thoughts) that we have about a particular problem and, even more important, that we have about ourselves and our ability to deal with the problem. The therapist would then help us look at how these particular thoughts or beliefs about ourselves, given this problem, are influencing our feelings and actions in both positive and negative ways. Together, we would explore how these thoughts and feelings have propelled us into certain types of action or inaction (e.g., being stunned, frozen, or stuck in "darkness"). Cognitive questioning would also explore the deeper beliefs or "truths" that we carry about ourselves and our pasts and how these are guiding our thoughts, feelings, and actions today. For once we notice and recognize the patterns of our thinking, we then have a choice to consciously stop and "change the channel" to some positive options. These options could include remembering more positive aspects of the day that we might have overlooked and looking forward with problem-solving ideas and an action plan. By switching the mind's preoccupation from the negative thoughts to more positive, calming thoughts, we are, in effect, changing "the spell" that the mind is caught up in.

CBT approaches usually give particular thinking strategies to us to bring greater awareness of how our thoughts and beliefs might be overly focused on a particular worry or problem. So, how might a CBT therapist bring this awareness to a client?

At the start of a CBT session, the psychotherapist does what is known as a *mood check-in*. Usually he or she asks something like, "On a scale of zero to ten (with zero feeling terrible and ten feeling great), where would you say you are today? What level have you generally been at, lately?" This would be done at the beginning of every session, and thus would not only help the therapist gauge any changes or improvements over time, but also help the client become more consciously aware of negative thinking patterns that can be altered.

Homework (practice to be done at home or outside the psychotherapist's office) is another tool that the CBT therapist uses to assist the client in "changing channels." Homework might be to have the client review events at the end of each day and estimate how often the mind was preoccupied with the particular difficult issues he or she is struggling with.

Another CBT strategy is to have the client say "Stop!" loudly to himself every time he notices "worry thoughts" are consuming him. This is one way the client can gain control over the things he can influence and let go of the things he can't.

So, how does CBT fit into Harry's life? It could be concluded that Harry's belief and trust in his life's purpose and the others around him are what seem to keep his thoughts on the positive and helpful side. Somehow knowing or believing in the "Greater Good" and believing that those he trusts are fighting for this, too, is a strong source of encouragement for Harry. He seems to recover well from each major life-threatening crisis, and so we might conclude that Harry's thoughts and beliefs about his apparent destiny would seem to be quite positive and hopeful, as he does remarkably well at rebounding and recovering from all the disasters thrown at him. He does not let worry or negative thoughts, in particular, take over his thinking and consume him. He is somehow able (again, often with the help of "therapist" Dumbledore) to notice and catch his negative thoughts and beliefs and turn them around—which is the essence of CBT. By realizing and carefully watching how negative thoughts get us stuck and feeling miserable, we can then stop them and switch to more realistic positive ones. But to change this negative "spell" that we Muggles often cast on ourselves and switch it to a positive "spell" takes more than a wave of a wand: it takes the practice of catching and switching every chance we get, until it becomes our new habit. Then we are in charge of our mind, rather than under the spell of negative thoughts.

EYE MOVEMENT DESENSITIZATION AND REPROCESSING (EMDR) TREATMENT FOR TRAUMA OR POST-TRAUMATIC STRESS DISORDER (PTSD)

Given what Harry has gone through in his life so far, probably the most difficult or traumatic moment was his first major shock: receiving his scar. Not only was the pain of the injury itself harrowing, but, even worse, it happened as he was witnessing the violent death of his parents. Although Harry doesn't seem to show any signs of trauma, we can never really know. What might he be repressing? What might the rest of us do if we encountered even one of the major traumas that Harry has been through in his life, from dragons to demons?

When people show signs that a past traumatic, dangerous experience is still a major bother to them (e.g., sleepless nights, having awake dreams or vivid memories of an accident that is constantly on their mind and that constantly stresses them), it is called Post-Traumatic Stress Disorder (or PTSD).

One unusual but well-researched and effective treatment method for PTSD has been in use for more than fifteen years: EMDR (Eye Movement Desensitization and Reprocessing). In EMDR, the client is systematically encouraged to remember the most difficult aspects of a particular traumatic event while the therapist has the client move his eyes from side to side, following his fingers or a light bar, back and forth, over and over again. It has been shown that when we move our eyes to the left, the right side of the brain is stimulated, and the opposite happens when we move them the other way. Studies of

EMDR have found that when the brain is stimulated back and forth between its two hemispheres while the client remembers a traumatic moment or encounter, the brain seems to overcome the tense feelings and thoughts that have been of such bother to them about the past accident, abuse, or traumatic moment. Of course, it can take several sessions for the client to work through the trauma, but this method has had remarkably positive results. Some might say magical results, for after years of feeling and thinking of old traumas with intensity and stress, many people have been able to recover quite dramatically and completely (Note: Although this method originally used and still emphasizes moving eyes, the simultaneous stimulation of each side of the brain can also be accomplished by sounds or by touch to alternating sides of the body).

The first part of the EMDR method has the client close his eyes as the psychotherapist guides him to relax and remember a time when he was feeling relaxed, safe, and content. Remembering this picture and relaxing is the fundamental method or "magic" that gives the client a peaceful place or memory to focus on while he processes the trauma by being exposed to it through memory visualization.

Like the pessimistic stories that clients first tell about themselves in narrative therapy, and also like the counterproductive thoughts they can have about themselves in CBT, the same negative, self-blaming thoughts about the present circumstances and the future are often a large hindrance to people suffering from PTSD. So, these, too, need to be addressed. However, in EMDR they are reviewed by using the bilateral eye movement and allowing clients to see what changes come up in their thoughts and their feelings without any direction from the psychotherapist. Only when a client notes that he can review the traumatic experience(s) with little to no disturbance, and that he has a positive idea about himself in relation to the trauma, is the treatment successfully complete.

Obviously, Dumbledore never performed EMDR on Harry, so this is one area in which our comparison breaks down. However, Harry does have ongoing past memories or visions from his parents in that special Mirror of Erised, and even more violent flashbacks of his parents' deaths when he is confronted with Dementors. These flashbacks could be a sign that Harry is suffering from a bit of PTSD. Also, because Harry was very young at the time of the trauma, he may be experiencing some shock or dissociation, where the person mentally blanks out (mentally runs away) in the face of the traumatic stress to survive. EMDR often brings out these memories to be realized and healed. It might be interesting to imagine how EMDR might work in helping Harry process and overcome this most disturbing and emotional event.

When using EMDR with a person who has been exposed to multiple shocking events (like Harry), the psychotherapist always goes to the first traumatic event that a person has encountered, even though this might not be the particular or recent traumatic experience that is bothering him. In Harry's case, the first trauma was undoubtedly when he experiences his first encounter with Voldemort, sees/senses his parents' death, and receives the pain with that terrible, life-long scar. However, Harry, being an infant at the time, may only have sensory memories of this, but the increasing pain and shock that he still experiences at Hogwarts, when Voldemort is around, appears to trigger the old trauma. Thus, to get the full benefit of EMDR we may need to take Harry through each and all of his shocking encounters one at a time, from oldest to most recent, including the abuse and neglect from the Dursleys.

1. The therapist would set up a relaxed, safe place for Harry to remember and visualize. He or she would teach Harry to breathe deeply, relax his body and face, and remember a happy, safe moment in his life—perhaps his first meal around the Weasleys' dinner table. The therapist would have Harry intensely focus on this pleasant memory, perhaps for ten to fifteen minutes (and would also encourage him to practice this method daily or nightly, as needed). In EMDR this is known as "a safe place"— almost as good as Harry's Invisibility Cloak!

2. With gentle observation as to what arises in the client's mind and memory as EMDR stimulation is used, the pressure seems to dissolve, and recalling the memory can finally be done in relaxation. Thus, after establishing a relaxed, safe place with Harry, the therapist would ask him to visualize and remember the specific most difficult moment of that traumatic event. It is possible that Harry might have a flashback because of this traumatic memory and almost feel as though he was living

that shocking moment all over again. Recalling that disturbing scene might bring up intense emotions of love and sadness as well as fright and severe pain.

3. Next, the therapist would ask Harry, "How bothersome (on a zero to ten scale, ten being the highest) is it when you think back to that first moment with you, your parents, and Voldemort?" (if this was the event of focus).

4. Another variable that is measured when practicing EMDR is how the client thinks of or views himself as a result of the past trauma. This second pre-measure is taken on a scale from one to seven. Most clients, at the beginning of treatment, have a low score on this, as they usually feel guilty and are very negative in how they see themselves relative to the trauma. In Harry's case, how does he feel about himself and how he handled the situation? Does he think he should have prevented it? Does he feel guilty that he has survived and his parents haven't? Most of us would prefer to see ourselves as brave and having done our best under the circumstances; however, when we are still affected by trauma, we can rarely see these positives in ourselves.

5. Once the therapist has noted the client's pre-treatment scores, he would be ready to start the eye (or sound or touch) stimulation (as described above).

6. After EMDR is complete, the therapist again asks the rating questions to measure the amount of discomfort the client is having and how he now sees himself when thinking of the traumatic event. Eventually, when treatment of PTSD is effective, the client should feel little to no emotional disturbance when thinking of the trauma. For Harry, this would be a great benefit—the less stressful his emotional burden, the stronger he can be to meet his next inevitable horrific and shocking encounters with dangerous creatures and villains.

MINDFULNESS TRAINING/ACCEPTANCE AND COMMITMENT THERAPY

Mindfulness:
Similar to CBT but with a twist of its own, mindfulness training is focused not on actively changing the negative thoughts that we

have of ourselves or our situation, but just *noticing* and *accepting* our thoughts and feelings in relation to our circumstances, as if from a distance, without judging ourselves. Thus, the goal of this method is to remain calm and not get flustered, no matter what life throws at us. The roots of this approach developed long before any psychological methods. In fact, they are estimated to be 2,700 years old and attributed to the teachings of Gautama the Buddha. What might such an ancient philosophy have to teach us, and what does that have to do with Harry Potter?

As Harry has gone through all of his major and scary encounters with what seem to be unnaturally calm thoughts and feelings, perhaps he has unconsciously been using this method or something like it. Because Harry, by necessity, must constantly be vigilant and aware of the dangers around him, he almost intuitively stays in the present moment. By casting his own spell of protection around himself and focusing on the apparent calmness he finds within while facing life's difficulties and uncertainties, Harry seems to be using a form of mindfulness.

Acceptance and Commitment Therapy (ACT):

The "acceptance" part of this reasonably new approach is similar to the "mindfulness" listed above. However, the "commitment" part is added on.

The goal of this therapy is to encourage clients who are "stuck" somewhere in their thinking, feeling, or actions to be less rigid and to practice what we call psychological flexibility. The commitment component steers clients toward reasonable action plans based on their values and away from old patterns of action that defeat them and make them feel miserable. Thus, ACT attempts to balance these two strategies: first, acceptance/mindfulness of those aspects of life that are not helpful or are not in the client's control, and, second, focusing on the actions that *are* able to be influenced or changed by the client.

Possible Mindfulness/Acceptance/Commitment Strategies for Harry's New Problem:

At the time of this writing (August 2006), we Harry Potter enthusiasts are awaiting Rowling's next and final novel, and all of us are likely asking ourselves one big question: How will Harry cope without Dumbledore? For a moment, let us imagine that Dumbledore's death in Book Six has left Harry bereft. He may blame himself, feel guilty, or feel emotionally and mentally paralyzed. How might a therapist using the mindfulness, acceptance, and commitment strategies help Harry to work through his grief and cope with the loss of his mentor? A mindfulness and acceptance/commitment approach would help Harry try to improve his psychological flexibility using the following principles:

1. *Contact with the Present Moment.* The therapist would help Harry to look around him and see the world as it actually is, without Dumbledore, and not as he thinks it should be. He would be encouraged to notice what is going on in his life *right now* instead of becoming stuck in the past or worrying about the future. For example, the therapist might ask, "When self-blaming thoughts or doubts come into your mind, what can you focus on to keep you alert and in the present, Harry?" and then help him to figure out a constructive focus.

2. *Acceptance.* The therapist would also gently help Harry accept that Dumbledore is gone, and that he can't change that fact. A therapist using this method will ask questions to help Harry realize for himself that railing against the unfairness of Dumbledore's death and saying, "It shouldn't have happened this way!" only weakens him and makes him less able to cope with his life as it currently is. He might say to Harry, "Dumbledore was your friend, your mentor, and a source of strength in your life. Now that you must live without him, what of your life, purpose, and destiny will you need to keep in mind?"

3. *Action Plan.* The therapist would try to help Harry keep moving in the right direction. He might ask, "What specific actions can you take to stay strong and not let this loss weaken your spirit? What would Dumbledore want you to focus on at this time? What commitment can you make today for an action that will bring you closer to your goal of helping good to overcome evil?"

If Harry has a plan and method to stay psychologically flexible, mindful of the present, and focused on his plan for the greater good, the pain and losses he has faced could become an asset rather than a setback. Each time Harry is able to see his tragedies and challenges as a learning experience and is able to deal with the realities that life throws at him, he strengthens himself and is better able to be of service and move toward his ultimate goal. This lesson applies to all of us—if we really notice what is actually going on around us, accept life as it is, and use that information to progress through committed action, we are more likely to stay psychologically flexible and achieve emotional balance.

HARRY POTTER THERAPY

This is a method that I developed for those people suffering from mild to moderate levels of anxiety, worry, or stress, on the one hand, or mild to moderate levels of low mood or depression on the other. While this essay does not replace seeing a psychologist, psychiatrist, or physician for high levels of these problems, it can always be added to and enhance any other treatments for these conditions, without any of the bad side-effects that medications can sometimes have.

In general, this method focuses on helping us keep our emotional equilibrium when events (and our feelings about those events) seem as though they are spiraling out of control. You may have heard of Daniel Goleman's term "emotional intelligence"; this refers to the ability in our brain to be aware of our feelings and our ability to keep them in balance rather than let them be in charge and take over our thoughts and actions. Through Rowling's novels, we see how Harry navigates through very rocky physical and emotional terrain without ever losing a healthy sense of himself; perhaps we, too, can employ some of the same methods to help us in our sometimes dark and scary journeys through life and our interactions with our own Dark Lords and Death Eaters.

My approach with Harry Potter therapy uses some of the same strategies that Harry himself uses to overcome his enemies, while also incorporating some of the proven therapeutic techniques we have mentioned.

Let's look at some of the Harry Potter themes that might be useful here:

- *Bravery and courage*—the willingness to face one's problems and daring to trust and be vulnerable when sharing our story with a therapist.
- *Self (instinct) wisdom*—looking inside oneself for answers; remembering times one has triumphed and using those same skills to triumph again, rather than complaining, playing the victim, and blaming others.
- *Elder wisdom or guidance*—building and using the cheering team of family and friends (from narrative therapy), as well as the guidance of the therapist himself.
- *Hope and encouragement*—focusing on building the positive story rather than the negative past problems; constructing action plans to move forward and grow.
- *Being patient during difficult times*—mindfulness and focusing on the present moment; learning to accept difficult situations and work with them rather than reacting in an unhealthy way.

We could also look at the theme of "magic" and see how it might be useful in keeping our emotional balance and regulating our stress levels. When working with clients, I call this magic *Potions or Spells of Thought*—those things that we pay attention to from others, or the constant, ongoing ideas or beliefs that we tell ourselves about a situation and how it's going to turn out. For example, if we tell ourselves that we are never going to be successful in passing our math or socials course, it is as though we are casting a negative thought-spell or taking our own poison—we are setting ourselves up for failure. Another way in which we practice "black magic" on ourselves is when we tell ourselves something like, "I must get into that course or my life will be ruined!" Then, if for some unfortunate reason we don't get into the course, we have cast a spell for some very upsetting feelings and thoughts.

The true magic, the kind I try to create in therapy, is to turn these spells of thought into more positive, practical ways of thinking and feeling: accepting ourselves for how we have done things so far, noticing and observing our negative thoughts and becoming more mindful, and making a conscious decision to try more positive strategies in the future—thus creating the kind of "good magic" that can change a client's life. With the right tools and lots of practice, we can learn to cast "good magic" spells of thought that enhance our lives, rather than "black magic" spells that drag us down.

One tool that I find useful in helping my clients learn to cast good spells is use of the following exercises:

Harry Potter Therapy Exercises:

Step 1: Find a comfortable, quiet place to be for the next fifteen minutes (or longer if possible). Sitting comfortably (or lying down if using this to fall asleep), gently close your eyes or look down on the floor with a soft, unfocused gaze (no eye strain).

Step 2: While your eyes are closed, place your hand on your stomach to check for deep, slow diaphragm breathing; when you inhale, the stomach should gently and fully fill up and continue to the upper chest. Hold your breath for a second before gently pulling the stomach in as the breath is exhaled fully and held out for a second, and then repeat the cycle. If possible, inhale through the nose and exhale through the mouth, as if breathing out through a straw. Once you have this cycle going, you can bring the hand on your stomach to a more comfortable position.

Step 3: Remember a time or an experience you had when you were quiet, peaceful, and relaxed (e.g., a favorite sunset you'll always remember). Keeping your eyes closed and your breathing deep and slow, focus your mind on this peaceful memory for as long as you can.

Step 4: Now, with your eyes still closed and the deep diaphragm breathing going, bring to mind one of the important people who guide and supporte Harry (e.g., Dumbledore, Sirius, Hagrid, McGonagall, or even his parents). You might even choose Harry himself. Imagine this character standing by your side and gently whispering words of encouragement in your ear. What would this person be saying to you? Well, if you are suffering from anxiety, you might imagine hearing words like, "Take it easy; you can be brave now with me here; keep remembering your courage; remember we are all with you now to cheer you on," etc. Or, if you're feeling down and miserable, you might imagine them saying, "It's okay, hold on, things will get better; they always do," or, "Remember your courage and bravery; remember your inner wisdom; don't listen to those bad thought spells. Find the vision or picture of what you can do about this." If you could imagine having a meeting with all of Harry's mentors to look for solutions to this problem, what do you think their ideas would be?

Like any change in our lives, learning to cast positive spells of thought instead of negative takes PRACTICE. Thus, to get the most benefit from Harry Potter therapy, it is best to practice it regularly, even daily, in order to be in top shape for when you might really need it.

Particularly for young school-aged boys these days, there seems to be an ever-stronger pressure to be physically aggressive and maintain a "tough" posture as the only method to gain acceptance. Harry Potter can be a great model for those boys who don't fit that mold, where bravery and courage to face ourselves and reality can be more heroic than bullying and aggression. All of us, though, no matter what our age, could benefit from Harry Potter therapy and Harry's model of bravery, courage, and trust. Long live that image and may the story continue forever!

NEIL MULHOLLAND, Ph.D., was born and raised in Glasgow, Scotland. He is presently a senior psychologist in child and family psychiatry at the Glenrose Rehabilitation Hospital in Edmonton, Canada, and consults to several health teams in the region. He also runs a small private practice for kids and adults, where he often uses Harry Potter as a therapeutic tool. In 1979, after spending ten years in the deserts of Arizona and New Mexico, Dr. Mulholland graduated from Arizona State University. He then returned to Vancouver, Canada, and spent twenty years there before moving to the prairies of Alberta. According to the online quizzes, he's a bit of a Mr. Weasley.

REFERENCES

Narrative Therapy:
Morgan, A. *What is Narrative Therapy?* Dulwich, Australia: Dulwich Ctr. Pub., 2000.
White, M. and D. Epston. *Narrative Means to Therapeutic Ends.* New York: Norton & Co., 1990.

Cognitive Behavior Therapy:
Friedberg, R.D. and J. M. McClure. *Clinical Practice of Cognitive Therapy with Children and Adolescents: The Nuts and Bolts.* New York: Guilford Press, 2002.

Rapee, R.M. et al. *Helping Your Anxious Child*. California: New Harber Pub, 2000.

EMDR:
Shapiro, F. *Eye Movement Desensitization and Reprocessing*. New York: Guilford Press, 1995.
Van der Kolk et al. *Traumatic Stress*. New York: Guilford Press, 1996.

Mindfulness/Acceptance-Commitment Therapy
Eiffert, G., M. McKay, J. P. Forsyth. *ACT on Life, Not on Anger*. Oakland, CA: New Harbinger Pub., 2006.
Germer, G. K., R. D. Siegal, P. R. Fulton. *Mindfulness and Psychotherapy*. New York: Guilford Press, 2005.
Hayes, S. C. et al, (eds). *Mindfulness and Acceptance*. New York: Guilford Press, 2004.
Orsillo, S. M. et al, *Acceptance and Mindfulness: Based Approaches to Anxiety*. New York: Springer, 2005.

Rippetoe explores the magic of cognitive theory, a potent technique for helping patients with their psychological issues. This essay discusses the destructive power of negative thinking and the different ways we can actually form our thoughts and beliefs in ways that cause us problems. The power of cognitive thinking in fighting these erroneous thoughts and the relationship between cognitive therapy and spell casting is explored.

PATRICIA A. RIPPETOE, PH.D.

Defense Against the Real Dark Arts

AT THE BEGINNING of *Harry Potter and the Half-Blood Prince*, both wizarding and Muggle worlds are in upheaval. Fear and gloom pervade both universes as a dismayed Prime Minister of Great Britain stands in his Downing Street office with the newly deposed Minister of Magic, Cornelius Fudge, and Fudge's successor, Rufus Scrimgeour. Upon hearing word of Lord Voldemort's return and the ensuing mayhem, the Prime Minister gazes hopelessly for a moment at the pair of them, then finally blurts out in frustration: "'But for heaven's sake— you're *wizards*! You can do *magic*! Surely you can sort out—well— anything!'" (*Half-Blood Prince* 18). By the time the Prime Minister speaks these words, Harry Potter is about to begin his sixth year at Hogwarts School of Witchcraft and Wizardry, where he will continue his Defense Against the Dark Arts studies. Yet, despite Harry's five years of Dark Arts study (albeit with some pretty incompetent professors), Voldemort is more powerful than ever, and the final showdown between the two looms ominously. And, as *Half-Blood Prince* closes, Harry knows, in refusing Scrimgeour's protection, that the Ministry can't sort out his problems any more, it seems, than his beloved Dumbledore could.

But Harry has learned a great deal at Hogwarts—about himself, his parents, his teachers, and about Voldemort. However, insight into the early lives of his family and Tom Riddle is not the most important thing that the Boy Who Lived has acquired in his years at Hogwarts. In learning to fight Voldemort and the Dark Arts, Harry has also learned to fight more unlikely monsters—the fear, anger, anxiety, and depression that have at times haunted his thoughts and feelings since we've known him. And whether or not, in the end, we Muggles are ever forced to stand against Voldemort, many of us battle the dark veils of fear, depression, and anger just as terrible as Harry's.

Harry Potter has fought his darkest thoughts with powerful spells. But Muggles haven't the ability to flick wands and recite incantations to dispel negative feelings, though they affect us the way joy-thieving Dementors and lurking Boggarts afflict the hearts and minds of the wizarding community. Yet luckily, some of Harry's most potent spells mimic techniques Muggle psychologists and other qualified psychotherapists use in a highly successful form of treatment—*cognitive therapy*.

ERRONEOUS THINKING

Cognition refers to thought, knowledge, and belief. The central construct of cognitive therapy (Beck) is that emotions are largely determined by what we believe is true about ourselves, the world we live in, and the future. But, if cognition is flawed—if our self-talk is illogical, unrealistic, or distorted—the result can be a range of negative emotions that leads to unhappiness, bitterness, and alienation. To see how belief can affect emotion, look at a situation that occurs early in *Harry Potter and the Order of the Phoenix*.

The Dursleys have been lured from Privet Drive by a bogus awards competition. Harry is alone in the darkened house and hears a loud crash. He bolts from his bed and snatches his wand. He is on alert, ready to fight, but his heart is in his throat and it's thumping uncontrollably. Soon, he realizes that the crowd of murky shapes gathered at the foot of his stairs is a rescue party. And, when Harry recognizes the voice of his old friend, Professor Lupin, we are told his heart "leapt," and he pockets his wand (*Order of the Phoenix* 47). He does this because his original belief has changed. Recognizing his friends alters his earlier, incorrect assumption (that a dangerous break-in was occurring) to a correct perception based on accurate knowledge (that he is in receipt of an unconventional visit from trusted friends). His interpretation of the event moves him from the faulty belief, "I am in danger," to the correct one, "I am safe," and his emotions follow. Therefore, Harry's initial fear and subsequent relief are completely dependent on his perception of the visitors.

Muggles can be as frightened as Harry is that night. What if, before you go to bed, you sling a large robe over your closet door? Then, waking up in the middle of the night, you glance toward the closet where a dark shape looms. Imagine your initial reaction. You would probably spring up, your heart would race, your palms might sweat, and the hair at the back of your neck might prickle. These are all symptoms of fear. And, although you have no wand to grab, you reach for something with which to protect yourself—or you prepare to flee. But an instant later, you remember—the robe. What happens then? You immediately calm down, your heart rate slows; and, although you want to kick yourself for not remembering the robe, you can lie back down and return to sleep. Yet what has changed? The robe is still there—it is still the same shape, size, and color. The only thing that has changed is your interpretation of it. At first you incorrectly perceived a threat, and your emotions responded appropriately with fear and the desire to fight or flee. When you realize it is a robe, your inaccurate belief in imminent danger disappears and fear vanishes.

When our cognitions are so incorrect that they negatively affect the way we see our world, our future prospects, and ourselves, they become destructive. Troubled emotions such as depression, anxiety, and inappropriate anger can result. Numerous practitioners and researchers have identified a great number of cognitive distortions that lead to self-defeating thoughts and resulting painful feelings (Ellis, Beck, & Westermeyer). David Burns, M.D., a psychiatrist and researcher of cognitive therapy, also discusses numerous thought errors in *Feeling Good: The New Mood Therapy*. Below is his list of the most common errors, and from them we can see that cognitive mistakes aren't limited to the Muggle world:

All-or-Nothing Thinking

This thought error is also known as black-or-white thinking, and it occurs when there is no self-forgiveness for being less than perfect. The middle ground doesn't exist, and if you are not a hero you are a failure. In *Order of the Phoenix*, this cognitive distortion is painfully evident in Harry's thinking following his mission to rescue Sirius Black. After the disaster at the Ministry, Harry is inconsolable because he could not save his godfather. He believes he has failed completely, although he succeeded that night in fighting powerful Death Eaters, protecting his friends, and surviving Voldemort's possession of him.

Overgeneralization

In this cognitive error, you believe that if a situation produces negative outcomes once, then that situation will produce a negative result every time. Think of Ron Weasley's overwhelming fear in assuming the Keeper position on Gryffindor's Quidditch team. During tryouts, he proves he is a good player, but during training, Ron is flustered by Slytherin heckling and makes numerous mistakes. Ron's playing deteriorates because he believes he will continue to embarrass himself as Keeper. It isn't until Ron alters his self-talk to "*[Y]ou can do this*" that he gains the confidence to lead Gryffindor to the winning cup (*Order of the Phoenix* 704).

Mental Filter

This thought distortion occurs when you dwell on negatives and filter out positives in a situation—even if the positives outnumber the negatives. In *Half-Blood Prince*, Hermione seems unable to rejoice in the fact that she achieves ten O's and one E on her O.W.L.s. Ron accuses her of being disappointed in her grades and, although she denies it, we know she has focused only on her slightly less-than-perfect E in Defense Against the Dark Arts rather than her multitude of O's.

Discounting the Positives

With this erroneous thought, you believe that your positive achievements, accomplishments, and qualities aren't really that important. In *Half-Blood Prince*, Neville Longbottom, who has always struggled at Hogwarts, receives on his O.W.L.s an O in Herbology and an E in both Charms and Defense Against the Dark Arts. But he is still miserable and anxious as he confers with Professor McGonagall about his course schedule. The high scores are not valuable to him because his formidable grandmother convinces him his best subject is a "soft option" (*Half-Blood Prince* 174). Only when Neville discovers that the august Mrs. Longbottom failed *her* Charms O.W.L. does he believe he has accomplished something important.

Jumping to Conclusions

Two forms of this thought distortion are (a) *mind reading*—assuming people are rejecting you without any evidence that they are, and (b) *fortune telling*—an incorrect prediction that things will turn out badly without any real evidence that they will.

Assuming you do not have Professor Trelawney's elusive gift of second sight and that you have not mastered the Legilimens Spell, you cannot read minds. But often we believe we know what others are thinking and reach incorrect conclusions. In *Order of the Phoenix*, Harry makes an incorrect assumption regarding Dumbledore's aloofness toward him. He feels abandoned and neglected by the headmaster and doesn't consider alternative explanations for Dumbledore's behavior. Harry's faulty belief contributes a great deal to his anger in his fifth year because he believes Dumbledore has rejected him—despite all Harry has done to fight Voldemort's evil.

Although in *Harry Potter and the Prisoner of Azkaban* Hermione disdains Professor Trelawney's Divination class, in *Order of the Phoenix* we find her unwittingly engaging in fortune telling—the second kind of conclusion jumping. By her fifth year, she is one of Hogwarts's best students ever. Yet, she has worked herself into a state of tremulous anxiety and irritability over her O.W.L. exams. She has never failed nor, we know, will she ever fail at her studies. But it is obvious that she is predicting a catastrophic outcome if she doesn't over-study, even forecasting that one mistranslation on her Ancient Runes exam could make the difference between passing and failing.

Minimization/Magnification

In this sort of unrealistic thinking, molehills become mountains and, alternatively, enormous mountains become molehills where huge positives are reduced to inconsequential occurrences. As we saw,

Neville minimizes his O.W.L. grades because his grandmother convinces him he did well in soft subjects only.

But when it comes to their son Dudley, Uncle Vernon and Aunt Petunia are good examples of flawed thinking that magnifies small difficulties by believing them to be huge disasters. After Harry and Dudley's Dementor encounter in *Order of the Phoenix*, Dudley is sick and shaken but seems fine. Yet, Vernon and Petunia react irrationally, screaming, raging, and threatening to call the police. They inflate perceived harm to Dudley to catastrophic proportions and treat their bullying son as if he were an invalid.

Emotional Reasoning

This distorted thought tells you simply that you are what you feel. If you feel foolish, you are a fool. If you feel guilty, you must be guilty of something. In *Prisoner of Azkaban*, during Harry's first encounter with a Dementor, his reaction is extreme—similar to Muggle descriptions of severe panic attacks and overwhelming depression. After the encounter, he also experiences other negative emotions—shame and humiliation. He worries that his heightened reaction to the Dementors means he's weak or delicate, and when Lupin prevents Harry from tackling the class Boggart, Harry's spirits sink even lower. He begins to reason that if his unique reaction to the Dementor causes him such extreme anguish, there must be something flawed in him. It isn't until Lupin explains that Harry's response to the Dementors is more acute because of his early childhood traumas that Harry alters the belief that he is weak.

"Should" Statements

These are unrealistic standards we set for ourselves that usually end in beliefs of failure and inadequacy when we cannot achieve them. Throughout the Harry Potter series, Hermione obviously makes numerous unrealistic demands on herself. We can almost hear the internal dialogue running through her thoughts: e.g., she *should* get all O's on her O.W.L.s; she *should* effortlessly handle triple coursework in year three; she *should* have gotten her Polyjuice Potion correct (*Harry Potter and the Sorcerer's Stone*); she *should* be able to effect house-elf reform (*Harry Potter and the Goblet of Fire*). She clings stubbornly to these expectations—standards no one demands of her but herself—and is miserable on the rare occasion when she cannot live up to them.

Labeling

In this cognitive distortion, you equate a single act or event with who you are as a person. Therefore, if you make a mistake, you are stupid. If you don't get a coveted job, you are a loser. In *Order of the Phoenix*, Harry reluctantly admits to himself he believed the prefect's badge should be his. Because of his belief, he feels ill-used, angry, and jealous when Ron receives it. Based on this event, Harry mistakenly labels himself overlooked and unappreciated without regarding the mountain of evidence for why he is important. It isn't until Harry discovers that his idealized father wasn't a prefect either that Harry's spirits brighten. He cannot label his brave father a loser, therefore Harry can't possibly be one either.

Personalization/Blame

The cognitive error of personalization occurs when you blame yourself for things over which you have no control. Recall how Harry, in *Prisoner of Azkaban*, blames himself for losing the Gryffindor/ Hufflepuff game when struck senseless by Dementors during the match. Although Harry has no power over the Dementors' effects, he is sick with humiliation because of his perceived inadequacy.

In distorted blaming, you blame others for things for which you are at least partially responsible. Countless times in the Harry Potter series, Draco Malfoy shirks responsibility for his wrongdoing (e.g., the hippogriff incident in *Prisoner of Azkaban*). Why? Because Draco mistakenly believes he is entitled to do what he wants with impunity, and because he perceives himself as a member of a superior class.

Catastrophizing

This is one of the earliest illogical thoughts to be identified and was first described by Ellis, one of the fathers of cognitive therapy. Catastrophizing is an illogical cognitive leap from one's comfort zone to immediate disaster before you have any evidence that the worst-case scenario will actually happen. In *Prisoner of Azkaban*, when Harry's anger inflates Aunt Marge to near-explosive proportions, he panics and races from Privet Drive. Having broken the Ministry's restriction of underage magic, he believes he will be expelled, arrested, and cast out of the wizarding world as a criminal. Harry believes in the worst-case scenario for his actions without any evidence that the worst will happen to him. He doesn't reason based on the evidence: Marge's vicious provocation; the fact that he has Dumbledore's respect and protection; the Ministry's policy of giving alleged wrongdoers a hearing.

COGNITIVE THERAPY

Wizards and Muggles are alike in experiencing illogical thoughts that influence emotion. However, when cognitive distortions become so destructive of happiness that one is overwhelmed by anxiety, hopelessness, or inappropriate anger, it's time to seek help in changing flawed thinking—just as Harry solicits Remus Lupin to help him fight the overwhelming terror the Dementors inflict on him. To do this, Harry uses the powerful Patronus Charm (*Prisoner of Azkaban*). But Muggles are more like wizards than you might guess in how we remedy troubled emotions.

If mistaken thinking leads to negative emotion, then altering beliefs to follow a more realistic, rational train of thought will produce positive feelings. For us Muggles, unable to wield charms and enchantments, cognitive therapy strives to eliminate the distorted beliefs, assumptions, and predictions (e.g., Burns's aforementioned list) that result in common emotional problems. Cognitive therapists accomplish this by teaching clients to recognize these errors—which frequently become automatic and habitual—then replace them with more realistic interpretations of events. As a result, the cognitive therapist gives his or her client permanent tools for discarding and replacing distorted thoughts long after therapy sessions are over. Unlike many Freudian-based therapies, which troll the unknown of the unconscious mind for insights, the cognitive therapist actively partners with her client to alter conscious thought. For obvious reasons, some psychologists refer to this process as cognitive restructuring

Cognitive therapy's effectiveness has been demonstrated in a multitude of research studies (Beck). For example, recent research (DeRubeis et al.; Hollon et al.) found that cognitive therapy was as successful as medication in treating moderate to severe depression, and that cognitive therapy's effects were more long-lasting than those obtained from a time-limited course of medication only. A review of controlled clinical trials in the United States, Great Britain, Germany, the Netherlands, and Sweden (Clark) shows that cognitive therapy is also a very effective treatment for panic disorder with a 74 percent to 94 percent success and longevity rate.

Therapists employ many techniques to change illogical thought patterns. Some of the most common train clients to question the evidence for a belief, to de-catastrophize by challenging the inevitability of the worst-case scenario, to explore less grave consequences and explanations for events, and to examine "the gray area" rather than only black-or-white options. Dr. Martin Seligman, in his book *Learned Optimism*, urges illogical thinkers first to examine if the evidence justifies a negative belief. Second, he suggests you search for possible explanations for an outcome or event other than the one that is most negative for you (this might have helped Harry in year five as Professor Dumbledore distances himself from Harry). Third, he recommends—even if the evidence exists and your interpretation of it is correct—that you question your conclusions.

For example, as *Half-Blood Prince* ends, things truly are grim. Dumbledore is dead; Hogwarts will be shut down; some of the finest Ministry wizards have been murdered; the Order of the Phoenix is in chaos after Snape's betrayal; and, because of the Horcruxes, Voldemort has several leases on life. It would be easy for Harry to believe it's hopeless and give up. But Harry doesn't come to that conclusion. Despite all the evidence for despair, he believes there is hope and he will go on until Voldemort is dead.

COGNITIVE MAGIC

Cognitive restructuring, once learned, is a skill always possessed, and its effects continue long after those of medication, which treats symptoms but does not change the underlying thought processes causing them. Similarly, in Harry's world of wizards, once a spell is learned, it is a skill forever possessed—far longer than time-limited potions and more useful than the insights Harry gains from Dumbledore's Pensieve. Remember in *Goblet of Fire* when an under-prepared Harry struggles to learn the elusive Summoning Charm for his Triwizard dragon challenge? At the time, he doesn't realize that his enduring mastery of it will aid him much later in the story as he barely escapes the resurrected Voldemort.

But the similarity between spell casting and cognitive therapy doesn't end with their relative permanence. Many of the powerful spells and charms Harry learns require more than an incantation and flick of the wand. To be successful, they require cognitive focus and strength of thought. As Hermione patiently teaches Harry the Summoning Charm, she tells him to "'concentrate'" (*Goblet of Fire* 345). But a frustrated Harry replies that he's trying but "'a great big dragon keeps popping up in my head…'" (*Goblet of Fire* 345). Until he eliminates this image, he cannot master the charm. In that same volume, the faux Mad-Eye Moody casts an Imperius Spell on Harry, but Harry does not succumb. Why? Harry stops before he jumps to the desk, then cognitively challenges faux-Moody's command, telling himself it would be illogical and silly to obey. Because Harry fights to keep his rational beliefs intact, Moody is ultimately unable to control Harry's mind. Also, in *Half-Blood Prince*, by directing cognition, sixth-year students begin learning the advanced art of nonverbal magic in casting incantation-free spells. Among the most difficult is Apparition. To accomplish the spell, students attack a complex cognitive process—the three D's. As they practice, Instructor Twycross teaches them to fix their minds on Destination, to be Determined to occupy that destination, and to move with Deliberation. To Susan Bones's chagrin, she splinches from her left leg because her mind, Twycross explains, was insufficiently "'determined'" (*Half-Blood Prince* 385).

However, some spells borrow more deeply from cognitive therapy by requiring wizards actually to change or replace thoughts. The rudiments of the Riddikulus and Patronus Charms, first described in *Prisoner of Azkaban*, demonstrate clearly the necessity—even in the wizarding world—for changing thought processes to master powerful defenses against the Dark side. Professor Lupin has a solution for terror when the class Boggart shape-shifts into each student's greatest fear, and his ensuing lesson on the Riddikulus Charm is lifted directly from cognitive therapy. For the spell to work, each student must restructure his or her thoughts to perceive the feared object as comical. If the student self-talks and alters his or her belief in apparent danger, the Boggart will disappear. This spell is similar to de-catastrophizing in cognitive therapy, i.e., questioning evidence and generating alternative explanations to help change misconceptions about negative feelings and events. But in *Order of the Phoenix*, Mrs. Weasley's fears for her family are quite rational. So, when the Boggart at Grimmauld Place causes her to catastrophize about their deaths, she cannot cognitively generate any alternatives to this possibility—much less a comical one—and her Riddikulus Charm is unsuccessful. As a result, poor Molly, wracked with anguish, succumbs to the Boggart.

When it comes to Dementors, Harry's fear is reasonable, too. As third-year classes begin, he has already suffered the Dementors' dreadful influence, and they provide Harry with some of the darkest times in his six years at Hogwarts. By reliving the overwhelming terror of his parents' murders, he is overcome by negative emotion and despairs of happiness. But the wise Lupin has a solution for Harry's fear in the powerful Patronus Charm, and once again its success depends on altered cognition. A Patronus represents what healthy, rational minds need to survive unhappiness, e.g., hope, happiness, optimism, and the desire to persevere regardless. It is a shield against Darkness that works only if the caster focuses intently on happy memories. But as Harry learns the charm, he has difficulty concentrating. His mother's screams still haunt him, and his Patronus is initially feeble. Then, in altered time, when Harry witnesses himself producing the stag Patronus, he finally changes his beliefs and perceives himself as strong and capable of so much happiness that he successfully produces his own Patronus against hundreds of attacking Dementors (*Prisoner of Azkaban*).

In *Order of the Phoenix*, we see Mrs. Weasley fail at the Riddikulus Charm. But why doesn't Harry, who becomes so adept in the advanced magic of the Patronus Charm, master Occlumency—another powerful cognitive skill that seals a wizard's mind against magical intrusion? If Harry had successfully learned this spell and shielded his thoughts from flawed beliefs, he would have prevented Voldemort from manipulating him with the inaccurate mental images that ultimately contributed to Sirius's death.

Harry's failure to learn this spell is tragic, but the explanation is simple. Muggle therapy and wizard mentoring require more than technique. A good therapeutic relationship between psychologist and client is essential for change to occur. And, as Harry's Occlumency teacher, Snape was functionally a therapist—probing Harry's thoughts and challenging him to alter his cognitions. But the animosity, mistrust, and disrespect between them screamed against the healthy therapeutic relationship, which fosters mutual trust, confidence, empathy, and respect. As a result Harry, sadly, did not—would not—learn the spell.

On the fourth floor of St. Mungo's Hospital for Magical Maladies and Injuries, there must be wizarding equivalents to the cognitive therapist; I hope that the healers there have enough of Arthur Weasley's curiosity about Muggles to learn from their non-wizarding counterparts. And although the courageous Longbottoms and the disturbingly blank Gilderoy Lockhart still languish on that locked ward, their minds broken by powerful magic, I like to think that many wizards are treated and cured on Ward Four. These patients would be treated with counter-hexes that attack the curses of Dark thought and overwhelming emotion. There should be as many of these spells as there are Muggle strategies for identifying and changing the flawed thinking that results in negative emotion. Perhaps Professor Trelawney—miraculously—developed a counter-divination spell to prevent patients from believing they know what the future holds. Or maybe Madam Pomfrey whipped up a comforting spell for the lonely and unsure who lack belief in their abilities. And it's possible that Professor Flitwick perfected a cognitive-error charm that displays in elaborate, glittering diagram the errors in a low-spirited witch or wizard's thinking.

Wizards and Muggles alike make errors in thinking, and the Dark Arts that Muggles confront are as frightening and overwhelming as what Harry must ultimately face. And although wizards alone are gifted with magical abilities to fight the evils they encounter, we Muggles aren't out of luck. Witches and wizards must always worry about curses and counter magic. But fortunately, once we Muggles learn to eliminate illogical and distorted thought, we no longer need worry what new weapons the enemy will use against us.

The great appeal of the Harry Potter series is the idea of a secret world whose inhabitants possess special powers to fight darkness. And, in the Harry Potter books, the wizarding world and the Muggle world must never collide. But fear, anxiety, and depression don't differentiate between wizard and Muggle. Harry, by using powerful magic, has learned to defend quite well against the negative feelings that still strike him.

How comforting to know that a bit of the wizarding world is available to us Muggles, and that in times of great Darkness we, too, can learn, from a good cognitive therapist, to cast spells against the Darkness.

———

PATRICIA A. RIPPETOE, Ph.D., is a clinical psychologist and fantasy writer. She obtained her Ph.D. in psychology from the University of Alabama, and her research on protection motivation theory and breast-cancer detection was named the psychology department's outstanding dissertation for 1985. As an assistant professor in the University of Alabama at Birmingham Medical Center's department of psychiatry, she taught psychology students at the graduate level, as well as psychology interns and psychiatry residents. For the last eighteen years, Dr. Rippetoe has treated hundreds of adult patients in solo practice using cognitive therapy techniques. In 2005, she was admitted to the annual Viable Paradise Workshop for writers of science fiction and fantasy. She is available for consultations at St. Mungo's (send owls to office, please), and hopes one day to find her way to Platform 9¾.

REFERENCES

Beck, A.T. *Cognitive Therapies and the Emotional Disorders*. New York: International Press, 1976.

A. T. Beck, "Cognitive Therapy: Past, Present, and Future," *Journal of Consulting and Clinical Psychology* 61 (1993): 194–198.

———, "The Current State of Cognitive Therapy: A 40-Year Retrospective," *Archives of General Psychiatry* 62 (2005): 953–959.

Burns, D.D. *Feeling Good: The New Mood Therapy*. Avon Books, 1999.

D. M. Clark, "A Cognitive Approach to Panic Disorder," *Behaviour Research and Therapy* 24 (1986): 461–70.

Clark, D. M. "Panic Disorder and Social Phobia." In D. M. Clark and C. G. Fairburn (Eds.), *Science and Practice of Cognitive Behaviour Therapy*. New York: Oxford University Press, 1997.

Robert J. DeRubeis, Steven D. Hollon, Jay D. Amsterdam, Richard C. Shelton, Paula R. Young, Ronald M. Salomon, John P. O'Reardon, Margaret L. Lovett, Madeline M.Gladis, Laurel L. Brown, and Robert Gallop, "Cognitive Therapy vs. Medications in the Treatment of Moderate to Severe Depression," *Archives of General Psychiatry* 62 (2005): 409–416.

Ellis, A. *Reason and Emotion in Psychotherapy*. New York: Lyle Stuart, 1962.

Ellis, A. "Rational Emotive Behavior Therapy." In M. Hersen & W.H. Sledge (Eds.), *Encyclopedia of Psychotherapy*. San Diego: Academic Press, 2002.

Steven D. Hollon, Robert J. DeRubeis, Richard C. Shelton, Jay D. Amsterdam, Ronald M. Salomon, John P. O'Reardon, Margaret L. Lovett, Paula R. Young, Kirsten L. Haman, Brent B. Freeman, and Robert Gallop, "Prevention of Relapse Following Cognitive Therapy vs. Medications in Moderate to Severe Depression," *Archives of General Psychiatry* 62 (2005): 417–422.

Rowling, J. K. *Harry Potter and the Sorcerer's Stone*. New York: Scholastic Inc., 1998.

———. *Harry Potter and the Prisoner of Azkaban*. New York: Scholastic Inc., 1999.

———. *Harry Potter and the Goblet of Fire*. New York: Scholastic Inc., 2000.

———. *Harry Potter and the Order of the Phoenix*. New York: Scholastic Inc., 2003.

———. *Harry Potter and the Half-Blood Prince*. New York: Scholastic Inc., 2005.

Seligman, Martin E.P. *Learned Optimism: How to Change Your Mind And Your Life*. New York: Simon and Shuster, 1998.

Westermeyer, Robert. *Kicking Depression's Ugly Butt*. St. Louis: Quick Publishing, LC, 2004.

SUGGESTED READING

Burns, David D. *Feeling Good: The New Mood Therapy*. New York: Avon Books (revised ed.), 1999.

Burns, David D. *The Feeling Good Handbook*. New York: Plume (revised ed.), 1999.

Seligman, Martin E. P. *Learned Optimism: How to Change Your Mind And Your Life*. New York: Simon and Shuster, 1998.

Seligman, Martin E. P. *Authentic Happiness*. New York: The Free Press, 2002.

Westermeyer, Robert. *Kicking Depression's Ugly Butt*. Quick Publishing, St. Louis: LC, 2004.

Uncredited. "Harry Potter Encyclopedia: Spells." *MuggleNet Home Page*. <http://www.mugglenet.com/info/other/spells.shtml>.

Green asks: Do the Harry Potter books encourage us to be disobedient? Does Dumbledore encourage Harry to resist the influence of leaders and peers? The scientific research shows that we are disturbingly willing to obey leadership, even when asked to do things that are clearly wrong. However, having friends who stand by us no matter what, such as Harry had, can help us stand up to make our own choices, in spite of pressure or bullying.

MELANIE C. GREEN, Ph.D.

Resisting Social Influence
Lessons from Harry Potter

Resisting SOCIAL INFLUENCE can be terribly difficult—but it can also be incredibly important. In the world of Harry Potter, just as in our own world, heroism comes from standing up for one's beliefs, even if that means going against the group or breaking the rules.[1] This focus on moral courage is clear from the beginning of J. K. Rowling's series. In the very first Harry Potter book, *Harry Potter and the Sorcerer's Stone*, the last few points awarded to Gryffindor House, the ones that push them over the edge to win the House cup over the hated Slytherins, are awarded to Neville Longbottom (a classmate of Harry's, better known for his forgetfulness and blunders). Did Neville single-handedly face down the evil villain Voldemort? Did he battle a fearsome magical creature? Did he perform an amazing spell? No, none of the above. Neville

---

[1] Indeed, this very emphasis on following one's heart even if it means breaking school rules is part of why some parents want the Harry Potter books banned from schools or libraries—because the books, in some sense, celebrate disobedience.

earned those points for his attempt to stop Harry, Ron, and Hermione from sneaking out of the dormitory. In Dumbledore's words, "'It takes a great deal of bravery to stand up to our enemies, but just as much to stand up to our friends'" (*Sorcerer's Stone* 306).

How and when are people able to resist pressure from others? There's no magical solution to this problem (although parents of teenagers would certainly rest easier if they could give their offspring an Anti-Peer-Pressure Potion). Courage is certainly part of the story, but social psychology tells us that features of the situation can have a powerful effect as well. In other words, what is going on around us can be as powerful an influence on our behavior as our own internal beliefs.

POWER

Let's begin at the beginning. How does someone exert control over another person in the first place? Social psychologists have identified five different bases of interpersonal power: reward power, coercive power, legitimate power, expert power, and referent power (French & Raven). Each of these types of power are on display in the world of Harry Potter.

Reward power is just as it sounds: the ability to provide help, benefits, or other rewards ("positive reinforcement," in psychological language). The teachers at Hogwarts have this kind of power. They can award points to the different Houses, thus helping them win the House cup at the end of the year.

Coercive power is the flip side—the Dark side, if you will—of reward power. Instead of providing rewards, people with coercive power have the ability to deliver threats and punishment. Of course, these types of power are not mutually exclusive. (The Hogwarts teachers can take points away as easily as they can award them.) But the biggest wielder of coercive power in Harry Potter is Voldemort himself, along with his crew of Death Eaters. Their willingness to use Unforgivable Curses to kill and torture is a powerful source of influence throughout wizard society—so powerful that wizards fear to even speak Voldemort's name.

Legitimate power often stems from a person's role or position, such as being the leader of an organization. This power is based in shared values. Subordinates believe that the leader has a right to exert influence, and willingly follow along. Oliver Wood, the captain of the Gryffindor Quidditch team, holds this kind of power. The players show up for practices when he schedules them and take his lead on team strategy.

Expert power is just like the old saying: knowledge is power. Harry shows this kind of power when he leads the secret Defense Against the Dark Arts lessons (Dumbledore's Army) in *Harry Potter and the Order of the Phoenix*. Some of the students who show up for the first meeting in the Hogshead bar are skeptical about following Harry's leadership, but once they hear about his success against dragons, Dementors, and the Dark Lord himself, they're convinced. Of course, Hermione exerts this type of power as well. Although Ron and Harry may call her a know-it-all, they are often willing to follow her lead, because they realize she reads and remembers more of their lessons than they do.

Referent power comes from being liked or admired. It includes charisma and fame. Dumbledore's influence over Harry does not stop when Dumbledore is gone from Hogwarts (as in *Order of the Phoenix*, when Dolores Umbridge takes over as headmistress); rather, it is Harry's respect and affection for the older wizard that makes him, as Rufus Scrimgeour says, "'Dumbledore's man, through and through'" (*Harry Potter and the Half-Blood Prince* 348).

Exploring these different types of power highlights another important point: sometimes it is best *not* to resist social influence. In everyday life, there are benefits to obeying the police, following directions from the boss, and getting along with the group. After all, if no one obeyed rules, society would descend into chaos and anarchy. If we never followed what other people were doing, we would miss out on valuable learning opportunities. But a key distinction is understanding when power-holders are using their influence for good rather than evil.

Sometimes one source of power masquerades as another. In *Order of the Phoenix*, Dolores Umbridge has the trappings of legitimate power. She has an imposing title (Hogwarts High Inquisitor) and claims to speak for the Ministry of Magic. However, it becomes clear that most of the other professors at Hogwarts do not view her authority as legitimate at all. Instead, people follow Umbridge's orders because of her coercive power—her ability to fire teachers she does not like (Professor Trelawny), to bar students from their favorite activities (banning Harry and the Weasley twins from the Quidditch team), and even imposing physical harm (making Harry write lines with his own blood). Coercive power has its limits, though: if people feel they can disobey without being punished, they will often do so. For instance, the other professors don't help Umbridge when the Weasley twins set off a barrage of fireworks in the hallways.

Of course, an individual can hold more than one type of power. Dumbledore has legitimate power through his role as headmaster of Hogwarts, expert power due to his intelligence and wizarding skill, and referent power due to the affection and admiration that others feel for him. Harry's fame as the Boy Who Lived sometimes gives him referent power (think of Colin Creevey following him in wide-eyed admiration!), and his growing mastery of magic gives him increasing expert power. Understanding what type of power a person holds helps us predict who will follow that person's direction and what the consequences of that power will be. Using coercive power can create resentment, whereas expert power typically does not. Reward and coercive power may only work in a specific circumstance (when a teacher is watching), whereas referent or legitimate power may be more far-reaching.

JUST DO IT

Even if we know where power comes from, we are still left with the question of how people go about resisting social influence. Let's take the most straightforward idea: maybe Harry is able to defy authority figures and his peers because of his morals and beliefs alone. What does psychological research have to say about that possibility?

Research on attitudes and persuasion tells us that some types of attitudes are more likely to lead to behavior than other types. Think about your feelings toward a particular brand of ballpoint pens (or quills, if you prefer). You probably don't care much. If someone gave you a pen that wasn't your favorite brand, you probably wouldn't throw it down in disgust and refuse to use it. If you had to talk about why a particular pen is your favorite, you probably wouldn't have much to say. But now think about your attitude toward your favorite Harry Potter character, your political party, or a food you hate. You probably know exactly how you feel about these attitude objects. For most of us, attitudes toward ballpoint pens are what psychologists call *weak attitudes*. These opinions are easily changeable and do not necessarily predict behavior. On the other hand, we also have *strong attitudes*, such as our politics, food preferences, or favorite characters. These attitudes are important to us, we hold them with certainty, and they come quickly and easily to mind (Petty & Krosnick). Strong attitudes lead to attitude-consistent behavior; if we can't stand Cockroach Clusters (a particularly unappealing type of wizard candy), we'll avoid them every time we go to Honeydukes Sweetshop.

Thinking hard about or elaborating on an attitude object helps to create a strong attitude. Harry has certainly spent a lot of time thinking about Voldemort. In fact, you might even say that Harry is obsessed with him.

Direct experience with an attitude object also helps to create a strong attitude. Unlike almost all the other students at Hogwarts, Harry has gone head-to-head with Voldemort and his Death Eaters. He does not have to rely on rumors or stories in the *Daily Prophet*, the wizarding newspaper. Each confrontation with Voldemort strengthens Harry's understanding of Voldemort's evil.

And as for importance, it is hard to imagine a more significant event than having one's parents murdered. Voldemort changes Harry's life in a fundamental way and is a continuing threat not only to Harry's very existence, but to the wizarding way of life as a whole. If that doesn't create a strong attitude, it's hard to imagine what would.

So, Harry has a rock-solid strong attitude and a clear idea of the right thing to do: defeat Voldemort. It's as simple as choosing good over evil. Right?

Well, not quite. Strong attitudes are a good start, but research in social psychology tells us that it often takes more than just *knowing* the right thing to *do* the right thing.

ILLUSION OF INVULNERABILITY

One obstacle to resisting illegitimate influence is the failure to recognize our vulnerability to it. We think that others might be fooled by persuasive attempts or lured in by conformity pressures, but that we ourselves are far too wise to fall for these tactics. (Communication researchers refer to this as the "third person effect.") For instance, one study of energy conservation messages gave people one of four reasons to conserve: to help the environment, to save money, to benefit society, or because conservation was common in their neighbor-hood. Which of these appeals do you think recipients said was *least* convincing? Right, the "everyone else is doing it" message. But which one led to the *most* conservation (as measured by people's actual elec-tricity use)? Surprise—it was the "everyone else is doing it" message. People often do not realize how much their actions are determined by the actions of others (Cialdini).

In *Harry Potter and the Goblet of Fire*, Percy Weasley, Ron's pomp-ous older brother, is so sure of himself that he does not even realize that his boss (Mr. Crouch) is under the spell of a Death Eater—surely an illegitimate authority!

How can people overcome this illusion? Just telling people that the illusion or bias exists does not seem to solve the problem. A bet-ter way is to demonstrate to people that they have been fooled be-fore. A study by social psychologist Brad Sagarin and his colleagues (Sagarin, Cialdini, Rice, & Serna) showed people an ad with an il-legitimate authority—a model (someone with no real credentials or knowledge about the stock market) dressed as a stockbroker adver-tising a financial service. Most people were taken in by this ad, find-ing it at least somewhat convincing. When they learned about their mistake, they were less likely to be persuaded by later ads featuring illegitimate authorities.

Ginny Weasley demonstrates this "once bitten, twice shy" princi-ple: after falling prey to Voldemort's old diary in *Harry Potter and the Chamber of Secrets*, she warns Harry against following the scribbled instructions in the margins of his Potions book in *Half-Blood Prince*. She has learned not to trust mysterious books—but of course Harry, having not had the same experience, does not heed her advice.

Sometimes, though, just recognizing that we are vulnerable is not enough—we need a little more help to resist social pressure.

I GET BY WITH A LITTLE HELP FROM MY FRIENDS

A series of studies by Solomon Asch demonstrated the power of group influence in the laboratory. In these studies, an unsuspecting partici-pant thinks he is going to be part of a visual perception experiment. He arrives at the laboratory and is seated at the end of a table with five other participants. They are told that their task is simply to look at a set of lines on a card that the experimenter holds up and say which of three other lines matches a target line. Pretty easy, right? Sure, it seems that way at first. They each give their answer out loud, going around the table. But then something strange happens. After a few rounds, the other participants start giving the wrong answer. They all say B when anyone with half an eyeball could see that line C is the one that matches the target. And then on the next card they give the wrong answer again, and then again on the following round.

What's going on here? In Harry Potter's world, we might think that the other participants had fallen under a Confundus Charm! But in reality, the "other participants" were actually all working with the experimenter, and the study was not on visual perception at all. Instead, what Asch really wanted to know was how people would respond to this conformity pressure from others. Would the participant follow the evidence of his own two eyes, or would he cave in and give the same wrong answer as the others in the group?

In this case, the "eyes" didn't have it: 75 percent of the people in Asch's study conformed (gave the same wrong answer as the others) on at least one round, and one-third conformed on the majority of the trials.

The fear of being the odd man out, of looking foolish and being embarrassed, was too much to resist. Social psychologists call this *normative social influence*, the desire to fit in with and be accepted by others. Indeed, Harry himself illustrates the pain of being different: think of all the times he flattens down his hair over his scar and wishes that he could be just like the other kids, or yells at Ron and Hermione when they do not seem to understand what he is going through. And much of the Dursleys' behavior is motivated by what the neighbors might think of them. They hate magic because their association with it would mark them as abnormal.

Social psychology tells us that the situation can be a powerful influence on how we behave. Asch made one slight change to the situation and reduced conformity considerably—he gave the participant an ally, one other person who was going against the group. It didn't matter whether this ally gave the right answer; even if he gave a different wrong answer from the group, conformity was still reduced. Being one of two outsiders is a much different experience from being the only one.

For Harry, the fact that Ron and Hermione stand by him and believe in him is an incredibly important source of support. They not only help him get through physical and mental challenges (like overcoming the obstacles guarding the Sorcerer's Stone), but they also help him stand up for himself. In contrast, Ginny becomes vulnerable to Voldemort's tricks—writing in Tom Riddle's old diary, which eventually leads her to open the Chamber of Secrets—at a time when she feels all alone and as if no one understands her. In *Order of the Phoenix*, the Sorting Hat reminds the students that they must stick together. The Hat's wisdom is far-reaching: friends and allies are important ingredients in resisting social pressure, as well as fighting enemies.

UNDER MY SPELL

In the wizarding world, the Imperious Curse—a powerful and unforgivable spell—makes people obey the commands of others, even leading innocent people to commit murder. In our world, social influence does not always require such an all-encompassing force. In perhaps the most famous set of studies in social psychology, Stanley Milgram showed that people would obey authority, even when that authority went against some of their most fundamental values.

In Milgram's study, a participant arrived at a laboratory at Yale University, along with a pleasant, middle-aged man. The experimenter explained that the study was about the effect of punishment on learning. The participant was "randomly" selected to be the teacher, and the other participant was to be the learner. The learner was to memorize a list of word pairs, and the teacher was to quiz the learner on the words and administer electric shocks to the learner when he missed a word. The teacher received a sample shock of forty-five volts as a demonstration of how the shock machine worked. The shocks started at fifteen volts and increased fifteen volts each time, up to a maximum of 450 volts. The upper end of the shock board was labeled "Danger: Severe Shock" and then simply "XXX." The learner was seated in another room, but the teacher and learner could communicate through an intercom.

At first, the experiment went smoothly. The learner had some correct responses and then some incorrect responses, and then began to make more and more errors. As the teacher moved up on the shock board, the learner began to protest. At 120 volts, the learner exclaimed that the shocks were painful. At 150 volts, he refused to go on and yelled, "Get me out of here!" At 270 volts, he screamed in agony—and after 330 volts, he fell chillingly silent.

If the teacher tried to discontinue the procedure, the experimenter responded with a series of commands, starting with, "Please go on," and escalating to, "It is absolutely essential that you continue," and "You have no other choice; you must go on."

If you're encountering this study for the first time, stop and think for a moment. How many people do you think would continue to give shocks under these conditions? The answer stunned even Milgram: almost two-thirds of the people (62.5 percent) obeyed until the end. The majority of subjects—average Americans—kept delivering shocks to a man who was screaming in pain, a man who may even have died as a result of their actions.

How can we explain this? Did Milgram just happen to get a bunch of Death Eaters in his study? Are people just more evil than we think? (And before you start to think that Milgram himself was evil, you should know that the learner was actually an actor working for the experimenter, and he never received any shocks.)

The people in Milgram's study did not relish harming another person. In fact, it was just the opposite—even those who obeyed until the end showed clear signs of discomfort and anxiety. They would ask the experimenter to stop the study, but did not maintain their resistance when the experimenter instructed them to continue. These individuals were caught between their desire to not hurt another person and their initial agreement to participate in the study to help advance science. They did not want to incur the disapproval of the experimenter. And furthermore, the moral problem snuck up on them—they were not asked to go into the laboratory and give a dangerous shock to another person immediately. Instead, there was a slippery slope. After giving thirty volts, it was hard to justify why one shouldn't go up to forty-five volts, and so on. (By the way, this gradual initiation into more and more harmful actions is the same way that genocides begin and torturers are trained.)

By doing variations on this study, Milgram found that subtle changes in the experimental setup evoked different levels of obedience. Bringing the participant closer to the "learner" (or the "victim," we might say) reduced obedience. And moving the authority further away also reduced obedience.

In *Half-Blood Prince*, Draco has sworn to kill Dumbledore and has spent the school year trying to do so in indirect ways (a cursed necklace, a poisoned bottle of mead). But up in the tower, face-to-face with his intended victim, Draco cannot bring himself to do the deed. Voldemort—the authority—is far away, and seeing Dumbledore in the flesh is too much for Draco.

WHAT ELSE COULD I DO?

Although they could have stopped at any time, participants in the Milgram study may have felt that they had no choice but to continue giving the shocks. (For a thoughtful discussion of the nature of "responsibility" in the Milgram study and its real world analogues, see Sabini & Silver.)

In her study of rescuers, individuals who saved Jews during the Holocaust (often at great personal risk), Kristin Renwick Monroe (1994) found that these individuals also describe themselves as having had no other choice. The way that individuals perceived themselves relative to others (as part of a larger whole of humanity or as one person powerless against larger forces) defined the options available to them.

Near the end of *Harry Potter and the Prisoner of Azkaban*, Wormtail (Peter Pettigrew) makes this claim when trying to explain why he betrayed Harry's parents to Voldemort: "'Sirius, Sirius, what could I have done? The Dark Lord...you have no idea...he has weapons you can't imagine'" (374). He continues, "'He would have killed me, Sirius!'" (375).

Harry's personal history may make him feel as though he does not have a choice in fighting Voldemort, a perception that is only strengthened by the prophecy revealed at the end of *Order of the Phoenix*: "*NEITHER CAN LIVE WHILE THE OTHER SURVIVES*" (841). However, as Dumbledore explains to Harry in *Half-Blood Prince* (512), "'You see, the prophecy does not mean you *have* to do anything.... In other words, you are free to choose your own way, quite free to turn your back on the prophecy!'" Indeed, freedom is a theme throughout the series. In *Chamber of Secrets*, Harry worries because the Sorting Hat considered putting him in Slytherin and thinks that he only went to Gryffindor because he asked not to be put in Slytherin. But Dumbledore explains that asking was the important part: "'It is our choices, Harry, that show what we truly are, far more than our abilities'" (333).

BACK IN THE REAL WORLD

Rowling celebrates courage over brains—our heroes come from Gryffindor, not from Ravenclaw. She also shows us the value of friendship and the power of a strong attitude. Seeing these truths played out in the stories of Harry and his friends can be a powerful influence in itself. Sometimes a narrative, even one set in a fantasy land, is far more compelling than all the lectures in the world (Green, Strange, & Brock).

The lessons of Harry Potter, and of psychology, can provide guidelines for real life. We may not have to stand up against an evil wizard, but a glance at a news report shows that we may be faced with other choices: following or resisting a boss who engages in crooked accounting, taking part in or reporting the torture of prisoners, going along with discrimination or speaking out against it. These choices require moral courage, to be sure, but the situations we find ourselves in—with allies or without, face-to-face with authority figures or those who will suffer from our choices—can make our actions easier or more difficult.

AUTHOR NOTE

This essay is dedicated to the memory of John Sabini, my friend, mentor, and fellow Harry Potter fan.

MELANIE C. GREEN, Ph.D., is an assistant professor at the University of North Carolina, Chapel Hill. She received her bachelor's degree (in psychology and literature) from Eckerd College and her Ph.D. in social psychology from Ohio State University. She wishes she could have attended Hogwarts as well, but the owl with her admission letter must have gone astray. Her research explores the persuasive power of narratives, which gives her a perfect excuse to read books such as the Harry Potter series.

REFERENCES

Solomon E. Asch, "Studies of Independence and Conformity: A Minority of One Against a Unanimous Majority," *Psychological Monographs* 70 (1956): 416.

Robert B. Cialdini, "Basic Social Influence is Underestimated," *Psychological Inquiry* 16(4) (2005): 158–161.

French, J. and Bertram H Raven. "The Bases of Social Power" In D. Cartwright (Ed.), *Studies in Social Power*. Ann Arbor, MI: Institute for Social Research, 1959. 150–167.

Green, Melanie C., Jeffrey J. Strange, and Timothy C. Brock. *Narrative Impact: Social and Cognitive Foundations*. Mahwah, NJ: Lawrence Erlbaum Publishers, 2002.

Milgram, Stanley. *Obedience to Authority: An Experimental View*. New York: Harper and Row, 1974.

Kristen Renwick Monroe, "'But What Else Could I Do?': Choice, Identity, and a Cognitive-Perceptual Theory of Ethical Political Behavior," *Political Psychology* 15(2) (1994): 201–226.

Petty, Richard E. and Jon A. Krosnick. *Attitude Strength: Antecedents and Consequences*. Mahwah, NJ: Erlbaum, 1995.

Sabini, John and Maury Silver. "Destroying the Innocent with a Clear Conscience: A Sociopsychology of the Holocaust." In Neil J. Kressel (Ed.), *Political Psychology: Classic and Contemporary Readings*. St. Paul, MN: Paragon House Publishers, 1993. 184–245.

Brad J. Sagarin, Robert B. Cialdini, William E. Rice, and Sherman B. Serna, "Dispelling the Illusion of Invulnerability: The Motivations and Mechanisms of Resistance to Persuasion," *Journal of Personality and Social Psychology* 83(3) (2002): 526–541.

Pahel compares the development and progressive trials that Harry has had to face, from the abuse of the Dursleys, to the struggles and pain from Voldemort, to the stages that an abused person may have to face in the specific treatment of psychoanalysis. Each phase of psychoanalysis and the factors that really help clients is compared to the growth and support that Harry is given as he grows up and faces his trials at Hogwarts.

LAURIE J. PAHEL

Harry Potter and the Magic of Transformation

HOPE FOR TRANSFORMATION abounds. With every step in development there is the push toward growth and alteration. Infants become less attached to their mother. Children yearn to fill their parents' shoes. Maturing individuals feel compelled to seek education, credentials, new relationships, and possessions. Such achievements may fail to provide lasting satisfaction or relief; the remedies often prove to be superficial and easily overpowered.

Who desires an extreme conversion or a simple transformation? Neurotic individuals struggling with conflict at work and home. Traumatized people afraid to trust anyone. Delusional patients looking to escape their internal enemies. Harry Potter fleeing to wizardry school. Yes, Harry Potter—the adolescent of J. K. Rowling's creation who has pitched this high-tech society into frenzied excitement over real paper-and-ink books. There must be some reason that Harry Potter has obtained such wide appeal. Like most important issues, the explanation for Harry's popularity is multi-faceted. Psychoanalytic principles may be helpful in examining this phenomenon. Harry Potter himself deserves psychoanalytic exploration.

Entering psychoanalysis, in fact, may appear to the ordinary person (Muggle) as magical and outrageous a feat as gaining admission to Hogwarts School of Witchcraft and Wizardry. Who on earth would enter into a treatment that required one to attend appointments four to five times a week over many years, to trust a previously unknown professional with one's innermost thoughts, to remember and discuss dreams as if they were important, and to pay money for this so-called privilege? It sounds an awful lot like going to Hogwarts to learn magic. Harry is called to enter training at Hogwarts and is carried there by Hagrid when the Dursleys neglect to help Harry with this task. But the ordinary person enters psychoanalysis at his own bidding and is driven only by painful experiences in relationships, failures at the work-place, self-deprecating thoughts, and anxiety from past traumas.

Psychoanalysis changes a person through the deep attachment and relationship that develops between the patient and the psychoanalyst. The patient initially responds to the psychoanalyst in ways similar to how the patient responds to people in his or her everyday life. Often the patient's current patterns of relating are based on dysfunctional relationships from the past. The patient has no idea that he or she perpetuates these unhealthy patterns. The psychoanalyst gently points out these patterns and then prompts, even prods, the patient to respond differently and in healthier ways in the therapeutic relationship. For these new ways of relating to be sustained, the patient needs many years of "practice" with the psychoanalyst. The patient is ready to leave the psychoanalyst when these positive changes feel permanent. After finishing psychoanalytic treatment, the patient grieves the absence of the analyst as if the analyst has died. The patient, however, has internalized the work with the analyst and functions in a more healthy fashion overall.

Harry Potter's story serves as a useful metaphor for childhood abuse and neglect and for recovery through psychoanalytic treatment. Leonard Shengold refers to the importance of metaphor in making "psychic connections of force and meaning" (Shengold 297). The psychoanalytic sojourn can be as exciting, mysterious, and arduous as Harry Potter's transformation at Hogwarts School of Witchcraft and Wizardry. J. K. Rowling demonstrates a sophisticated understanding of psychological processes in her vivid storytelling. Harry Potter gains strength and independence by doing hard work and by facing fearsome challenges. Proponents of psychoanalytic treatment believe that in-depth, often-painful analytic processes are necessary to provide meaningful, long-lasting relief from symptoms. Irwin Hoffman depicts the analyst as wielding "special power" and as displaying "magical" attributes; he views these as inherent qualities within the asymmetrically powerful analytic relationship (Hoffman 10, 84). In this essay I compare Harry Potter's rescue from abuse by entering Hogwarts with the traumatized patient's hope for recovery within psychoanalytic treatment. Also, from a psychoanalytic perspective, I explore Rowling's thoughtful depictions of emotional and interpersonal processes.

THE ABUSE

Rowling succinctly describes the deprivation and abuse inflicted upon Harry Potter within just a few introductory chapters of each book. From the overwhelming trauma of witnessing his parents' murder and of being attacked himself, one-year-old Harry is delivered onto the doorstep and into the harsh, unloving hands of the Dursley family. Family members consist of "horse-faced and bony" Aunt Petunia (sister to Harry's mother), "large and neckless" Uncle Vernon, and "pink, and porky" cousin Dudley (*Harry Potter and the Chamber of Secrets* 4). The Dursleys require that he live "in a dark cupboard" (*Harry Potter and the Sorcerer's Stone* 20), ignore him on a daily basis, forget all of his birthdays, withhold food from him, and isolate him for prolonged periods of time in his small, windowless room as punishment. From the clutches of a true murderer, Harry is delivered into the hands of ignorant and selfish "soul murderers"—"soul murder" is a term ascribed to severe childhood trauma and neglect (Shengold 16). Somehow, Harry draws upon innate psychological strengths, protections bestowed upon him by wizards, and his own inherent wizard abilities in order to endure unbearable circumstances. Harry recalls that even when unaware of his wizard capabilities his powers literally leak out:

> [E]very odd thing that had ever made his aunt and uncle furious with him had happened when he, Harry, had been upset or angry.... Chased by Dudley's gang, he had somehow found himself out of their reach...dreading going to school with that ridiculous haircut, he'd managed to make it grow back...and the very last time Dudley had hit him, hadn't he got his revenge, without even realizing he was doing it? Hadn't he set a boa constrictor on him? (*Sorcerer's Stone* 58).

Who in the reading audience can resist entering into fantasies with Harry? Imagine the delirious surprise, yet horrible fear, in the happenstance that a revenge fantasy should magically come true. Could there be a safer venue to imagine retribution than through a book written for children?

Despite the extreme neglect and abuse he suffers throughout childhood, Harry perseveres. Certainly, clinicians encounter unexplained hardiness in some patients, individuals who seem able to tolerate abuse that would easily crush others:

> One comes across the unexpected in these people...alongside the scars and distortions produced by terrible childhoods there are some strengthening effects: some survivors appear to have derived from their experiences adaptive powers and talents that helped them survive (Shengold).

Harry receives venomous care from the Dursleys, and yet he endures. Many victims of childhood abuse and deprivation never make it to a clinician's doorstep. Just as Harry persists until help arrives, some victims of childhood trauma survive, seek treatment, and recover despite severe adversity and numerous obstacles. Some people, certainly including Harry Potter, build upon innate strengths and develop amazing capacities to withstand years of torment.

Why is Harry left to live with the Dursleys when magic is available? Ironically enough, the charm Dumbledore placed on Harry as an infant requires that he live with his only remaining blood relative, Aunt Petunia. Dumbledore explains, "'Your mother's sacrifice made the bond of blood the strongest shield I could give you'" (*Harry Potter and the Order of the Phoenix* 836). And so powerful wizards do not intervene on Harry's behalf as the boy suffers the abuses inflicted upon him by the Dursleys. This passivity is analogous to the inherent difficulty of acknowledging the childhood abuse and neglect around us (Herman). The tragically unavoidable placement of the boy with the Dursleys keeps Harry Potter's story real despite the enchanted environment. As evil wizardry erupts into the Muggle world in the sixth volume, the Muggle Prime Minister declares to the wizard Minister of Magic, "'But for heaven's sake—you're *wizards*! You can do *magic*! Surely you can sort out—well—*anything*!'" The new Minister of Magic, Rufus Scrimgeour, replies, "'The trouble is, the other side can do magic too, Prime Minister'" (*Harry Potter and the Half-Blood Prince* 18). The unstoppable nature of evil ruining the lives of innocent victims links Harry's abuse with victims in today's society who've suffered childhood trauma and neglect. In either world, often there is no magic that will prevent or unveil the abuse a helpless child may suffer at the hands of relatives, who have an extreme amount of power.

Wizards intervene only once Harry turns eleven—the age at which wizards may begin training. Then Harry embarks, with intervention from the necessarily giant-of-a-man Hagrid, on the journey leading away from his onerous growing-up years. Likewise, the troubled patient entering treatment turns away from his perpetual emotional suffering. The abused patient's decision to enter treatment is an essential beginning toward recovery (Shengold). It requires extraordinary courage to forgo what is familiar, even when it's abuse, for the anxiety-provoking unknown. Harry hardly requires "seduction" away from the Dursleys, yet he must "surrender" to Hagrid's benevolent kidnapping without knowing what changes will follow (Maroda 16). Harry and the patient start their journeys knowing only that they want to leave the pain behind. They begin the hard work of discovery, learning, and reparation.

THE ESCAPE

Hope abounds for Harry's well-being because of his rescue into the safety of Hogwarts. Likewise, the adult victim of childhood neglect and abuse entering psychoanalysis may dare to hope for improvement. Harry may recover under the persistent ministrations and benevolent instruction of Professor McGonagall, Headmaster Dumbledore, and Groundskeeper Hagrid, to name only a few amongst many generous caregivers at Hogwarts—some mortal, some ghost.

With escape from abuse and deprivation comes the uncovering of truth. Hagrid starts to unravel Harry's story for him. At the age of eleven Harry learns that his birth parents died in the selfless act of saving his life. He finds out that they died fighting the evil Lord Voldemort, not just to protect him, but for the good of all wizards. Up until that time Harry believes the Dursleys' story that his parents died in a car crash. Harry never fits into the Dursleys' world—what a relief to find out that he truly is different from them. Most elementary school-aged children fantasize that they don't really belong to their own family—that, like Harry Potter, they were born of nobler parents (Freud). Living the fantasy through Harry's eyes, in a story in a book, may be a safe way for young readers to explore these magical hopes. Escaping into the fantasy, however, may be necessary for some children to survive severe abuse and deprivation because there is no hope for actual escape.

Harry almost doesn't make it to the safe haven of Hogwarts. Uncle Vernon thwarts him unceasingly and prevents him from opening his acceptance letter to the school. A magical force multiplies the acceptance letter deliveries to exponential rates. Letters follow Harry no matter how many ways Uncle Vernon attempts to intercede. Freud warns that family members will oppose and prohibit a close relative from entering psychoanalytic treatment (Freud). The letter deluge that piles around Harry compares to the patient's burdensome search to relieve his symptoms. Many a mishap is possible given the debilitating nature of the patient's suffering; people seeking help are vulnerable to exploitation (Hoffman). Uncle Vernon's repeated attempts to prohibit Harry from going to Hogwarts exemplify the power of a patient's resistance, both internal and external, to entering appropriate treatment. Perhaps the enormous figure of Hagrid is analogous to the force necessary to combat such strong resistances to starting psychoanalysis.

Platform 9 ¾ is the elusive portal through which the prospective Hogwarts student must enter to begin the journey. A parallel may be seen with the individual struggling to start an analysis once it has been recommended. Finding Platform 9 ¾ is like finding a psychoanalyst. Within any community analysts are retired, do not have openings, do not have available hours that are convenient, or are not able to offer manageable fees. So, just as Harry must search to find the platform, so must patients search to find an appropriate analyst. Furthermore, negotiating the details of analytic treatment resembles the quandary that Harry faces as he searches for Platform 9 ¾:

> Harry was now trying hard not to panic. According to the large clock over the arrivals board, he had ten minutes left to get on the train to Hogwarts and he had no idea how to do it; he was stranded in the middle of a station with a trunk he could hardly lift, a pocket full of wizard money, and a large owl (*Sorcerer's Stone* 91).

Mrs. Weasley's advice about entering the platform serves Harry just as well as it could serve the patient about to start psychoanalysis: "'Don't stop and don't be scared you'll crash into it, that's very important. Best do it at a bit of a run if you're nervous'" (*Sorcerer's Stone* 93). Once on board, the train delivers Harry away from his known tormentors, but is delivering him to an unknown destination and toward unforeseen future adversaries—difficult propositions at best. Likewise, the patient cannot predict what awaits him or her in the course of treatment. Initially there is elation in receiving the invitation to join Hogwarts just as there may be relief in having psychoanalysis recommended as treatment. Once the entry is made, however, there is trepidation about the uncertainties that lie ahead.

THE FATHER

At last Harry arrives at Hogwarts and at last the psychoanalytic treatment begins. Dumbledore is the "greatest headmaster Hogwarts has ever had... [his] powers rival those of He-Who-Must-Not-Be-Named at the height of his strength" (*Chamber of Secrets* 17). The parallels between Professor Dumbledore in Harry's life and the psychoanalyst in the patient's life hardly need elaboration. The steadfast presence of the analyst for soul-murdered patients is "a kind of miracle that has considerable ameliorative power" (Shengold 313). Dumbledore is the all-knowing, all-powerful, paternal figure of Hogwarts. Only he has the power necessary to counter the threatening Dark forces in the wizarding world. It is Harry's unwavering trust in the professor's goodness and power that saves his life when facing Voldemort in the *Chamber of Secrets*. Dumbledore informs Harry, "'You must have shown me real loyalty down in the Chamber. Nothing but that could have called Fawkes to you'" (*Chamber of Secrets* 332). (Fawkes is the phoenix essential to Harry's rescue in this particular Voldemort encounter.) The patient with a history of abuse or neglect will engage in treatment only if he, on some level, believes that the analyst has fortitude, is well-trained, and is trustworthy. If these are not real attributes of the analyst, the treatment will certainly fail.

Harry so idealizes the professor that it is not until his fourth year that Harry sees Dumbledore as capable of feeling dark emotions or as showing signs of aging. Near the end of the fourth book Harry sees "no benign smile upon Dumbledore's face, no twinkle in the eyes behind the spectacles. There was cold fury in every line of the ancient face" (*Harry Potter and the Goblet of Fire* 679). Shortly after this scene, Dumbledore "looked as old and weary as Harry had ever seen him" (*Goblet of Fire* 696). In the sixth volume, Rowling portrays Dumbledore in the final year of his life as injured and more vulnerable. These changed perceptions are essential. Viewing Dumbledore as more human (with apologies to wizards) and less all-powerful helps Harry to build upon his own strengths—that he needn't live under Dumbledore's watchful protection.

Harry's first trauma originates with the murder of his good, loving parents. Tragically, Harry faces this trauma again and again as father figures are killed in front of him—first Sirius Black, his godfather, and then Dumbledore, his beloved headmaster and tutor. Despite his apparent aging, Dumbledore does not die a natural death—he is killed by an apparently disloyal, possibly double-crossing Snape. The last phase of psychoanalysis is called *termination*, the phase of treatment which results in an abrupt cessation of seeing the psychoanalyst. The analyst becomes dead, figuratively, to the patient. The good professor becomes dead, permanently, to Harry. The patient at the end of treatment and Harry at the end of volume six must stand alone, taking the necessary steps toward autonomy.

Dumbledore's death appears final, accented by Fawkes's mourning song and then permanent departure from Hogwarts. Lord Voldemort, however, resurrects himself after each thought-to-be fatal attack on him. He will not die. He personifies evil in Harry Potter's world. Voldemort, Dumbledore informs Harry, leaves more than the scar on Harry's forehead. The evil Lord unintentionally transfers some of his powers onto the infant Harry during the fatal attack, the attack that kills Harry's parents. Harry Potter struggles with this knowledge: "Voldemort put a bit of himself in *me*?" (*Chamber of Secrets* 333). Thus, Harry struggles to accept that he, like everyone, has the capacity for both good and evil. Just as the potential for aggression and rage will always exist, so will Lord Voldemort persist. The most frightened wizards are quickest to believe that Voldemort has perished; they cannot even speak his name, thus the alias "He-Who-Must-Not-Be-Named." They live in a state of denial. Harry, however, is not afraid to call him by name or to think about him. He does not repress the dreams about Voldemort; rather, he uses them to increase his awareness of present circumstances. Harry does not shirk from, nor solicit, difficulties. Likewise, the patient in treatment will develop a greater capacity to deal with what or who torments, challenges, perplexes, and tempts him.

THE MOTHER

Motherhood perplexes the sturdiest of maternal souls at times. Harry Potter has a host of "mothers" in his life: his all-loving, saintly birth-mother Lily Potter, the depriving and cruel Aunt Petunia, the stern yet comforting Professor McGonagall, and the openly loving and generous Mrs. Weasely. Professor McGonagall plays an essential care-taking role in Harry Potter's life. She blends into the storyline in an unassuming, nearly invisible manner—until the reader endeavors to pay special attention to Minerva McGonagall. It then becomes apparent that the emerald-green-robed professor is everywhere. She is the stalwart taskmaster who is in charge of Gryffindor House, the dorm equivalent where Harry lives at Hogwarts. Just like the psychoanalyst who treats many patients, Professor McGonagall has many students entrusted to her for safekeeping. Harry's welfare depends on her care and attendance. He takes her concern for granted like the patient who is able to take the analyst's careful attention for granted.

Mrs. Weasley (Harry's best friend Ron's mother) more than makes up for the lack of outward affection provided by Professor McGonagall. Harry meets the Weasleys for the first time when he is trying to find Platform 9 ¾. Mrs. Weasley bakes Harry homemade sweets, knits him sweaters (the best ones, according to her children), and attends Harry's special events, such as the final task of the Triwizard Tournament. Harry expresses sincere delight when Mrs. Weasley arrives to see him compete in the tournament. In response to Harry's inquiry about whether the Dursleys will attend, Mrs. Weasley "refrained from criticizing the Dursleys in front of Harry, but her eyes flashed every time they were mentioned" (*Goblet of Fire* 616). Mrs. Weasley treats and protects Harry as if he were one of her own children. Certainly, no substitute can make up for the lack of adequate maternal care, but there can be corrective experiences that help an individual work through early losses (Viederman). A patient may receive reconstructive nurturance through the intimate relationship with the analyst and then through subsequently healthier friendships. Mrs. Weasley portrays the warm, nurturing, selfless mother, and she complements Professor McGonagall's representation of the protective, though less flexible and more frustrating, care-taking mother. Perhaps many maternal figures later in life are required to construct adequately the essential totality of an absent or impaired original mother.

Good meals usually accompany adequate mothering. The myriad complex meanings and uses of food in our culture far exceed the purpose for nourishment. Some of the most tender or the most despairing moments in a lifetime may include ritual meals or food deprivation. Rowling takes food to new celebratory heights and to neglectful lows in her young hero's life. If a little magic can spice up an everyday meal, imagine what it can do for holidays and special events. The Great Hall is where meals are served at Hogwarts. The magnificence of the meals begins with this setting:

> Harry had never even imagined such a strange and splendid place. It was lit by thousands and thousands of candles that were floating in midair over four long tables, where the rest of the students were sitting. These tables were laid with glittering golden plates and goblets. At the top of the hall was another long table where the teachers were sitting.... Harry looked upward and saw a velvety black ceiling dotted with stars. He heard Hermione whisper, "It's bewitched to look like the sky outside." It was hard to believe there was a ceiling there at all, and that the Great Hall didn't simply open on to the heavens (*Sorcerer's Stone* 116–117).

The deprivation imposed by the gluttonous Dursleys on Harry Potter stands in stark contrast to Hogwarts feasts. On a zoo trip, the "Dursleys bought Dudley and [his friend] large chocolate ice creams at the entrance and then, because the smiling lady in the van had asked Harry what he wanted before they could hurry him away, they bought him a cheap lemon ice pop" (*Sorcerer's Stone* 26). When cousin Dudley finally is placed on a strict diet after having "reached roughly the size and weight of a young killer whale," Aunt Petunia makes sure that Harry gets even less to eat than Dudley (*Goblet of Fire* 27). In yet another eventually futile effort to prohibit Harry from returning to Hogwarts after summer vacation, Uncle Vernon locks Harry into his bedroom and "fitted a cat-flap in the bedroom door, so that small amounts of food could be pushed inside three times a day" (*Chamber of Secrets* 22). Harry becomes accustomed to the ache of hunger while living with the Dursleys. Hogwarts meals, however, are satisfying and delicious:

> The dishes in front of him were now piled with food. He had never seen so many things he liked to eat on one table: roast beef, roast chicken, pork chops and lamb chops, sausages, bacon and steak, boiled potatoes, roast potatoes, fries, Yorkshire pudding, peas, carrots, gravy, ketchup.... The Dursleys had never exactly starved Harry, but he'd never been allowed to eat as much as he liked. Dudley had always taken anything that Harry really wanted, even if it made him sick. (*Sorcerer's Stone* 123).

The ability to control food portions and to manipulate mealtime events provides tremendous power and apparent pleasure to an abuser. Harry Potter must yield to the Dursleys' sadistic control over food while under their roof. The nurturance provided Harry by magical Hogwarts feasts and tasty Mrs. Weasley care-packages compensates for the deprivation inflicted by the Dursleys. Usually not so easily repaired, the patient may experience enough sustenance in psychoanalytic treatment to begin to acknowledge and to recover from a past tainted by insidious cruelty.

THE STRUCTURE

Harry is introduced to Hogwarts with a ritual that all neophytes must undergo when entering the castle for the first time. This ritual resembles the birth process. The new students are gathered into boats and must cross a lake to reach the castle:

> The little boats carried them through a curtain of ivy that hid a wide opening in the cliff face. They were carried along a dark tunnel, which seemed to be taking them right underneath the castle, until they reached a kind of underground harbor, where they clambered out onto rocks and pebbles (*Sorcerer's Stone* 112).

Now reborn into the world of wizardry, Harry may begin his transformation.

In every book, Harry Potter encounters and prevails over each daunting ordeal within the steadfast safety of Hogwarts. The physical structure itself defies unwanted intrusions. Outside there stands a "pair of magnificent wrought iron gates, flanked with stone columns topped with winged boars" (*Harry Potter and the Prisoner of Azkaban* 87), and "[t]he entrance hall was so big you could have fit the whole of the Dursleys' house in it...the ceiling was too high to make out, and a magnificent marble staircase facing [the new students] led to the upper floors" (*Sorcerer's Stone* 113). The enormity of the castle suggests that all things may be held, contained, and studied within its walls. A sense of limitless security is essential within the treatment of patients who have been neglected and abused (Shengold). Harry may explore his innate powers and traumatic past freely within the confines of Hogwarts. The same may be said for the patient in treatment.

There is no question in this metaphor for childhood abuse and deprivation that Hogwarts serves as a therapeutic structure. The title of the second book, *Harry Potter and the Chamber of Secrets*, names a force detrimental to any treatment structure—secrets. Students protected by Hogwarts are in danger when the Chamber of Secrets is opened. This open chamber impairs the safety of the castle just as secrets jeopardize the process of treatment. Harry confronts the open chamber; the patient chooses truth. Each remains safe within a protective structure.

REPARATION

Coincidentally or not, as Voldemort continues to terrorize Harry Potter and his fictional world, terrorists increasingly threaten the real world. As each new book is released, reviewers warn that the Harry Potter story grows darker, more violent—cloudier with the usual storms of adolescence but even more threatening with Voldemort growing in power. Both Harry Potter and his readership have to deal with more intense, more confusing political and life experiences. As Dumbledore debriefs Harry Potter after the murder of Harry's beloved Sirius Black, "Harry felt the white-hot anger lick his insides, blazing in the terrible emptiness, filling him with the desire to hurt Dumbledore for his calmness and his empty words" (*Order of the Phoenix* 823). Harry Potter expresses rage unlike anything he has demonstrated earlier. Even his admiration and idealization of Headmaster Dumbledore cannot deflect his anger and guilt over Sirius Black's death. Harry grows closer to entering young adulthood, where aggression, hostility, and violence in us and around us cannot be denied. Like the wise, seasoned psychoanalyst withstands—even welcomes—the patient's rage, Dumbledore listens to Harry without argument or coddling. There are no good answers after all. How does one deal with the destructive violence of Voldemort? How does one deal with the deeds of terrorists who feel righteous in their actions?

Harry's readership waits expectantly, even anxiously, to see how Harry deals with Dumbledore's murder and Snape's betrayal. Shortly before the great headmaster's death, Dumbledore explains to Harry, "'Don't you see? Voldemort himself created his worst enemy, just as tyrants everywhere do! Have you any idea how much tyrants fear the people they oppress? All of them realize that, one day, amongst their many victims, there is sure to be one who rises against them and strikes back!'" (*Half-Blood Prince* 510). This, then, is the terrible and powerful prophecy that Harry Potter embraces. He, whose parents and beloved parent figures are murdered by Voldemort and his followers, alone has the authority to avenge the damage done by Voldemort. Individuals who have been traumatized and victimized by others face the gift and the curse of such a prophecy. Some victims never have the strength or the opportunity to face their abusers. Psychoanalysis and psychotherapy allow the lucky few who ever enter treatment to evaluate whether such a confrontation could ever be possible. We have yet to see whether Harry avenges the deaths of his loved ones or dies trying. It's usually not so black and white—justice or death. Victims, however, who confront their abusers in a safe and legal manner, are likely to experience reparation of a deeply healing nature.

ENDING OR BEGINNING

The Harry Potter books are magical escapes into a world where good usually overcomes evil, where deserving people sometimes win, and not all heroes survive. The revelry and safety of the stories may be safe reconstructive experiences to readers who are familiar with childhood trauma. Diving into these fantasies right along with Harry imparts hope that, with diligent work and deliberate thoughtfulness, transformation is possible.

What would have happened if Harry Potter had finished his adolescence in a dark room under the stairs? He would have had no outlets for or even an understanding of how to express his budding wizardry talents. Harry would have been more vulnerable to Lord Voldemort's attempts at converting him, if not killing him outright, to join his group of evil followers. Attention, care, or consideration from anyone would have been better than the abuse and deprivation Harry would have continued to suffer if he'd not been removed from the Dursleys' home. Likewise, when someone falters before the recommendation for psychoanalysis or doesn't know where to look for help, natural talents are wasted and despair becomes entrenched. Worse still, those in pain may be converted to live in darkness and to inflict upon those weaker than they are the very traumas afflicted upon them. Transformative experiences through Harry Potter fantasies and within psychoanalytic treatment offer hope. There is magic, but mostly hard work, in transformation.

LAURIE J. PAHEL is a psychiatrist and psychoanalyst in private practice in Chapel Hill, North Carolina, as well as an adjunct faculty member of the University of North Carolina in the department of psychiatry. She is also a mother of three children and has read aloud each Harry Potter book at least twice—so far.

REFERENCES

Bollas, C. "Dead Mother, Dead Child." *The Mystery of Things*. London: Routledge, 1999.

H. Craige, "Mourning Analysis: The Post-Termination Phase," Accepted for publication: *Journal of the American Psychoanalytic Association*. 2000.

Freud, S. "Family Romances." Vol. 9 of *The Standard Edition of the Complete Psychological Works of Freud*. W. W. Norton & Co., 2000 (1900). 237–241.

——. "Recommendations to Physicians Practicing Psycho-Analysis." Vol. 12 of *The Standard Edition of the Complete Psychological Works of Freud*. W. W. Norton & Co., 2000 (1912). 111–120.

Gove, P. B. Ed. *Webster's Third New International Dictionary—Unabridged*. Springfield: Merrian-Webster Inc., 1993.

T. G. Gutheil and G. O Gabbard, "The Concept of Boundaries in Clinical Practice: Theoretical and Risk-Management Dimensions," *American Journal of Psychiatry* 150(2) (1993): 188–196.

Herman, J. *Trauma and Recovery*. New York: Basic Books, 1997.

Hoffman, I. Z. *Ritual and Spontaneity in the Psychoanalytic Process—A Dialectical-Constructivist View*. Hillsdale: The Analytic Press, Inc., 1998.

Maroda, K. J. *Surrender, and Transformation—Emotional Engagement in the Analytic Process*. Hillsdale: The Analytic Press, Inc., 1999.

Rowling, J. K. *Harry Potter and the Sorcerer's Stone*. New York: Scholastic Inc., 1998.

——. *Harry Potter and the Chamber of Secrets*. New York: Scholastic Inc., 1999.

——. *Harry Potter and the Prisoner of Azkaban*. New York: Scholastic Inc., 1999.

——. *Harry Potter and the Goblet of Fire*. New York: Scholastic Inc., 2000.

L. Shengold, "Is There Life Without Mother?" *Psychoanalytic Quarterly* 69 (2000): 445–464.

——. *Soul Murder—The Effects of Childhood Abuse and Deprivation*. New York: Ballantine Books, 1989.

———. *Soul Murder Revisited—Thoughts About Therapy, Hate, Love, and Memory.* New Haven, CT: Yale University Press, 1999.

Tyson, P. and R. L. Tyson. *Psychoanalytic Theories of Development—An Integration.* New Haven, CT: Yale University Press, 1990.

Vaillant, G. E. *The Wisdom of the Ego.* Cambridge, MA: Harvard University Press, 1993.

S. C. Vaughan and S. P. Roose, "Patient-Therapist Match: Revelation or Resistance?" *Journal of the American Psychoanalytic Association* 48(3) (2000): 885–900.

M. Viederman, "The Real Person of the Analyst and His Role in the Process of Psychoanalytic Cure," *Journal of the American Psychoanalytic Association* 39 (1991): 451–490.

Psychologists turn their attention to *The Simpsons*, one of America's most popular and beloved shows, in these essays that explore the function and dysfunctions of the show's characters. Designed to appeal to both fans of the show and students of psychology, this unique blend of science and pop culture consists of essays by professional psychologists drawn from schools and clinical practices across the country. Each essay is designed to be accessible, thoughtful, and entertaining, while providing the reader with insights into both *The Simpsons* and the latest in psychological thought. Every major area of psychology is covered, from clinical psychology and cognition to abnormal and evolutionary psychology, while fresh views on eclectic show topics such as gambling addiction, Pavlovian conditioning, family therapy, and lobotomies are explored.

smartpopbooks.com | BenBella Books

From situational ethics and tribal loyalties to stress and body image, this collection of essays employs cutting-edge psychology to delve into the dynamics of the hit television show *Survivor*. Containing new thoughts and theories on the past thirteen seasons of the show-which many consider the mother of reality television-this analysis looks at the root behaviors and emotions that come to light while people are being filmed competing for a large sum of money while stranded on a deserted island.

Available August 2007

smartpopbooks.com | BenBella Books

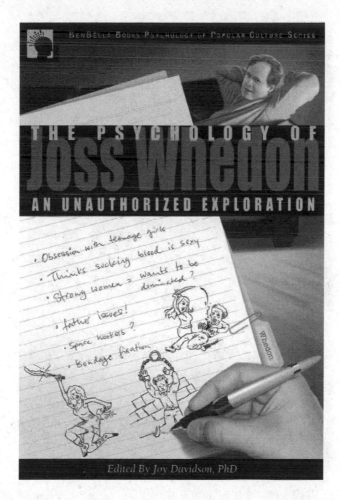

Joss Whedon—creator of the wildly popular *Buffy the Vampire Slayer*, its spin-off *Angel*, the short-lived series Firefly, and the feature film it inspired, *Serenity*—takes a seat on the couch in this in-depth examination of the psychological gravity that has captivated his deeply devoted fan base. Whedon fans will enjoy a discussion of issues that are both funny and profound, from the significance of Angel's mommy issues and the best way to conduct government experiments on vampires to what could drive a man to become a cannibalistic Reaver and the psychological impact of being one girl in all the world chosen to fight the forces of darkness.

Available December 2007

smartpopbooks.com | BenBella Books

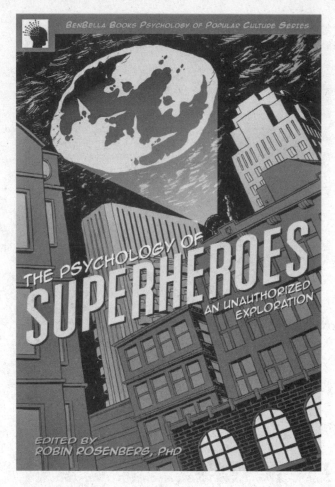

Unmasking superhuman abilities and double lives, this analysis showcases nearly two dozen psychologists as their essays explore the minds of pop culture's most intriguing and daring superheroes, including Spider-Man, Batman, Superman, and the X-Men. Exposing the inner thoughts that these reclusive heroes would only dare share with trained professionals, heady experts give detailed psychoanalyses of what makes specific superheroes tick while answering such questions as Why do superheroes choose to be superheroes? Why is there so much prejudice against the X-Men mutants? What makes Spider-Man so altruistic? and Why are supervillains so aggressive? Additionally, the essays tackle why superheroes have such an enduring effect on American culture.

Available March 2008

smartpopbooks.com | BenBella Books